MW01119705

Elizabeth B. Silva
TECHNOLOGY, CULTURE, FAMILY
Influences on Home Life

Palgrave Macmillan Studies in Family and Intimate Life
Series Standing Order ISBN 978–0–230–51748–6 hardback
978–0–230–24924–0 paperback
(*outside North America only*)

You can receive future titles in this series as they are published by placing a standing order. Please contact your bookseller or, in case of difficulty, write to us at the address below with your name and address, the title of the series and one of the ISBNs quoted above.

Customer Services Department, Macmillan Distribution Ltd, Houndmills, Basingstoke, Hampshire RG21 6XS, England

Adoption, Family and the Paradox of Origins

A Foucauldian History

Sally Sales
University of East London, UK

palgrave
macmillan

First published 2012 by
PALGRAVE MACMILLAN

Palgrave Macmillan in the UK is an imprint of Macmillan Publishers Limited,
registered in England, company number 785998, of Houndmills, Basingstoke,
Hampshire RG21 6XS.

Palgrave Macmillan in the US is a division of St Martin's Press LLC,
175 Fifth Avenue, New York, NY 10010.

Palgrave Macmillan is the global academic imprint of the above companies
and has companies and representatives throughout the world.

Palgrave® and Macmillan® are registered trademarks in the United States,
the United Kingdom, Europe and other countries.

ISBN: 978–0–230–27625–3

This book is printed on paper suitable for recycling and made from fully
managed and sustained forest sources. Logging, pulping and manufacturing
processes are expected to conform to the environmental regulations of the
country of origin.

A catalogue record for this book is available from the British Library.

A catalog record for this book is available from the Library of Congress.

10 9 8 7 6 5 4 3 2 1
21 20 19 18 17 16 15 14 13 12

Printed and bound in the United States of America
by Edwards Brothers, Inc.

Maybe the target nowadays is not to discover what we are but to refuse what we are ... we have to promote new forms of subjectivity through the refusal of this kind of individuality that has been imposed on us for several centuries.

Michel Foucault

For Rose Helena

Contents

Acknowledgements

It was during my time at the Post-Adoption Centre in the mid- to late 1990s that I first began to grapple with the issues about open adoption that this book attempts to unravel. I owe an enormous debt of gratitude to colleagues at the Centre, who over an eight-year period provided a space and structure within which I could explore the complex field of contact in contemporary adoption. It was through discussion with Centre colleagues that I first really understood the structuring dominance of attachment theory in the debates around open practices. I wish to particularly acknowledge my association with Rose Dagoo, a passionate advocate for openness and a wonderfully supportive training partner. My work at the Centre would not have been possible without significant funding from the Nuffield Foundation and the Kings Fund. I finally owe an equally large debt of gratitude to the many Centre users of the Mediation & Contact service whose experiences and brave participation helped foster and shape my own thinking about this complex field of practice.

During the course of my time at the Centre I met many inspirational social workers and chief amongst them is Lynne Lehane, whose modesty means her own unique contribution to this contentious field has remained largely unacknowledged. She probably has no idea how inspiring her own practice has been for me in the writing of this book.

I want to particularly thank the participating local authority who gave me generous and open access to their adoption archive. The manager and the post-adoption staff were always available for discussion and always willing to answer my questions.

The University of East London has been a facilitative and supportive place for thinking through the issues in this book. I warmly acknowledge Professor Phil Cohen, whose own work on adoption was an inspiration. I am hugely indebted to Professor Maria Tamboukou, whose generosity with her profound knowledge of Foucault was enormously helpful at a critical point in the project. The London Foucault circle that Maria convened was an important forum for exploring some of the ideas in Part II.

Colleagues at the Site for Contemporary Psychoanalysis have fostered my passion for Foucault and the relevance of his late work for rethinking the psychoanalytic clinic. Many thanks to them for the opportunities of airing some of these ideas in seminars. Angela Kreeger, Madhu Nandi, Ilric Shetland and Peter Wood, members of a Foucault study group, helped me to think about how Foucault might be central to a radicalising of the psychological self.

I am very grateful to my editors at Palgrave Macmillan: Philippa Grand, Olivia Middleton, who initially commissioned the book, and Andrew James, for supporting its completion. I owe particular thanks to the anonymous reviewers whose feedback helped me to rethink and clarify some important arguments in Chapter 1.

My greatest debt is to Ilric Shetland, who quite simply allowed me to get lost in the work without demand or complaint.

Sally Sales
Cornwall
December 2010

Part I

A Genealogy of Adoption
1926–2000

1
Introducing the Study

The following are two extracts from an English guide for adoptive parents, written in 1959:

> It is always wise to avoid using the expressions 'your own mother' or 'your real mother'. Even 'your other mother' makes it sound as if the child has two mothers, whereas he only has you. One good way to put it is 'your first mother'. There is no emotional feeling about the word 'first'. The child knows 'first' as something which comes and goes. (Rowe, 1959, p. 140)
>
> It is rare for a happily adopted child to wish to look up his adoption records and even more rare for him to try to find his first parents. If they do it usually means that something has gone wrong in their home and they are searching for a satisfaction that they have not yet found. An intense and long-continued interest in his original parents is a sign that all is not well and the child may need professional help. (ibid., p. 147)

Some 30 years later, in 1992, the following notes were recorded in the adoption file of two brothers:

> I feel that contact with mum will be beneficial to the boys especially R, if it is predictable, well planned in advance and limited to once or twice a year. Since mother has become accustomed to visiting the children unannounced at their present address, it may be appropriate for contact to take place outside the home and to be organised by an outside organisation like Thomas Coram Foundation.
>
> Some contact to mother's extended family should also be encouraged but limited to exchange of pictures and letters once per year.

> This level of contact should ensure that the boys keep in touch with their family of origin without unsettling their long-term placement.

The stark opposition evoked by these two pictures of adoption speak to a certain break or transformation in how adoption was practised. Put simply, adoption was once closed and it then became open. This is well illustrated by the two examples above; the 1959 guide consigns the child's biological family to the dead past, emptied of emotional significance and without a role to play, whereas the 1992 adoption file describes an adoption which includes the biological family through visits, letters and photographs. In the space of three decades adopted children's needs and emotional capabilities have been completely reconfigured. The clean break with the past approach has been replaced with an adoption experience that far from deleting the past endorses and provides continuity with it. It could be said, then, that adopted children live their histories differently in the contemporary era. At some point in the late 1980s the nature of what it means to be adopted changed. The study that follows is an attempt to interrogate this apparent change in contemporary adoption practice.

The starting point for my research arose during the time I spent working for the Post-Adoption Centre in the mid- to late 1990s, researching the use of mediation in contemporary open adoption. The Post-Adoption Centre is a small, independently funded charity engaged in pioneering work in the area of post-adoption services. The Centre wanted to develop a service to facilitate the making and maintaining of open adoptive placements, a growing part of adoption work since the beginning of the 1990s. As a newcomer to adoption, having no professional background in the field, I enthusiastically endorsed this recent innovation of keeping adopted children in some form of contact with their families of origin. However, I quickly discovered that the introduction of openness was both controversial and unpopular. When approaching local authority adoption teams I encountered an intense opposition to my work and a vociferous questioning of the practice of open placements. I very quickly found myself engaged in the most controversial debate in contemporary adoption: whether it was beneficial for adopted children to have continuing contact with their family of origin.

On leaving the Centre I wanted to pursue in a more detached setting the questions that had insistently preoccupied me during my work of the previous eight years: why is openness in adoption so controversial and contested? What is being questioned when adopted children sustain some kind of contact with the families who no longer parent them? However, as my research progressed, I began to be intrigued by altogether different questions: what compelled the adoption profession to introduce a practice that was in such opposition to their views about adopted children's welfare? How could this paradoxical development of implementing a practice that is then contested be understood? It would appear that the adopted child's biological family is in a paradoxical position within contemporary adoption – their involvement is both evoked and contested. I began to wonder whether this paradox was constitutive of adoption, rather than simply an effect of contemporary openness. In order to think about this question I turned to the history of adoption.

Histories and descriptive studies of adoption (Kornitzer, 1952; Goodacre, 1966; Kornitzer, 1968; Benet, 1976; Teague, 1989; Triseliotis et al., 1997; Parker, 1999) chart a changing and contradictory relationship to the family of origin since adoption's legal inception in 1926. The full legal severance of adoption was only reluctantly achieved in 1949 suggesting that early policy makers wanted to sustain a certain place for the family of origin within the adopted child's life. Yet at the same time there was a growing trend to achieve a full substitute home for the adopted child. After the Second World War, this trend to accomplish a far-reaching substitute family continued, but there were also practices unsettling the supposed closed status of adoption of this period. There were practices that invited the participation of the biological family, such as third-party and direct placements and practices that sustained the biological family's presence within the adoptive home, most importantly the practice of telling children they were adopted. In the 1970s when adoption was expanded to include older children from care, the same tensions around birth family involvement persisted. This was the era of permanency planning where adopted children's welfare was understood to require a 'psychological parent' as full substitute for the biological parent they had lost. However, this manifest severance with the family of origin was compromised by the 1976 Adoption Act, which allowed adopted adults access to their birth records for the first time, thus opening up a previously closed archive. By the 1990s adoption had become 'open', with an apparent embracing of practices that directly involved the biological family. But as already discussed, these practices were contested and their implementation resisted.

It would seem from even this brief historical overview that adoption practices have sustained a paradoxical place for the family of origin within diverse and changing policies at different historical periods. Returning to my opening two vignettes, this paradoxical positioning of the family of origin can be clearly seen in both 1959 and 1992.

It is clear that even in the so-called closed era of 1959 that closure with the child's past was not absolute. The adopted child knew something of his or her adoption and knew that there were not only other parents elsewhere, but records of this other life before adoption. However, this knowledge had to be divested of any emotional attachment, an acknowledged kinship bond that left no enduring mark. Something similar can be glimpsed in the 1992 vignette. Here there was an apparent open embracing of the children's biological family, with the mother even having visits, but, crucially, only if the visits were kept separate. The birth mother could not visit the children in their new home once they had been adopted, even though she had visited the same house when the children were still being fostered. It reads as if former attachments needed to be redefined as more marginal and more distant once the adoption order had been made.

Whilst a considerable passage of time separates these two vignettes, they share a far-reaching continuity in terms of the position the birth family occupies in the adoption narrative. In both 1959 and 1992 there was a move to remake a child's history into an event emptied of any emotional intensity, while, at the same time, evoking its continued significance.

I am making two points here; first, that there might be more continuity of practice in these two eras than the usual histories relate, and, second, that an approach that emphasises hidden continuities of practice, rather than manifest discontinuities, may better help to understand the contested status of contemporary open adoption. Such an approach would run counter to the usual commentaries the profession has produced. Histories of adoption are usually narrated and interpreted in terms of this opposition between closed and open; whilst there are divergences of interpretation, the majority of commentators tell the history from within this framework.

The most common version of adoption history is that it had moved from a closed to a more open practice by the era of the 1990s. Such accounts trace a progressive opening up of adoption through the course of its history, documenting an increasing move to include the formerly excluded biological family. The primary emphasis of such historical accounts is to illustrate how adoption has progressively improved through time from its crude and inexperienced beginnings in 1926 to an increasing expertise and professionalism post war (Kornitzer, 1952; Goodacre, 1966; Kornitzer, 1968) to the contemporary era of open placements – a narrative of progressive enlightenment:

> From the time of the Adoption Act 1926, there has been a gradual trend for adoption to become increasingly open. Adopted people have been given more and more information about their backgrounds

and origins. Adoptive parents have been given increased knowledge about their children's early years and they have been encouraged to be open in acknowledging and discussing adoption with their children. (Howe and Feast, 2000, p. 10)

In the above extract the history of adoption is presented as one of incremental improvement, with elements that disrupt such a narrative covered over or erased; for example, this account simply omits the oppositions and resistances to adoption open practices that have been present throughout the history.

The other, less cited account of adoption describes a pre-war period of more open and consensual practice that was regulated by post-war legislation to achieve a more closed and exclusive approach (Ryburn, 1992b, 1998; Cretney, 1998). Some commentators hold the view that the later practice effectively 'drew a veil of secrecy over adoption' with any 'loopholes' from the earlier era progressively closed (Smith and Logan, 2004, p. 7). Within this perspective, regulation is understood to have had a restrictive effect on a previously fluid and encompassing practice. This approach reads the history for examples of open practice that have been made marginal by a conservative and closed adoption profession; so 'legal adoption, in the form in which we currently practise it, has always included the practice of openness and contact' (Ryburn, 1999, p. 514). The contemporary move towards openness is understood as a welcome, but never sufficiently developed step. Within this kind of account, openness is understood as a good and progressive practice that a closed profession has resisted, with the implication that practice needs to be 'freed' or 'enlightened.'

The difficulty with both the positions outlined above is how they characterise adoption history within a reductive opposition – from closed and secretive to open or its reverse. This opposition is an inadequate description to characterise the myriad and contradictory practices that addressed the adopted child's relationship to its birth history. Traditional adoption commentaries cannot account for the simultaneous emergence and deployment of both inclusionary and exclusionary forms of practice around the place of the birth family in adoption work. Most importantly, these accounts do not locate adoption within the wider field of western kinship where the blood tie occupies a foundational place.

Adoption and western kinship practices

There has been a proliferation of anthropological work on western kinship in recent years, in particular exploring the emergence of new reproductive technologies and their contribution to rethinking the ways that children come into and belong to families. Whether by adoption or by technological innovation, these artificially achieved families certainly rewrite the originary place of the blood tie for those growing up outside of their biological blood line. However, even within these radical ways of achieving family, the kinship origin remains a foundational source of knowledge and truth. Franklin (1997, pp. 20–1), in her study of in vitro fertilisation (IVF), discusses the insistent place that biological reproduction occupies for western conceptions of the family: 'it continues to be the case that biological facts of human reproduction or "the facts of life" occupy a privileged explanatory status.' The rooting of identity in an originary biological heritage appears to be an abiding practice at the heart of western kinship.

This link between individuality and kin relatedness has been a well-explored theme in contemporary sociological and anthropological literature. In a recent book, the sociologist Steph Lawler (2008) claims that individuality, that sense of *being* an individual, is itself a middle-class practice and one that has progressively informed the template for working-class identity. The establishment of this form of middle-class identity was central to the emergence of adoption and Chapter 2 will explore this historic convergence in detail; for now, I just want to highlight one of the central elements in middle-class kinship formation. Strathern (1995, pp. 14–15), in her now classic study of middle-class English kinship, draws attention to the paradox that is installed at the heart of middle-class identity formation: 'We might consider then how the particular social relationship of parent and child generates the image of the child, not just as son or daughter but as a unique individual …. Individuality would thus be both a fact of and "after" kinship.'

The dual demand that Strathern identifies – to be both like and unlike one's familial origin – has been profoundly consequential for how adoption has been practised since its legal inception in 1926. In a culture where the accomplishment of individuality is tied to kin relatedness, the state of being adopted will immediately be rendered problematic. The separation from original kin that adoption installs will always put into question the adopted subject's capacity to become a 'full individual'. There is, then, a dual and contradictory message at the centre of adoption practices: provide the child with a new foundation, but simultaneously sustain the old foundation of the family of origin. This has produced an enduring terrain of controversy and contestation throughout the history of its implemented practice.

This study is an attempt to understand the complex and changing historical location of adoption within wider kinship practices in the

United Kingdom. It has emerged out of a profound dissatisfaction with existing commentaries and histories that seem to offer no account of the problematic and paradoxical place of original kinship in the field of adoption. It was this dissatisfaction with existing explanatory frameworks that led me to the work of Foucault. His way of 'doing' history – genealogy – opened up new possibilities for rethinking both the place of history and practice that could more fruitfully address the paradoxical and contested place of contemporary open adoption.

Introducing a genealogical approach for adoption

> The object was to learn to what extent the effort to think one's own history can free thought from what it silently thinks, and so enable it to think differently. (Foucault, 1986, p. 9)

Foucault's genealogical approach is a strategy for disturbing and unsettling the commonplace ways we see ourselves and our worlds. His object, as the above quotation makes clear, is to destabilise the routine and conventional ways that certain histories in the west have been told in order to recover the conflicts, differences and other buried voices that those histories have eclipsed or submerged. Foucault's own genealogies took familiar objects – prisons, sexuality – and made them strange and unfamiliar by using a mode of analysis that worked to both unravel the self-evident and disturb assumptions (Hook, 2007, p. 142). In the paper 'Two Lectures' (1980), Foucault describes genealogy in the following way: 'What it [genealogy] really does is to entertain the claims to attention of local, discontinuous, disqualified, illegitimate knowledges against the claims of a unitary body of theory which would filter, hierarchise and order them in the name of some true knowledge' (ibid., p. 83).

Foucault's target in all his work was the apparently unalterable truths produced by certain stabilised forms of cultural knowledge, which worked to marginalise and exclude other forms of knowledge. For example, the object of knowledge, sanity, operates by both defining and excluding all those who do not fit into its regulatory hierarchy, the so-called mad and insane. As Hook (2007, p. 140) lucidly explains, the importance of recovering 'buried historical contents and subjugated knowledges' lies in their potential to disrupt the dominant and unitary narratives that impose their singular truths on the cultural field. Genealogical analysis is, then, not to do with discovering objects of knowledge, but about investigating the practices through which objects of knowledge are constituted in order that we might think differently about that object. The 1971 essay 'Nietzsche, Genealogy, History' is usually understood as the moment when Foucault prioritised genealogy, leading to a foregrounding of the analysis of cultural practices. For the purposes of this study, the essay elaborates a way to undertake historical research without falling into what Dreyfus and Rabinow (1982, p. 118) describe as the errors of 'presentism' or 'finalism'. Briefly, these approaches root historical enquiry in a relationship to a historical origin – one reads either the past into the present or the present into the past. Dreyfus and Rabinow argue that Foucault's genealogical approach goes in an altogether different direction, where the distinctions between surface and depth, origin and event, are effects of a particular way that power is organised and deployed in cultures of the west (ibid., p. 82). Foucault's genealogies are as much about the development of history as a mode of being as they are about the analysis of a particular historical period or era. Drawing on Foucault's work, this genealogy of adoption will trace the development and deployment of history itself in adoption practices as well as analyse the historical continuities and changes in those practices (Steedman, 1994, pp. 77–81).

In 'Nietzsche, Genealogy, History', Foucault compares his own genealogical method with that of more traditional historical approaches, contrasting what he terms traditional history and effective history. Traditional history is rooted in constants and absolutes; it has a teleological and developmental movement and focuses on rediscovery; it attempts to homogenise whole periods, causally linking disparate elements together and totalising divergent trends and events. The field of adoption has largely recounted its own histories within this kind of framework. In contrast, Foucault describes effective history as 'vertical' or synchronic, with its focus on the haphazard, the random, the contingent and the new: 'History becomes effective to the degree that it introduces discontinuity into our very being – as it divides our emotions, dramatises our instincts, multiplies our body and sets it against itself' (Foucault, 1998a, p. 380). Such an approach would involve an active consideration of those elements that rupture, break, mutate or transform the continuous line of descent tracked by traditional historical narratives. The focus then is not on understanding a person or an event by going back to an origin, but on describing the constellation of factors that contribute to a given position in time, an approach that will work to describe localised relations. This approach is a challenge to the traditional historical accounts that the field of adoption has generated.

Central to Foucault's genealogical approach are the two concepts of descent and emergence. Both these terms have a proximity to history, but with some critical differences that are very relevant for this project and I will briefly outline them in turn. The tracking of descent is not about discovering a singular originating identity:

> Genealogy does not pretend to go back in time to restore an unbroken continuity that operates beyond the dispersion of forgotten things...on the contrary to follow the complex course of descent is to maintain passing events in their proper dispersion; it is to identify the accidents, the minute deviations...the errors...the faulty calculations that gave birth to those things that continue to exist and have value for us. (Foucault, 1998a, p. 374)

The genealogist does not impose coherence on complexity by either the restoration of some connection with the past or the imposition of a diagnostic category; rather, the genealogist allows the complexity free play, without such closure – maintaining events in what Foucault describes as their proper dispersion. If we apply this to the field of adoption, then here is an approach that pays attention to the complex play of events in the present that shape the emergence of open and closed practices. Such an approach will trace out what contributes to the current emergence of a practice, rather than attempt to explain the practice in terms of some earlier history.

The other key genealogical term is emergence. By emergence Foucault is talking about the process whereby something comes into being – 'the moment of arising'. He is describing an approach that can account for the emergence of particular phenomena at a particular moment, with the emphasis on episodes that erupt rather than belong to a developmental process: 'We should avoid accounting for emergence by appeal to its final term...developments may appear as a culmination, but they are merely episodes in a series of subjugations' (ibid., p. 376).

It is difficult to think about the concept of emergence without considering Foucault's ideas about power and knowledge – what it is possible to know and do within the systems of dominations within which we live. Here Foucault is drawing attention to the way that social practices emerge through the play of competing forces; the complex movement of power is therefore fundamental in grasping how Foucault characterises his genealogical approach: 'Genealogy...seeks to re-establish the various systems of subjection: not the anticipatory power of meaning, but the hazardous play of dominations' (ibid., p. 376). His focus is to show how a practice is constituted in the present through an analysis of the forces at play in the emergence of that practice. For example, the practice of telling adopted children that they were adopted emerged most forcefully in the post-war era as a paradoxical effect of other practices that aimed at making adoption more secretive and closed. Its emergence was an effect of a number of forceful and competing discourses – one about the fundamental importance of birth origins; one about the need to secure a singular identity; one about the harmful transmission of illegitimacy.

This discussion has emphasised the contribution that genealogy can offer to an adoption field characterised by linear and developmental readings of its history. Veyne (1997, pp. 160–1) clarifies the very different orientation that Foucault introduced into historical analysis:

> Everything hinges on a paradox, one that is Foucault's central and most original thesis. *What is made*, the object, is explained by what went into its *making* at each moment of history; we are wrong to imagine that the *making*, the practice is explained on the basis of what is made. (author's emphasis)

What Veyne captures in the above quotation is the constitutive place of social practices in Foucault's approach to history; it is the processes of making, and not the made, that is his focus. Veyne is also highlighting the constitutive role of paradox in Foucault's historical work, a dimension that makes it most relevant to my exploration of adoption. Writing in a similar critical trajectory, the feminist historian Joan Scott, in her study *Only Paradoxes to Offer*, understands the challenge that reading for paradox poses for more conventional historical analyses.

> Reading for paradox requires a different kind of reading than historians are accustomed to...this technically deconstructive way does not work comfortably with linear narrative or teleology; it tends to undercut those stories that establish the truth or inevitability of certain views of the world by eliminating accounts of conflicts and power within them. (Scott, 1996, pp. 16–17)

Scott elaborates a strategy for the reading of feminist struggle through identifying the paradox of sexual difference that both makes possible and impossible that struggle. In mobilising the concept of paradox, she draws upon two specific meanings, a proposition that is simultaneously true and false and a sign of the capacity to balance complexly contrary thoughts and feelings, whilst emphasising the unresolvable nature at the heart of the concept (Scott, 1996, p. 4).

In turning to my own study, it was clear that the place of original kinship would operate paradoxically in much the way that sexual difference operated in Scott's account. In contemporary western cultures the origin of birth is a dominant form of truth and knowledge through which subjects recognise and form themselves. If the truth of one's being is bound up with this kinship origin, then separation from that origin through adoption will produce an enduring need or wish to recover that truth. Since its legal inception in 1926, adoption practices have consistently produced the adopted child's biological origin as a prior truth and knowledge for the adopted child, whilst simultaneously installing a new set of truths in a new adoptive family, thus inaugurating adoption as a paradoxical form of substitute care. Original kinship makes adoption both possible and impossible in that it has to be both accepted and refuted.

For Scott reading material for paradox has a number of distinct strengths as a form of historical research, which are relevant to my own study (1996, pp. 174–5). First, it illuminates the specificity of unresolvable positions and so casts light upon the recurrent and continuous conflicts surrounding open practices. Second, historical accounts are made more complex and focused in a field prone to generalisations and simplifications. Finally, by subjecting adoption's paradoxes to critical scrutiny there is a more complex appreciation of the difficulties and conflicts that adoption generates.

In using Foucault's genealogical approach, I am wanting to disrupt the commonplace and familiar understandings of adoption in order to open up an enquiry about the conflicted and paradoxical position of open adoption practices. I will be arguing throughout this book that the field of adoption needs to go astray of its dominant understandings and think itself differently and Foucault has an exemplary methodology to engage in such a project. However, it is a methodology that brings a number of challenges for the social work field.

Genealogy and social work

Foucault brought together into a single fold the two poles of the social work profession that are traditionally kept apart, the micro and macro levels of the person and the environment. He made visible the linkage between individual and society: how institutional practices generate social identities, which in turn trigger new knowledges and practices. This approach is a profound departure from social work ways. (Chambon, 1999, p. 56)

The above commentator draws attention to the challenge that a foucauldian methodology poses for the social work field in collapsing the traditional separation between an outside reality and an individual subject. Social work's intellectual heritage has remained largely that of the Enlightenment, with its approaches – positivism, empiricism and humanism – rooted in a belief in progress, scientific method and the certainties and stabilities of human reason. Whilst some areas of social work have been more open to post-structuralist and post-modernist perspectives (see particularly Parton, 1991; Parton et al., 1997; Parton, 1999; Ferguson, 2004), the discipline of adoption has remained largely anchored within universalising and objectifying modernist methodologies, where an objective, verifiable, reality, is 'acted upon' by fully constituted human subjects.[1]

This overarching emphasis on a reliable and stable empiricism has certainly shaped the research culture in the field of adoption. The field has produced and continues to produce a proliferating and diverse literature. Thoburn, in her 1990 review of adoption research, identified eight different categories of adoption studies, making up a literature that she described as both 'voluminous and inadequate' (ibid., p. 4). This intriguing description suggests that this large output somehow falls short, that it does not provide an adequate account of the adoption field. Thoburn's eight categories certainly reveal an exhaustive attempt to cover the field, including historical accounts, guides to both the legal and social work systems, 'How to do it' books, consumer accounts, discussions and critiques of law and/or policy, descriptive studies of placement and agency work and research studies. Thoburn clearly thought in 1990 that this 'voluminous' literature was still not quite grasping some fundamental issue in the field of adoption, that the proliferating research studies speak to a continuing search for a way of 'explaining' adoption, a search that constantly eludes and so is continuously repeated.

This is clearly illustrated by the research on open adoption, a growing body of work that has been emerging since the late 1980s (Borland et al., 1991; Fratter et al., 1991; Ryburn, 1994, 1995, 1996; Fratter, 1996; Neil, 2000; Thoburn et al., 2000; Macaskill, 2002; Smith and Logan, 2004). These studies commonly conceptualise the problematic status of contact with birth family in terms of the adopted child's long-term wellbeing, setting up projects to measure whether such contact will help or hinder the child's development in its new adoptive family. In spite of the growing number of such studies, the call for yet more research, conducted on a greater longitudinal basis with a more rigorous methodology, continues. A recent adoption research survey by Quinton et al. (1997) characteristically concludes: 'so far the findings on contact do not give us *unequivocal answers*...we need *reliable information* to guide decisions on maintaining, supporting and evaluating contact' (ibid., p. 411, my emphasis).

The approach I will be taking in this study stands in marked contrast to that which currently dominates the adoption research field. This adoption research culture situates the individual subject as a unit of explanation and then reads that subject's experience as a reliable and stable indicator of practice. This can be clearly seen in the studies of open adoption, where participant's experiences are used as accurate data to assess whether an open practice is positive or negative for adopted children. Furthermore, these studies remain silent on the implicit measures that they use to categorise and assess individual experience. For example, the studies share a model of the well-adjusted child that is used as a measure for assessing open adoption practices. This measure works to normalise certain kinds of behaviour, for example, open practices help children bond with adopters, and to pathologise other kinds, for example, open practices evoke conflictual feelings towards adopters. Clearly, 'experience' is not a neutral research field, but one which is heavily constructed by certain normalising ideas about family life and parental attachment.

Following Foucault, this study will approach the problematics of open adoption in a very different way. A strength of Foucault's genealogical approach is how it works to expose the practices that shape and form individual experience. As Rose (1998, p. 23) neatly expresses it, Foucault takes what it is to be an individual as the 'site of a historical problem, not the basis for an historical narrative'. In terms of this project, my focus will not be the adoptive participant's experience, but the open practices through which that experience is formed. Consequently, this study will not be making any further contributions to 'measurable' research on open adoption, but instead will seek to understand what the need for such empirical certainty might signify about the place of open practices in the cultural field.

Writing a genealogy of adoption

Tamboukou, in her influential paper 'Writing Genealogies' (1999), identifies three stages in the writing of a genealogy. First, a conflictual problem is identified in the present. Second, the practices that relate to the problem are traced and, finally, a network of relations are formulated that can account for the conflictual status of the problem under investigation (ibid., p. 213). Relating this to my own genealogy of adoption, I have begun by identifying a problem in the present – the contested status of open adoption. This problem will then be unravelled by tracing historically those practices that relate to its conflictual status. Finally, this reading will generate a network of relations that will begin to account for the conflict. This final stage achieves a 'grid of intelligibility' (Dreyfus and Rabinow, 1982, p. 120) that draws into relationship diverse practices from the cultural field (Tamboukou, 1999, p.213), setting up surprising and unexpected connections.

In identifying adoption as my genealogical focus, I am choosing a subject that encompasses those elements that Foucault saw as important to any genealogical work. Dreyfus and Rabinow (1982, p. 120) clarify the foci that Foucault had for his own genealogies, 'cultural practices in which power and knowledge cross and in which our current understanding of the individual, the society and the human sciences are themselves fabricated'. Adoption is a set of practices that intersects with different and divergent institutions and bodies of thought – the law, the family, psychology, social work. As an object of knowledge that straddles the individual and the social, adoption is well placed to cast light upon the constitution of both personal and public spheres. For Foucault these spheres are inextricably linked, as Rose makes clear below:

> The apparently 'public' issue of rationalities of government is fundamentally linked to the apparently 'private' question of how we should behave, how we should regulate our own conduct, how we should judge our behaviour and that of others. (Rose, 1998, p. 77)

Rose links what Foucault would term disciplinary power, that is, how we are acted upon, and individualising power, that is, how we act upon ourselves. For Foucault, the western subject was always formed through this double movement of power and his genealogical works are complex explorations of these two distinct but related technologies of power and of the self. In *Inventing Our Selves*, Rose (1998, p. 26) defines a technology in the following way: 'Human technologies are hybrid assemblages of knowledges, instruments, persons, systems of judgement, buildings and spaces…one can regard the school, the prison, the asylum as examples of one species of such technologies.' He goes on to elaborate how technologies work: '[they] do not simply manufacture and manipulate, but…fundamentally order being, frame it, produce it, make it thinkable as a mode of existence that must be addressed in a particular way' (Rose, 1998, p. 54).

Following this definition, one could understand adoption as an assemblage of knowledges, judgements and practices that both impose and order a particular mode of being on subjects, but also enforce subjects to make themselves in particular ways. This study will trace how techniques of power and techniques of the self work together to produce the technology of adoption within a paradoxical field of deployment. My analysis will show that whilst techniques of power are certainly operative, these techniques are deployed within the instabilities of family relations, where their subversion or transformation is as likely as their implementation. The work of Judith Butler has been particularly helpful in analysing this complex movement of power in the field of adoption. I have drawn on her work in *Excitable Speech* (1997a) and *The Psychic Life of Power* (1997b) at specific points to explore both the productive effects of subjugation on marginalised identities and the public disenfranchising of certain forms of love and loss.

I will be undertaking this genealogy of adoption in two contrasting, but related ways. First, I undertake a genealogical analysis of adoption open practices from its legal inauguration in 1926 through to 2000. This analysis forms Part I of the study and is entitled 'A Genealogy of Adoption'. Second, I conduct a detailed examination of the adoption files of one urban local authority in the period 1989–2000. This exploration forms Part II and is entitled 'The Open Archive'. I will conclude this introductory chapter by outlining the trajectory of my analyses in both Parts I and II of this study.

My historical analysis in Part I will be undertaken through a reading of four distinct narrative perspectives from the adoption field – official policy documents and commentaries, descriptive histories, research studies and user guides for parents and professionals. As my analysis will explore, most of the open forms of practice emerged through the disciplinary terrain of social work practice and get variously defined and implemented within the instabilities of the biological and adoptive familial settings. Whilst the law did sometimes direct the operation of open practices, that direction would often be contested through the normalising operations of social work. Foucault elaborates how differently disciplinary power and the law regulate: 'The discourse of discipline has nothing in common with that of law, rule or sovereign will. The disciplines may well be the carriers of a discourse that speaks of a rule, but this is not the juridical rule ... but a natural rule, a norm' (Foucault, 1980, p. 106). What Foucault describes can be clearly observed in the field of adoption, where laws instructing open practices are rendered impotent by the disciplinary procedures of social workers, whose interventions close down the involvements that the law has permitted. A good example is the pre-war practice of informed consent, a legal requirement that adoption workers both contested and refused to operate. However, it is also conversely the case that open practices contest legal procedures, opening up a field of involvement that the law has worked to prohibit. An obvious example here is the post-war practice of third-party and direct adoptions, where adopters and birth family commonly met and exchanged personal details. This practice was operating in opposition to a legislative directive to conceal adopter's identities, and worked to unsettle the legal move to normalise fully adoptive family life in this period. My analysis will trace the complex movements of power in the field of adoption, showing how juridical and disciplinary rule work together to both permit and prohibit open practices, creating a field of considerable discursive complexity.

Openness in adoption signifies all those practices that disclose the substitutive status of adoption as an experience. The starting point for a genealogy of open practice is to identify the different ways that such disclosure operates. I have identified the following different types: verbal disclosure, where the substitutive nature of the adoption experience is revealed through talking; documentary disclosure, where written information about adoption is transmitted either to the adoptive family or to the biological family; and participatory disclosure, where birth family members are actively and directly involved in the adoption experience. These different types of disclosure produced different forms of open practice at different historical periods. My analysis in Part I will map the emergence, deployment and disappearance of these different forms.

Chapter 2 draws on Foucault's analysis in *History of Sexuality* Volume I (1978) and explores how certain transformations in how power operated to regulate the family in the nineteenth century and worked to eventually produce adoption as an enduringly paradoxical form of childcare. Chapter 3 examines open practices in the period 1926–1945, tracing the inaugurating period of adoption work as it slowly emerged as a professionalised form of substitute care. I analyse the emergence, deployment and disappearance of different forms of pre-war open practices, as adoption acquired its paradoxical mode of operation. Chapter 4 takes these practices into the next period 1945–1970, showing how adoption was transformed into a closed and exclusive service for the provision of infants to infertile parents. I analyse how simultaneous with this move to make post-war adoption both secretive and confidential there were also practices that included the participation of the birth family, thus consolidating adoption as a paradoxical form of care in this period. Chapter 5 examines the period 1970–1985 and analyses how the convergence of adoption and public childcare in the 1970s worked to change the way that adoption was both structured and regulated.

I explore how an aggressively interventionist child protection discourse powerfully intersected with adoption's own exclusionary and inclusionary practices, laying the ground for the contested advent of 'open adoption' in the late 1980s. Chapter 6 covers the period 1980–2000 and traces the emergence of open adoption practices from out of the convergence of a number of paradoxical discourses that circulated in the 1980s. This discursive complexity produced the contested implementation of open adoption in the 1990s. I analyse the way that debates in support and against open adoption drew their arguments from the same technology of attachment.

Part II of this study is a more detailed and focused exploration of the era of open adoption 1990–2000. Whilst Part I of this study argues for a far-reaching continuity in both open and closed practices since adoption's legal inauguration, Part II considers whether the advent of open adoption marked the emergence of something particular and different. This question is addressed by drawing upon my work in the adoption archive of one urban local authority, where I analysed adoption files in the period 1989–2000 to trace the emergence and deployment of two forms of open adoption, letterbox and direct contact. Alongside this focus on tracing how these practices emerge, I also conduct an analysis of the different technologies of the adopted subject that are mobilised to account for decision-making about those practices. This latter analysis draws more directly upon Foucault's last work on technologies of the self, where he became more focused on how subjects form themselves within available regimes of truth/knowledge:

> One could take up the question of governmentality from a different angle: the government of the self by oneself in its articulation with relations with others (such as one finds in pedagogy, behaviour counselling, spiritual direction, the prescriptions of modes of living and so on). (Foucault, 1997b, p. 88)

Subjects of adoption, parent, worker and child, constantly articulate and produce themselves through a network of familial and professional relationships that are governed by particular regimes of truth. Foucault (1997c, p. 289) has been particularly concerned in his genealogies to trace out the 'problem of the relationship between subject and truth', showing how the modern self emerges out of certain familial and cultural injunctions to know the truth about one self: 'In every culture this self-technology implies a set of truth obligations: discovering the truth, being enlightened by truth, telling the truth. All these are considered important either for the constitution of, or the transformation of, the self' (Foucault, 1997a, pp. 177–8).

As I have already discussed, contemporary subjects form themselves through regimes of truth bound up with original kinship and the origins of birth, regimes within which adoption is paradoxically produced. In my local authority archive study I will be considering how far open adoption practices enable subjects to acquire and transform themselves in truths that are not reducible to the rules governing this technology of adoption. It is my contention that open adoption practices are indicative of a certain radical promise, a potential break with this dominant regime of truth/knowledge – that children developmentally acquire a singular original identity through living with their biological family consistently for the period of their childhood and adolescence. Adoption is an effect of the hegemonic position of the biological family, but also a potential resistance to its particular ways of inscribing belonging. My archive study considers how far open adoption practices further impel that resistance by generating a different technology of the adopted subject. In exploring this I will be drawing upon the following questions:

- Do these practices create new history or restage old history?
- Are children's biographies transformed or re-centred in former birth narratives by letter and direct contact?
- Are letters and photographs hermeneutical tools or do they operate differently?
- Does the transmission of information about birth family 'build up' an adopted child's prior history or construct new history?
- And finally how far do open adoption practices break with the dominant technology of adoption and produce a different kind of subject.

Chapter 7 introduces my local authority archive work and my use of Foucault's *Hermeneutics of the Subject* (2005). Chapters 8 and 9 explore how the local authority both define and implement the open adoption practices of letterbox and direct contact. Chapter 10 draws together the main research findings of this study. It also considers what relevance the study has to contemporary open practices in adoption social work today.

2

Family as Cause and Cure: The Emergence of Adoption

I want to begin this chapter by evoking a picture of the unmarried mother from the 1860s, taken from a study by the French historian Barret-Ducrocq (1992). She describes how in the mid-nineteenth century, unmarried and deserted working-class women approached the Thomas Coram Foundling hospital to have their illegitimate babies permanently or temporarily looked after elsewhere.

> The internal rules of the establishment required an unmarried mother wishing to place her child permanently, or for a limited period of time, to conform to certain criteria. She had to be able to show that her good faith had been betrayed, that she had given way to carnal passion only after a promise of marriage or against her will; that she therefore had no other children; and that her conduct had always been irreproachable in every other respect. She must also be without any sort of material aid. Finally the child had to be under one year old. This was thought the best way of ensuring that the children would be brought up under good conditions and of promoting the moral rehabilitation of single women deserted by their seducers. (1992, pp. 40–1)

Here we can glimpse some of the principles that will inaugurate adoption some 80 years later, the relinquishment of a child voluntarily for its moral 'good'; the rehabilitation of the fallen woman through such relinquishment; the archiving of the circumstances of the birth history; the securing of the woman's basically good nature; an assessment regarding her ability to support a child. However, at this time there was no move to regulate illegitimacy through the legal intervention of adoption. Illegitimate children would be either boarded out with substitute carers or more commonly placed in a residential institution. Yet, in the early 1920s, some 80 years later, the illegitimate child began to be understood as a 'problem' that adoption could address. What happened in that space of time to effect such a transformation in child welfare policy and practice?

The emergence of adoption as a solution to illegitimacy has to be understood as an effect of a number of transformations that took place in the nineteenth century. Drawing on Foucault's analysis in *History of Sexuality*, Volume I (1978), this chapter will explore those changes that were central to the eventual inauguration of adoption in 1926. The construction of illegitimacy as a social problem emerged gradually through the nineteenth century, gathering momentum within a complex matrix of other cultural transformations. The historical vignette from 1860 already signals a cultural concern with illegitimacy, responded to with a welfare practice to separate the illegitimate child from the immorality of its birth origins. For Foucault the concerns sketched out in this brief extract, bad blood, the primacy of sexuality, the irreducibility of childhood origins, the state as pastoral intervention, are the signifiers of new ways that power was operating to shape and form human experience in the Victorian era. This chapter will discuss how these changes not only led to the establishment of adoption in the 1920s, but how these transformations worked to produce adoption as an enduringly paradoxical form of childcare.

From sanguinity to sex: the new technology of sexuality

During the nineteenth century, you begin to see that sexual behaviour was important for a definition of the individual self ... the idea of characterising individuals through their sexual behaviour or desire is not to be found, or very rarely, before the nineteenth century. (Foucault, 1997d, pp. 127–8)

In the above interview Foucault is suggesting that the nineteenth century witnessed a transformation in how subjects were both understood and regulated. Prior to 1900, the illegitimate child and the fallen woman would not have been categorised as sexually deviant, but by mid-century both had acquired an identity rooted in unpermissible sexual practices, making guidance and welfare intervention necessary. In *History of Sexuality* Foucault is tracing how this new technology of sexuality emerged as an effect of what he termed bio-power, a concept that describes a process whereby individuals and populations are simultaneously regulated. Rabinow and Dreyfus (1982, p. 140) clarify how these two dimensions – control of the individual body and control of the species – are brought together through the construct of sex. 'Sex was a means of access both to the life of the body and the life of the species ... this new technology of sex ... combined in varying proportions the objectives of disciplining the body and that of regulating populations' (ibid., p. 146).

The nineteenth century produced sexuality as its dominant form of power by moving it into the home. The bourgeois family assumed a central position in this double move to regulate the life of both the individual and of the population, becoming the interchange, the meeting place, of the old system of alliance and the new one of sexuality (Foucault 1978, p. 108). As Foucault makes clear throughout *History of Sexuality*, the deployment of sexuality was initially bourgeois; the working class managed to escape its disciplinary and regulatory power for at least half of the nineteenth century (ibid., p. 121). The ways that sexuality was deployed through working-class culture was of fundamental importance to the eventual emergence of adoption and I will return to this at a later point. For the present, I want to focus on the deployment of sexuality within the middle-class family as this will have considerable bearing on how the working-class family was later transformed.

Foucault traces the emergence and establishment of the bourgeois family as a key site for the transmission of social values organised around the immediate blood tie of its membership: 'the bourgeoisie ... looked to its progeny and the health of its organism when it laid claim to a specific body. The bourgeoisie's blood was its sex' (1978, p. 124). This injunction to know yourself through your immediate familial blood tie was the central way that the expanding middle classes legitimated themselves in the new industrialised era. Strathern, in *After Nature* (1992, p.100), captures very well this bourgeois drive to secure the sanctity of the domestic space in the absence of any hereditary birth status: 'Middle-class culture could not be promoted through the rhetoric of birth ... it could not elevate family fortunes to noble estates. It addressed itself instead to small-scale connections and to the social self-sufficiency of the domestic unit.'

As the century progressed, there would be a multiplicity of projects linked to the production of the healthy bourgeois family unit and a constant war against 'the menaces of heredity' (ibid., p. 127). For the middle classes, a healthy sexuality was valued in the same way that the nobility valued the hereditary line of descent. Here, knowing who you were was inextricably bound up with knowing where you had come from. As Foucault (1978, p. 118) makes clear below:

> the analysis of hereditary was placing sex (sexual relations, venereal diseases, matrimonial alliances, perversions) in a position of 'biological responsibility' with regard to the species: not only could sex be affected by its own diseases, it could also, if it was not controlled, transmit diseases or create others that would afflict future generations.

This concern with preserving the sexual health of the bourgeois family led to a range of medical and political projects for managing marriage and birth for fear that sexual perversion would deplete the line of descent. Here truth and knowledge were bound up with the origin of birth – the importance of knowledge about one's origins and the importance of having a true origin. Within this, illegitimacy was constructed as a threat with all its uncertainties regarding the paternal origin and its challenge to the newly evolving marital family unit. Welfare practices that emerged to address the problem of illegitimacy were paradoxically situated in a culture where original kinship had assumed the status of truth and knowledge for the individual subject.

The emergence of childhood and the inner self

Foucault understood the production of sexuality and the production of childhood as inextricably connected emergences in the nineteenth century, transforming how subjects were both governed and understood (1978, p. 31). He elaborates this connection: 'in the nineteenth century sexuality was sought out in the smallest details of individual existence ... it was suspected of underlying the least follies, it was traced back into the earliest years of childhood; it became the stamp of individuality' (ibid., p. 146).

What Foucault traces in *History of Sexuality* is how the idea of the modern self, a subject with a childhood history rooted in the sexualised life of its parents, became established first in the bourgeois family. Securing an individual history was of fundamental importance in the establishment of the bourgeois family line, reflecting the nineteenth century's enormous concern with history as a mode of analysis and a way of organising life: 'the new mode of relation between history and life: in this dual position of life that placed it at the same time outside history, in its biological environment, and inside human historicity' (ibid., p. 143).

It was through the assumption of its 'historicity' that this new concept of the subject emerged, a subject who had acquired a childhood history through which self meaning was produced and embedded. Early life was now a point of origin and foundation, not only for the human subject, but also for the social order. Not only did the nineteenth century provide its citizens with a childhood history, but this history was understood as an internalised realm within the subject, a source of inner truth, knowledge and guidance. Carolyn Steedman (1994, p.

12) emphasises how throughout the period the essence of an organism, a body or a soul was felt to be interior and that this sense of interiority was fundamental in understanding the new technology of self that was taking shape: 'the modern self is imagined as being inside – the self within, created by the laying down and accretion of our own childhood experience, our own history, in a place inside.'

There was an increasing interest in the child as adult in embryo, with a nature that would need protecting, nurturing and educating if it was to achieve its full adult potential (Aries, 1996; Steedman, 1994). As the nineteenth century progressed, a more robust place was created for both the concept of childhood – a time-specific experience that all children should enjoy – and a family life that would ensure the production of the right kind of childhood development (Piper, 1999, p. 36). It was this recognition of the singularity of children's natures that led to an increasing move to separate children from adult company. The increasing importance of this separation, and what it implied about the corrupting effects of adults on children, would eventually lead to a whole range of welfare practices to protect children.

I want to now explore how this new technology of self was deployed into working-class life, as this deployment was central in establishing very particular child welfare practices. The possibility of adoption will depend on the ways that the working-class family was assimilated into the familial culture of the middle classes, becoming an object of both scrutiny and intervention by the 1880s. Foucault contends that the working classes were 'penetrated' by the new 'mechanism of sexualisation' at three key points, two of which emerged in the nineteenth century, the 1830s and the 1880s (1978, pp. 121–2). Following Foucault, my discussion will focus on these two latter moments of 'penetration'. What distinguishes these two periods is the very different ways that child welfare was constructed; in the earlier period intervention was always focused on children living outside of the family, whereas by the end of the nineteenth century, it became possible to intervene into children's lives within the family. Through exploring these two moments, it will become clearer how adoption became possible by the 1920s.

The deployment of sexuality into working-class life

1) Mid century – the family as cure

> The organization of the 'conventional' family came to be regarded, sometime around the eighteen-thirties, as an indispensable instrument of political control and economic regulation for the subjugation of the urban proletariat: there was a great campaign for the 'moralization of the poorer classes.' (Foucault, 1978, p. 122)

The mid-century campaign to 'moralise' the working classes turned around a range of social interventions that were aimed at establishing the new bourgeois family as a cultural measure for conduct and behaviour. Both Barret-Ducrocq (1992, p. 181) and Ferguson (2004, p. 29) describe the increasing move in the nineteenth century to bring the 'otherness' of working-class culture, with its more informal and communal attitudes to courtship, extra-marital sex and illegitimacy, into the dominant familial discourse of the era.

Foucault identifies two effects of industrialisation that were demanding this very specific form of surveillance by mid-century. First, acute problems of urban overcrowding leading to the spread of disease and, second, an accelerated development of urban industry requiring a stable and healthy labour force (1978, p. 126). Enclosing the urban poor within the family structure depended on establishing regimes that removed their presence from the streets and enforced the familiarisation of their lives. Foucault outlines how the supposed mid-century reforms, restrictions on child labour, public hygiene, housing, schooling, were effects of this move to bring the working classes within the new culture of family life (ibid., p. 126). There was a related move to stabilise the idea that children needed to be privately enclosed in the family home, reflected in legislation to reduce and then eradicate child labour and to separate children from adults in the poor law system (Parker 1990, p. 10).

It is important to emphasise here that the family, without support and intervention from the outside, was understood as a regulatory institution. As Fergusson (2004, p. 36) makes clear, the family was a civilising environment, in and of itself, which should inculcate the right kind of morality to the uncivilised urban poor: 'They [the working classes] were subject to new codes of social regulation that extolled the sanctity of the civilising home and the dangers of the street.' The relative newness of the bourgeois family made its claims of belonging far too precarious to allow outside intervention into its internal workings. The family occupied a place of foundational importance in Victorian society, but this place depended on its functioning as a private and autonomous unit. For much of the nineteenth century, intervention into its internal life was considered both undesirable and unnecessary. It was understood to be the right moral place for the raising of children, with parents the unproblematic transmitters of these moral values. Whilst it is clear that parents were held responsible for their children's natures, this is not in the modern sense of a psychological relationship. For much of the century it was the moral climate of family life that was considered important and this is central in understanding the move to assimilate the working classes into this familial culture – the poor would be regulated by the moralising regimes of family life, so the central issue was ensuring that the idea of family was established amongst the urban working classes. What happened within the family was not at this point a focus in welfare work.

The move to extend family life to the urban poor immediately produced those on its outside as a social concern. A key point in Foucault's analysis in *History of Sexuality* is how the family was always productive of what he terms 'peripheral sexualities'; it did not simply produce the promised norms of its apparent purpose (ibid., p. 47). Those living outside of the mainstream conjugal family were specified as separate and so constructed as problematic and in need of intervention. Foucault's argument is that such a move intensifies, incites and incorporates a whole cast of working-class figures to better control and regulate: 'This new persecution of the peripheral sexualities entailed an incorporation of perversions and a new specification of individuals' (ibid., pp. 42–3).

For the first time, then, a number of figures entered the cultural scene as 'welfare problems'. The welfare regimes that were focused on the street and the public space made visible a range of concerns that were constructed as requiring philanthropic and charitable intervention. The working child, the street child and the illegitimate child were increasingly produced as social problems because their position in the factory, on the streets and outside of the family made them un-childlike and dangerously 'other' to the prevailing moral order. It is important to emphasise two aspects to the emergence of early social work mid-century. First, as many commentators have noted (Parker, 1990; Piper, 1999; Fergusson, 2003) it was children visibly outside of any family structure who were the object of intervention and, second, the removal of children from the 'immorality' of non-family environments was a priority.

Up until the end of the nineteenth century, reformers did not clearly delineate between different categories of children in child welfare work. The illegitimate child, the orphaned child and the delinquent street child were all viewed as one group, outside the family and in need of intervention. What differentiated the illegitimate child was the way its position outside the family was understood, a difference that would eventually be central to how adoption was inaugurated. I will return to this below, but first I want to outline more generally the emergence of child welfare practices mid-century.

The philanthropic societies that emerged in the 1850s and 1860s developed their work with deserted and orphaned children with the express purpose of breaking them away from the immoral influences of their working -class backgrounds. Commentators have noted (Heywood, 1965; Packman, 1975; Parker, 1990; Triseliotis et al., 1995) that children who were separated from their home environments did not keep up ties or links with any member of their home community. Heywood (1965, p. 87) in commenting on this ethos cites the Mundella Committee of 1896 on the purposes of boarding out children: 'To aid it to forget its alien birth and to merge it in the foster family is a cardinal principle of boarding out.' It was the removal of the child from an immoral environment that was the central concern and finding a better environment the most pressing task. As parenting was not viewed as a psychological undertaking, but the provision of a certain moral culture, it was not necessarily new parents that the child was judged to need, but a new moral environment. Thus early child welfare work made the provision of a better moral environment the priority, something that could be offered by an institution, by emigration or by apprenticeship, as much as by boarding out with a family.

It was the *absence* of parents that made it possible to both remove the child into alternative care and break the child's links with its former life. I emphasise this because of the constitutive importance of parental presence or absence in the reaching of these decisions. Removal and severance were predicated on a parent being absent or dead. This was an era where parental responsibility was taken very seriously, both inside and outside the marital family. It was a tie not lightly broken and parents were under acute pressure to be responsible for their dependents. Indeed, the boarding out orders of 1870 and 1877 privileged the biological family as the place for the raising of children, even when not functioning well. George (1970, p. 26) cites an 1869 poor law report emphasising how fostering should not destabilise the fundamental place of the biological family: 'It is most important on all grounds to avoid severing or weakening in any way the ties of family, even where, owing to the character of the parents, it be thought that children could be benefited by removal from their control.'

It is clear that the idea of family as a morally curative and regulatory institution was too fundamental to the social order for its functioning to be questioned in any way. If children were living within a family setting, they could not be defined as welfare problems within the prevailing understandings of welfare mid-century.

It is at this point that I want to consider the position of the illegitimate child, who was differently situated in terms of family to the orphaned child or the street child. These latter welfare subjects had parents absent through death or desertion, whereas the illegitimate child commonly had a living parent present in their lives. Whilst the illegitimate child was outside the family and therefore a case for welfare intervention, there was a parent with responsibility for it. This presented the mid-century state with a problem: the severing of parental responsibility was not yet part of its regulatory or disciplinary function, yet illegitimacy was increasingly constructed as a contaminating and indelible legacy from which children needed saving. Here we see an altogether different strategy enter child welfare work and one which would gather momentum in social work practices over the next 100 years – parental consent to a child's removal. If we recall the extract at the beginning of this chapter, the unmarried mother is giving permission for the removal and placing of her child. This permission is central to the illegitimate child's reception into the institution, the permission signifying the relinquishment of parental responsibility. The State did not intervene directly to sever or remove parental responsibility, but its moralising discourses exercised coercive pressure on unmarried mothers to relinquish 'voluntarily' their responsibilities towards their child. This is well illustrated by Barret-Ducrocq (1992, pp. 155–6) in her discussion of the 1834 poor law's role in promoting the new family ethos and constructing illegitimacy as a moral danger. This legislation had a clause that withdrew the previous right to subsistence for unmarried mothers and their infants thus forcing able-bodied women to leave their children in the workhouse and seek work. This clause had a number of effects: it disciplined and punished those members of the social body that lived outside of its familial culture; it enforced an illegitimate child's separation from the contaminating effects of its immoral origins and it created a population of deserted children who could be more easily the subjects of welfare intervention.

It was already apparent that by mid-century there was an emergent paradoxical thinking in early child welfare work; the removal of children from a dead or absent parent was a routine practice, yet the responsibility of parents for children was not lightly interrupted. Whilst the placing of children into some form of substitute care might be absolute in that they were never reunited with their families of origin, their biological kinship would remain intact. Commentators often describe such arrangements as de facto adoptions, a term that speaks to a certain permanent change in parentage. However, the permanency of such arrangements never led to a transfer of parentage; this was an era that accorded such a foundational place to the blood tie of birth that it could not be severed in the way that adoption would eventually offer.

Given the idealised place that the family occupied for much of the century, it is paradoxical how little it figured in substitute care for children. Below I have summarised the four critical issues that worked to circumvent the family as a form of substitute care.

First, only children outside of the family setting had their lives open to intervention. The family occupied such an idealised position at the heart of society that its internal functioning was not for public scrutiny. It was anyway assumed that its functioning depended on an inviolable privacy. Social attention first focused on those errant figures outside the family – the immoral unmarried mother and the abandoned or deserted child. The family – even when its members were engaged in abuse or cruelty – was considered beyond public intervention. Second, and following on from the above point, matters of child welfare were more focused on cruelties of the public space, rather than cruelties of the domestic home. The quality of parenting was generally disregarded, while the focus of reform and intervention would be the immorality of the environment – the factory floor, the street, the slum dwelling, the illegitimate birth. Third, parenting was about providing the right moral environment and less about a psychological relationship. Reformers of the era did not understand child welfare in terms of early parenting and emotional attachments. It followed then that in child welfare work the priority would be the provision of a better moral climate and this could be found in an institutional setting as much as in a substitute family. Finally, for children deprived of the benefits of family life, substitute family care was still uncommon and when provided was only for children with no parental ties. The family was such an idealised and untouched space at the centre of Victorian society that it could not be easily simulated or substituted and its kinship ties not easily severed.

Clearly, this was not a culture where adoption was possible; there would need to be two transformations in the concept of family before adoption could become a substitute form of care: the family would need to become a place for public intervention and parenting would need to become a primary psychological task in the production of children's natures. This emergence of a self rooted in a formative and foundational familial origin would be fundamental to the shaping of child welfare policies at the end of the century, leading to the paradoxical possibility of adoption.

2) Late century – the family as cause and cure

> It was in the 'bourgeois' or 'aristocratic' family that the sexuality of children and adolescents was first problematised, and feminine sexuality medicalised; it was the first to be alerted to the potential pathology of sex, the urgent need to keep it under watch and to devise a rational technology of correction. (Foucault 1978, p. 120)

For much of the nineteenth century the family was the untouched moral centre of the social body, with pathology located outside of its idealised regulatory function. What Foucault describes above is a change in the way that the family was understood to operate, a change that made the family itself the site for pathology and dysfunction. This marked a very important transformation in how power operated. Foucault (2000b, p. 216) traces how the family moved from being a model *for* government to being an instrument *of* government, a move which will make intervention into the family both necessary and desirable: 'The family becomes ... the privileged instrument for the government of the population and not the chimerical model of good government.'

Class was a significant structuring force in how outside intervention operated to regulate family life; the middle-class family and the working-class family were subject to very different regulatory processes. Foucault (1978, p. 130) describes how the regulation of the middle-class family through the growth of psychological services and the regulation of the working-class family through child protection procedures were different, but simultaneous outside interventions: 'We must not forget that the discovery of the Oedipus complex was contemporaneous with the juridical organisation of loss of parental authority (in France this was formulated in the laws of 1889 and 1898).' The middle-class family would be subject to the medical/psychotherapeutic gaze, whilst the working-class family would be subject to a legal and policing intervention. I want to briefly outline the trajectories of these different forms of intervention, as together they made possible the eventual emergence of adoption.

The psychologising and problematising of family relations began with the middle classes and it was not until the post-war period that the working-class family 'acquired' a psychological life (see Chapter 4). This transformation to middle-class family relations was achieved through what Foucault has termed 'pastoral power'. This is a form of power that takes charge of the individual subject from the inside, regulating the production of a conscience, governing through the normalising techniques of welfare concerns and educational programmes. Put simply, regimes of self-governance became the primary way of regulating the middle-class subject. Campaigns to transform the sexual conduct of the bourgeois family targeted three specific areas – the sexuality of children, the sexuality of women and demography, the regulation of births (Foucault, 1978, pp. 116–17). What Foucault makes clear is how the bourgeois family would need outside intervention in order to regulate the precarious production of the right kind of sexual subject. Peripheral sexualities were now produced within as well as outside of the family, making intervention both necessary and vital. These errant by-products of family life – the hysterical woman, the masturbating child – were the subjects of all kinds of medical attentions: psychiatric consultation; incarceration; psychoanalysis.

A central family project was the production and disciplining of childhood sexuality, with the illegitimate child now understood as a product of a sexuality that had not been guided along the right and proper channels by parents within the family. Foucault (1978, p. 104) describes how in this period childhood became a paradoxical state, where the child was situated as both natural and unnatural in its sexual activity.

> Children were defined as 'preliminary' sexual beings, on this side of sex, yet within it, astride a dangerous dividing line. Parents, families, educators, doctors and eventually psychologists would have to take charge, in a continuous way, of this precious and perilous, dangerous and endangered sexual potential.

Here Foucault captures very well two narratives of childhood produced during this era. There was the child as innocence, the not yet sexual subject, and there was the child as sexually knowing, anticipating the sexual potential of its adult future. Illegitimacy, a signifier of a sexuality that had escaped from the civilising confines of the conjugal home, would be a dangerous exposure to this newly sexualised concept of the child.

Central to the transformation I am outlining would be the new way that parenting was understood, a transformation of fundamental importance to the emergence of new child welfare practices. Parents begun to be understood as active agents in the production of their children's natures and for this reason parenting – or rather mothering – assumed more and more importance. This new emphasis on parental responsibility made it possible to believe that the parent's virtues and vices would be transmitted to the child, for better or for worse. This marked a very important change for child welfare practices. Once it was established that parenting was responsible for the way that children were formed, it then becomes possible to construct the category of 'bad/failing' parent, who should not be allowed parenting responsibilities and from whom children should be protected. Furthermore, it also made possible the category good parent, who could operate as a substitute for those children in need of corrective psychological nurture. By the end of the nineteenth century the middle-class family had become the locus for both the production of normal sexuality and its pathological forms, a precarious and unstable site for the transmission of social values and rules, a space for the production of both failed and successful subjects. This was the point when the deployment of sexuality spread through the entire social body (Foucault, 1978, p. 122).

This emergence of the newly psychologised bourgeois family had little discursive effect on how working-class life was constituted:

> There was a long period during which children were regarded as essentially malleable, at least as long as they could be removed from detrimental surroundings and pernicious influences. They were thought capable of forgetting the past and making a new start, but that such 'renewal' required conducive environments in which retraining could be accomplished. (Parker, 1990, pp. 12–13)

Parker describes a very particular technology of the working-class subject, whereby original kinship was not constituted as a source of knowledge or truth and where the past was not operative in securing the present self. As the preceding section discussed, this technology can be clearly seen in the welfare practices that were operative right through the nineteenth century with working-class communities. Both institutional care and fostering deployed practices of removing and severing the child from its corrupt working-class environment. Whilst for much of the century the working-class family was *not* a site of intervention, it was clear that this technology would enable a child's unproblematic removal when such intervention emerged as desirable. By the late 1880s the removal of children from their working-class families became a new form of intervention, understood as neither troubling nor traumatising for the 'malleable' and unattached working-class recipient. Whilst separation and attachment were slowly assuming a central psychic role in middle-class mothering (Rose, 1989, pp. 158–61), within the working-class family the breaking of the parental relation was accorded little psychological significance in child removal practices. This enabled the welfare services to directly intervene into working-class family life in a very new way, as I will discuss below.

The two forms of intervention that I have outlined – a gentle pastoral intervention for the bourgeois family and a coercive policing intervention for the working-class family – speak to a considerable paradoxical transformation in how the family was understood. By the end of the century it had become a site for public intervention, a cause of childhood damage, but also a place of psychological transmission, a cure for childhood disturbance. I now want to trace how it became possible to intervene into the sanctity of the family by the end of the nineteenth century.

Commentators have drawn attention to a variety of social and political factors that led to the family becoming a target for public intervention. Williams (1989) identified a number of factors that put into question the previously laissez-faire approach to the family. She argues that there was a growing concern about the state of the family that had been produced by a number of international scenes where Britain was seen to be failing. Its industrial supremacy was being challenged by the United States and Japan; its imperial power was being rivalled by Germany; its army had been exposed as weak and inadequate in the Boer War and Irish Home Rule conflicts (1989, pp. 154–5). Williams argues that this crisis, coupled with a declining birth rate, focused attention on the family as currently failing in its role of efficient social reproduction. The solution was a range of welfare reforms, which saw the state more directly intervening to regulate and discipline domestic life, producing a new role for the family in general and motherhood specifically (ibid., p. 157). Mothering began to assume an increasingly symbolic role – mother of the race, the nation – reconfirming the sanctity of certain forms of the family and making those on the outside, that is, the illegitimate, the non-white, the failing parent, more marginal, more pathologised and in need of corrective intervention (ibid., p. 157). Williams describes the way that the working classes were led to identify with the project of nationalism and consequently reject as unpatriotic and un-English the liberatory political movements around class and race (ibid., p. 156). The relevance of this was that it became possible to define working-class families into discrete groupings – bad and failing or respectable and good, opening up the possibility of selective regulation of certain kinds of family life. The family was no longer a universal ideal, but retained the potential to become ideal with the right kinds of support and intervention.

From a more foucauldian perspective, Piper (1999, p. 39) interrogates why it took the Victorian reformers so long to intervene in matters of domestic abuse and cruelty, given both its prevalence and the existence of a reform agenda. She is not convinced that intervention into family life in the 1880s was necessarily because of threats to the moral order, a commonly cited reason by mainstream commentators. Neither does she subscribe to the other common view (e.g., Parker 1990) that the various reform agendas – the pioneering child welfare work of the Christian philanthropic societies; the suffragette movement, where the interests of women were closely allied to the welfare of children, and the introduction of compulsory education – led to the eventual perception of family abuses of children. She cites a long history of complete failure to intervene into the privacy of the family, arguing that such intervention was held to be a greater evil than child abuse, such was the status given to the family as an autonomous cornerstone of the social order. Piper argues that in order for the child to be seen as a victim of cruel parents, the family unit itself had to be constructed as a threat to the moral system 'greater than the threat posed by intervening in that family' (1999, p. 43). Thus intervention into the family, far from undermining or compromising its importance, paradoxically underlined that importance as so central to the social order that it could not be left to self-regulation: 'Various social and political anxieties prompted the construction of intervention in the family as a lesser evil than undermining the entire moral framework of society which is what might happen unless selected families were regulated' (ibid., p. 46).

It was not until the late 1880s that legislation was passed to allow intervention into the working-class family with the 1889 Prevention of Cruelty to and Protection of Children Act. 'What were previously seen as deaths explainable by disease and hazardous social conditions, began to be reframed in terms of a new conception of parental responsibility in child welfare' (Ferguson, 2004, pp. 37–8). This legislation immediately created a distinction that in terms of childcare provision had not been operative before; the illegitimate child became a separate category from the abused or neglected child. Whilst early child welfare agencies thought both illegitimate and abused children were in need of protection, this need was differently constructed by the end of the century. Welfare practices around illegitimacy were still consensual, the illegitimate child was relinquished and not removed from the care of its mother, whereas the abused or neglected child, for the first time, was taken into protective custody without the co-operation or permission of the biological parents. Up until this legislation children were only taken into the care of the state if deserted or orphaned, in other words, if parents were irreducibly absent. This legislation *made* parents absent by removing children from their care. Cretney (1998, p. 186) discusses this issue:

> The Poor Law Act 1899 provided that the guardians could in certain circumstances assume by resolution all the parents' rights and powers until the child reached the age of 18; and the guardians were then empowered to arrange for the child to be 'adopted'... the adopters acquired a measure of protection against any claim by the child's natural parents.

What was critical in the above situation was how the state held back from instituting a complete severance of parental responsibilities from those parents who were subject to state intervention against their wishes. The policy of removing children from the damaging association of their parents did not lead to the total severance that would be eventually offered by full legal adoption. The neglected or damaged child might well leave their family home, temporarily or permanently, but they did not lose their kinship status with that family. What they did lose, however, was any contact with that family.

This emergence of coercive intervention into working-class family life signified how far the family had become a site of radical reshaping, an open and porous social structure that could be changed. By the 1880s the family had been transformed into an institution that could be modified or replicated, making possible both intervention into the family and substitution for it. Indeed, as Foucault makes very clear, by the 1890s outside intervention was integral to its functioning as family – the boundaries of its privacy had been re-drawn to include a whole cast of public figures from doctors and health visitors to social workers and psychiatrists. Once it was possible to intervene into biological families, then the previously sacrosanct place that the parent occupied had been weakened; kinship was no longer its own authority, but subject to the intercession of outside authorities. Parenting was now a practice that required a whole range of supports because it was now regarded as central to the formation of a child's character.

By the end of the nineteenth century it began to be possible to think about a child's well-being in terms of the quality of its family life, whereas for much of the preceding era this link between child and parent was not only outside of public scrutiny, but also not theorised in psychological terms. The new centrality of parents in the production of their children's natures would have three effects: it would make parents responsible for the psychological disturbances of their children, it would make possible intervention into failing families to save children and it would make the family a substitute compensatory experience for children.

Illegitimacy was reconfigured in the light of these changes in how parenting was understood. The psychological responsibility of parents for children constructed illegitimacy as a sexually immoral transmission to a child, disturbing its sexuality into the wrong channels and making its removal to new parents a reparative necessity. This immediately opened up the possibility of substitute kinship.

However, the place of original kinship was considered so fundamental that it could only be relinquished with consent and not transferred against family wishes. As we will see below, adoption was inaugurated as a substitution for that which the illegitimate child lacked – a proper biological family. Yet, the open practices with the family of origin that adoption has always sustained worked to destabilise and expose this substitution, reinscribing the importance of the very blood tie that adoption was meant to replace and simulate. This emergence of the family as a paradoxical site, both cause and cure for social immorality and dysfunction, is central in understanding adoption's paradoxical inauguration. It is to this that I will now turn.

The inauguration of adoption

The vignette with which this chapter began described an unmarried mother seeking welfare help for her illegitimate child in the 1860s. At that time, the form of help on offer was the removal of the child from her care, but not the removal of her legal status as mother. The inauguration of adoption 80 years later would radically change this form of welfare support through not only removing the child, but also by severing its parentage. This radical intervention was neither easily nor quickly introduced. There was a caution and reluctance surrounding the introduction of legal adoption, reflected in the number of committees that were formed to debate its desirability at the beginning of the 1920s. This reluctance to introduce adoption was a reluctance to intervene so dramatically into the kinship ties of biological birth. As already discussed, welfare practices in this era were newly intervening into family life, but only to separate children from their parents, not to sever and transfer the kinship tie. Legal adoption marked a very new intervention into the life of the family at a time when the family was still very new to intervention.

The campaign for adoption legislation was led by the new societies that had been formed to provide a service to unwanted, usually illegitimate children. These early adoption societies had their origins in the philanthropic movements of the nineteenth century, a lineage which was central to how adoption would emerge. The strongly embedded child rescue ethos of these societies viewed the illegitimate child as much in need of saving as the abused or neglected child. The fledgling adoption societies had been campaigning for adoption in order to give greater legal security to parents who had taken in illegitimate children on a fostering basis.

Commentators (Kornitzer, 1952; Heywood, 1965; Benet, 1976; Triseliotis et al., 1997) have traced this demand for adoption to an increase in illegitimate births after the First World War. Heywood (1965, pp. 114–15) notes that in 1918 illegitimate births made up over 6 per cent of all live births, creating a pressing social problem. It is my contention that the introduction of adoption was less a response to a demographic increase in illegitimate births and more a reflection of the growing importance of the family in securing a certain kind of development based on a particular way of belonging. The adoption societies pioneered an adoption practice based on the careful reproduction of the heterosexual family unit. It was clear that their emphasis on legal status derived from this very particular conception of family life. This could be seen when the societies highlighted two major concerns if children's status was not secured by a legal transfer of parentage: Unscrupulous parents would reclaim their children when they became old enough to be economically useful and that there could be a return to the baby farming scandals of the nineteenth century (Tomlin Report, 1926, pp. 4–5).

Through citing the twin dangers associated with the fostering of children, the societies were making two clear points about the superiority of adoption as a form of family life. First, the child could be permanently rooted in a substitute family, beyond the claims of blood and, second, it would be loved as a kinship member, rather than wanted for the economic reward that it brought.

Clearly, such reasoning emerged from the new emphasis on parenting as central to the formation of children's natures. Children now not only needed protection from the attentions of 'bad parents', but the benefits of the loving environment provided by married 'good parents'. By the 1920s illegitimacy was constructed as sufficiently stigmatising to need its eradication by a legal transfer of birth heritage. This is exemplified by Heywood's (1965, p. 116) contention that the social stigma of illegitimacy was so great that it led to a neglect and deprivation of babies born out of wedlock. Adoption, through severing the child from its illegitimate origins, could offer a way to remove the taint of an immoral background, 'destroying' the fact of illegitimacy by creating a new legitimate status for the child (Ibid., p. 116). At the same time, it could protect a birth parent from the shame of having borne a child outside of marriage.

Adoption emerged as a form of regulatory and disciplinary power, aimed at solving the problems of illegitimacy for the health of the nation through the 'calculated management' of a new form of family life. Through conferring a new origin on the adopted child, that child would be safely re-rooted in the truth and knowledge bound up with its new familial identity.

One might think that such a conception of adoption would work powerfully against any open relationship with the biological family and promote a fresh start foundation to adoption. However, there were two concerns in circulation at the time that worked against a conception of adoption as a complete and closed solution to illegitimacy. First, the adoption societies and the parents who used their services were very concerned about the transmission of 'bad blood' to the child from its immoral origins and, second, there were worries that the legal introduction of adoption would sanction or even incite the immorality of having an illegitimate child and for this reason it should not be introduced (Kornitzer, 1952, p. 63; Howe et al., 1992, p. 11). This reasoning questioned whether the substitute adoptive family could really eradicate the flaws inherent in the original biological family. Could adoption prevent the transmission of bad blood to the child or is the child's history an irreducible and persistent presence defying adoption's substitutive power? There was a sense that the family of origin should remain responsible for the child and that this responsibility should not be severed lightly. One can begin to see here an emergent paradoxical relationship to the family of origin; their bad blood line was to be interrupted and substituted by adoption, but the substitution would only ever be partial and incomplete. The child's origins persisted and could never be entirely colonised by the replacement family experience.

Lowe (2000, p. 311) finds a persistent reluctance amongst the early adoption legislators for severing the child's original birth status. He comments on the strong sense in both the Hopkins and Tomlinson Committee reports that the child's difference from his or her adopters needed to be sustained through a preservation of the child's birth heritage. This privileging of the child's difference can be seen in a number of the recommendations, which, significantly, were mostly enacted in the first legislation. I want to focus on the two most significant.

The keeping of succession and inheritance rights within the natural family was recommended and then enacted in the 1926 Act, thus preventing the adopted child from complete assimilation into its adoptive family. Lowe (2000, p. 313) comments: 'given that succession rights were unaffected by adoption, one could say that all adoption did was sever the legal relationship between child and birth parents prior to death and in that sense adoption only *suspended* the parent–child relationship' (my emphasis).

As this chapter has traced, the emergence of a dominant middle-class culture in the nineteenth century depended on the protection of their blood line to secure their legacy for the future. This reluctance to interfere in the line of descent by preventing the transfer of inheritance rights speaks to an enduring need to continue to sustain the purity of their blood (Triseliotis, 1998a, p. 61).

This sustaining of the adopted child's original family ties was also endorsed by a clause that permitted an adoptee to marry their adoptive parent. The Tomlin Report (1925, p. 20) that preceded the 1926 legislation had been particularly insistent on this issue:

> *The blood tie cannot be severed* ... [The] existing prohibitions ... must remain and it is repugnant to common sense to make *artificial offences the result of a purely artificial relationship.* The relationship of guardian and ward does not today preclude intermarriage and the adopting parent will only hold the position of a special guardian ... [Accordingly], legalized adoption should have no effect in this regard at all. (my emphasis)

This is an important paragraph to interrogate, as it encapsulates a number of tensions in how the family and the position of the parent were understood at the beginning of the twentieth century. Clearly, the 1926 conception of adoption was not one where the kinship of blood could be fully substituted by a legal transfer of parentage. By keeping the familial ties of adoption 'artificial' the adopter could lay no claim to the position of parent. This opened up some radical possibilities. The adopted child would not be subject to the prohibition of incest, meaning a sexual relationship with their adopter was both possible and permissible. If the child's desire was not defined in oedipal terms, with all the prohibitions that regulate its appearance, then the cultural norm of exogamy would not be operative, making desire and marriage within the adoptive family a potential outcome.

From a contemporary perspective, where sexual abuse haunts every institutional and familial scene, this early conception of the adoptive family seems a strange kind of perversity. The free circulation of sexuality between children and adults that was incited in the absence of any oedipal prohibition worked to unsettle the dominant kinship structure of family. But, it is precisely because that kinship structure was considered to occupy such a central and foundational place that its transferability was profoundly in question in 1926. The legislators were clear that the blood tie could be neither severed nor simulated. What becomes interesting some 20 years later is how adoption did incorporate the incest taboo into its legal operation, suggesting that a fuller simulation of the blood tie became possible after the Second World War.

Conclusion

This chapter has traced the emergence of adoption in 1926 from out of the paradoxical place that the family had come to occupy at the end of the nineteenth century. What made the emergence of adoption possible by the 1920s was the new importance accorded to the family as a place for both promoting and safeguarding the development of children. However, adoption as a substitution for the 'real' family was problematically situated in a culture that privileged belonging by birth. Clearly, such a privileging worked to keep adoption 'artificial' and to sustain the biological family in a certain place of prior and continued importance. At the same time, adoption was meant to substitute for blood and worked to reform and eradicate the legacies of bad blood.

Adoption, then, was an effect of the hegemonic position of the family, but also a potential resistance to its particular ways of inscribing belonging. As a space for child rearing without or outside of the legitimation of the blood tie, adoption was a challenge to that dominant kinship arrangement, a radical possibility for a different kind of familial belonging. However, adoption also replicated, or reproduced biological kinship and so confirmed as much as it contested this culturally dominant arrangement.

It was this tension that would produce practices that engage or involve the adopted child's family of origin. As I will trace in the following chapters, adoption's paradoxical relationship to the blood tie of birth would operate to simultaneously include and exclude the adopted child's founding history, implementing and contesting practices of openness with that history.

3
Contested Involvements: Adoption before the Second World War

> If power is properly speaking the way in which relations of force are deployed ... should we not analyse it primarily in terms of struggle, conflict and war. (Foucault, 1980, p. 90)

I have prefaced this chapter with a quotation from Foucault that describes history as a war of competing forces, a movement whereby struggle and subjugation are dominant. The image of war is a good description to begin my analysis of open practices, as this earliest era is characterised by a war of two specific discourses that will be differently staged and fought throughout the history I will be tracing. The legal commentator Cretney (1998, p. 185) captures something of this inaugurating conflict:

> In 1926 ... adoption was essentially a process whereby, under minimal safeguards supervised by the court, a civil contract was registered and recognised ... it has now become a process largely administered by welfare agencies, from which contractual elements have almost disappeared.

Cretney is reflecting on what he understands to be a transformation in adoption practices from its legal inception to the present day. He is suggesting that adoption was initially 'contractual', that the parties involved reached agreements between themselves without much legal or social work involvement, but these more negotiated elements eventually disappeared. Cretney sees the period 1926–1939 as the era of contractual adoptions, an era where confidentiality, secrecy and the mediation of a professional adoption service did not characterise the field. His account evokes two different cultures of adoption in a historical relationship, one emerging at a cost to the other. My account will differ by understanding these two discursive formations as in continuous and simultaneous conflict. It isn't that the contractual discourse disappeared and the secrecy discourse emerged, but that they continued to operate together, structuring the field with richly conflictual practices. Before moving on to consider the emergence of these practices, I want to briefly consider the nature of the antagonistic forces at play in this early era of adoption.

Early history

There was in the 1920s continuing legislative reluctance to intervene into the sacrosanct life of the biological family. This could be seen in the caution with which adoption first entered the statute book, with legislation holding back from severing the adopted child's original birth status. As Chapter 2 discussed, this was most strikingly illustrated by the keeping of succession rights within the birth family and the non-recognition of consanguinity within the new adoptive family. This resistance to legally implementing a total transplant of the child to a new adoptive family had a number of effects on the position of the 'natural parents', whose involvement in the adoption process was actively sought. Over the next two decades this continuing involvement would slowly become a key area of contestation in adoption practice, as legislation eroded away the previous grounds for their presence. The arguments for legislating against birth family involvement were central to the much later debates around birth parent contact in contemporary adoption.

This reluctance by legislators to make adoption a full replacement was co-extensive with their resistance to the secrecy and confidentiality through which the early adoption societies wanted to operate their placements. It followed that if the adopted child still 'belonged' to its family of origin, then that family should be active participants in his or her adoption, giving an immediate role to practices of disclosure. The Tomlin Report (1925) that preceded the 1926 Adoption Act was already in conflict with the very different culture of the adoption agencies: 'They [the adoption societies] deliberately seek to fix a gulf between the child's past and future' (ibid., p. 8). The report goes on to critically discuss a policy of 'if the eyes can be closed to facts, the facts themselves will cease to exist' as 'wholly unnecessary and objectionable in connection with a legalized system of adoption, and we should deprecate any attempt to introduce it' (ibid., p. 8).

It was, of course, the 'fact' of the illegitimate child's immoral birth family that led the adoption societies to embrace practices of secrecy and confidentiality. Fixing a gulf between an illicit past and a new respectable future had long been the welfare response to the social problem of illegitimacy. What begins to enter the discourse in the twentieth century was a more public coming out of illegitimacy as a social welfare issue:

> The early publicity given to the work of the adoption societies was almost the first twentieth century advice to the community at large that girls ('quite nice girls') got into trouble and produced babies who were a social problem. The societies provided open and above board means for placing children honestly, whereas before all had been a dark and furtive exchange. (Kornitzer 1952, p. 65)

In this early era of adoption, infertility had not yet entered as a social problem that adoption could address. As Kornitzer points out above, adoption was a regulatory response to promiscuity and its consequence, illegitimacy. The focus was on securing an alternative home for the adopted child away from its immoral origins; at this point there was less regulatory interest in achieving a particular kind of home and no regulatory interest in adoption as a solution for infertile parents. The pre-war era was still marked by the nineteenth-century concern with the provision of a decent moral environment away from the corrupting effects of immoral practices, such as non-marital sexual liaisons. Parents did not yet strongly figure as a central element in the production of a particular kind of childhood subject, although the early adoption societies did advocate for married family life as the best placement for the illegitimate child. These emergent tensions can be seen in the very particular culture of pre-war adoption.

The Horsburgh Report of 1937, the first 'official' enquiry into adoption, describes an adoption culture markedly less regulated and more working class than that which characterised the post-war era. The case vignettes at the beginning of the report reveal the degree to which different kinds of families from a working-class background were adopting. These included 'labourer', 'hawker', unemployed and people dependent on pensions or benefits (Horsburgh, 1937, pp. 12–13). Age and marital status were not yet conditions or measures for adopting. The children were often older when placed and although there was a stress on good health and fitness (ibid., p. 14), there was a reported popularity for the toddler or school-age child, as it was clearer what kind of child the adopter was taking in. Adoption was still not popular in this era – only 4,000 orders were made annually on average – and mothers found it difficult to get their children adopted and were offered little support by the societies.

What is fascinating about this demographic profile is the way that it illustrates how the family was not yet a fully integrated part of the disciplinary society. As Chapter 2 explored, by the beginning of the twentieth century the family had become both a site for intervention with failing subjects and the primary space for the correct and proper production of moral subjects. Clearly, by the 1930s there was an emergent sense of the family as a welfare resource for adoption, a place where the socially marginal and excluded could be reabsorbed and re-normalised (Donzelot, 1997, p. 58). However, its function in these respects had not been stabilised and social groupings that fell outside of the family unit were active participants in adopting children. Triseliotis (1998a, p. 63) understands the dominantly working-class nature of pre-war adoption as an effect of the middle-class fears about 'hereditary and bad blood'. As Chapter 2 discussed, the emergent middle classes secured their line of descent through preserving a healthy blood line achieved by knowledge about its origins. The adoption of an illegitimate child would install both 'bad blood' and an uncertain or unknown genealogy into middle-class family life. Triseliotis (ibid., p. 63) sees these concerns not operating in working-class cultures, making adoption of illegitimate children possible for those communities.

The report also illustrates a tension between a regulated service and an autonomous adoption service. This tension will be a common feature of this analysis, as regulation of the family within a field of voluntarily relinquished responsibilities produced contradictory practices that had an enduring legacy for adoption work. In the pre-war era consenting to the adoption of a child brought with it responsibilities and involvements for the biological parent, as relinquishment did not achieve a complete dissolution of the original parental status. The voluntarily relinquished illegitimate child was a different welfare subject to the child of statutory intervention, where child protection concerns require its separation from its family of origin. This difference was most graphically illustrated by the way that consent to adoption operated – should a birth mother change her mind prior to the adoption order, then the child was returned to her care. I emphasise this because in the post-war era there was a drastic redefining of the consensual force of adoption which had effects on the position of the relinquishing parent.

In the pre-war era, there was a continuous conflict between the societies who wanted different and more restrictive regulation against a legislative body who wanted to keep the field of intervention as un-coercive as possible. The adoption societies argued that the low number of adoption orders was an effect of practices that kept the birth family involved. This argument reflected a new sense of the family as a space of privacy and self-enclosure essential for the raising of children. As we will see below, the call for regulation was usually to instigate practices that would exclude or make more marginal the different involvements of the family of origin in the adoption process. The Horsburgh Report (1937) was in part an effect of this demand for more regulation: 'The report ... noted how the home secretary had received a deputation asking for an inquiry into the "evils associated with unlicensed, unregulated and unsupervised adoption" in 1935' (ibid., p. iv).

The report goes on to describe the absence of a formal, standardised adoption service with the practice of placing children differing enormously from society to society (1937, pp. 15–16). The staff were not necessarily qualified and there were no standards of placement procedures. One of the effects of this report was to introduce some form of procedure and regulation into adoption work through the 1939 Act, including case committees to hear reports on children and adopters; registration of societies; probationary period; home visits; supervision of third-party and direct placements by local authorities; payments of money regulated by court. Here we can see beginning to emerge into the field of adoption the disciplinary procedures that will form the post-war service – methods of surveillance, interventions for measuring and standardising practice, procedures of observation and normalisation. Clearly, these disciplinary interventions will differently shape the post-war forms of open practice. However, in the pre-war era, where such disciplinary interventions were not fully operative, different possibilities for the emergence of open practices circulated.

In the pre-war era there were two discourses in continuous conflict: a discourse of consensual and contractual practice, in which birth parents were involved and consulted, and a discourse of secrecy, intervention and social work imposition, in which birth parents were excluded and marginalised. I will be arguing that these two discourses productively worked together to produce a richly controversial and paradoxical field of open practices. It is to this analysis that I will now turn.

Open practices

Provision of information to birth parents

This practice emerged with the introduction of legal adoption in 1926 and took two distinctive forms. I will describe these two forms before exploring in detail the different conditions of their emergence and subsequent contested deployment. First, there was the practice of giving birth parents information about the adopters – their name, their address, their religion and other personal circumstances. Second, there was the practice of providing information from a file kept by the agency. This information would not usually identify the adopters in any way, but would focus on the welfare of the adopted child. In the pre-war era it was the direct provision of information about the adopters that was the most common and most contested of these two practices and it is here that my analysis begins.

In understanding the emergence of this practice, it is important to understand the status that the adopted child's original family continued to hold in the pre-war era. The adopted child still 'belonged' to its family of birth, a belonging powerfully represented by inheritance rights and the structuring operation of incest. The early legislators were not only concerned to preserve the adopted child's blood tie, but were also concerned that any transfer of residual parental responsibilities was done consensually, not coercively. This gave rise to a crucial element in early adoption work – informed consent. What this meant in terms of practice was that a parent could only consent to an adoption if they had information about the future home and future parents with whom their child would be living. In other words, the biological parents would assess the adopter's suitability to adopt their child by having information in advance about the prospective parents (Creteny, 1998, p. 192). The information about the adopters was provided on the adoption consent forms, so that there was a clear link between consenting to adoption and having information upon which to base that consent.

What is striking here was that the assessment of the adopters was being undertaken by the family of origin, not the adoption agency. This practice worked to sustain the birth parent's involvement as parent and in so doing sustained the poor law tradition of parents being responsible for their children. For most of the nineteenth century the presence of a parent was always used to refuse or minimise the state assuming any responsibilities for that child. What is fascinating to observe in the 1920s was how the punitive poor law emphasis on parental responsibility was reversed in the field of adoption. Here the sustaining of responsibility worked in a productive way to keep an involvement for the biological parent against the adoption society's practice of complete severance of such involvement. The same reverse discourse will be at play when I discuss the practice of birth parents supporting their children.

The practice of providing information was immediately a terrain of contestation by the adoption societies that were in charge of its implementation. This was an instance of a practice instituted through legislation being contested through social work practice that effected a gradual redefinition of its place in adoption work. I want to examine the forms that this opposition took in the deployment of this practice.

There were two related concerns from the adoption societies about providing information: first, they claimed that prospective adopters were not applying for adoption orders because they did not want their personal details disclosed to the biological family and, second, such information invited the potential for the biological family to make a direct and unmediated communication with the adoptive family.

As I have already discussed, the adoption societies based their placement work on the necessity of separating the illegitimate child from its immoral origins. It followed that keeping the new placement confidential and secret was important and that providing information about the adopters to the family of origin would compromise the perceived need for an absolute break with the illegitimate child's past. Clearly, adopters were beginning to recognise confidentiality and secrecy as essential elements in their construction of themselves as substitute parents. Within this discourse birth parents' involvement was constructed as interference, an interference that would disturb the adopted child's possibility for a new, more morally correct beginning. The adoption societies cited the anxiety of adopters at the prospect of the disclosure of their name and address to the biological parents: 'they are afraid that the parent may disturb the child or may even attempt a mild form of blackmail' (Horsburgh Report, 1937, p. 18). The idea of the birth family as both an intrusive and destabilising force emerged simultaneously with the idea of adoption as a full and exclusive replacement for the illegitimate child's family of origin.

By the 1930s the societies argued that the practice of providing information was handicapping their work by not sufficiently excluding the biological family from the adoptive family's life. Their opposition to this practice took a very concrete form – they simply refused to provide information about the adoptive families. By the time of the Horsburgh Report (1937), it was found that parents were consenting to the adoption of a child with no supporting knowledge or information about the actual family with whom their child would be living. The Horsburgh Report noted that many of the societies had dispensed with consent forms that included adopter's details. Furthermore, the report commented upon the increasing use of blank forms, a practice which was justified with the argument that the best adopters were those that favoured confidentiality and secrecy (ibid., pp. 18–19).

The presence of a more consensual and contractual discourse was reflected by the Horsburgh Report, which was keen to uphold the biological families' participation through having real information about the adopters. The report (1937, p. 99) acknowledged how little such information was being transmitted, to the detriment of the biological parent:

> We have heard of a case where a mother genuinely anxious for the welfare of her child was refused all information as to its whereabouts by the society concerned and, from ignorance of the name and address of the adopters, was unable, by communication with them, to learn whether her child was alive and happy.

The societies' opposition to providing information was precisely to avoid a direct communication from the family of origin to the adopters. Yet in the above vignette, such communication was considered both welcome and expected, reflecting as it does a continuing maternal concern for an adopted child. For legislators of this period, the adopters were not so much replacing the family of origin, as working alongside them to care for their child at a time of difficulty. Within this construction of adoption, the biological family sustained their parental position and had concerns about their child associated with that position. These concerns were addressed and alleviated by the practice of providing information, which in this formulation was understood as involvement, not interference.

What is fascinating about the fate of this practice was how the counter-discourse that actively supported it in legislation was rendered impotent by the adoption societies' work. This was most graphically illustrated by the case of J M Carroll in 1931. This case involved a Catholic mother who had placed her baby with a protestant adoption society and then wanted to reclaim the baby on the grounds that she knew nothing about the adopters. The Horsburgh Report (1937, p. 19) cites the important judgement:

> It is scarcely necessary to point out that the form of consent which has already been given by the mother with the name of the applicant

absent is a nullity. It is clear ... that *parental consent can only be given to a specific adoption by a named adopter.* (my emphasis)

The judgement was in the mother's favour and in so doing upheld the centrality of her right as biological mother to the child. As Teague (1989, p. 62) comments: 'The effect of re: J M Carroll is clear. The majority verdict bound the court in future to consider a restated emphasis of the rights of natural parents to their children.'

Yet, in spite of this judgement in 1931, the adoption societies continued to evade the legal demand to transmit information about their placements. Their relentless opposition eventually worked to amend the legislation. In the 1936 Adoption of Children (summary jurisdiction) rules an amendment was made so that the information that was provided to biological families was restricted to the name of adopters only.

What seems important is that the consensual appearance of adoption remained, even when there was no information provided on which to base this consent. It has been argued by some commentators (Howe et al., 1992) that the apparently consensual basis of adoption was always masking the enormous social pressures that operated upon unmarried mothers; relinquishing a child for adoption implied a choice that was often not available. Again, what seemed important was that adoption was characterised as a consensual transaction to conceal the more insidiously coercive dimensions of its operation.

I now want to turn to the second practice: the provision of information to biological parents from a file kept by the agency. Unlike the first form, where information about the adopters was given directly, this form is a more indirect transmission. It relied upon a system of record keeping which would be administered by adoption professionals, who would take charge of what information was transmitted, to whom and at what time. There were two distinctive ways that information was stored in adoption work: first, information about the adoption order was recorded on an adopted children's register and, second, information about the child's birth history and birth family and information about the child's new family was held on a file about the adopted child.

This was a practice of archivisation. An archive works to gather information together in one place for the purposes of preserving, remembering, reproducing and repeating (Derrida, 1996, pp. 10–12). All these forms of archiving implicitly keep open the relationship between the child's adoptive status and its original birth status; by preserving the adopted child's first history the archive works to expose what it was inaugurated to conceal – the substitutive status of adoption. I want to discuss each of these forms of archiving and the contested practices that emerged.

The adopted children's register was administered by the Registrar General and was a list of all adoption orders granted. It omitted any reference to the child's original parentage, but then highlighted the child's adoptive status by marking all entries with the word 'adopted'. Information linking the adoption certificate and the original birth certificate was kept in a special registrar and access to it was by application to the court. Triseliotis et al. (1997, p. 7) comment on the inauguration of a system of secrecy: 'Provision that records of adoptions be sealed and that a new birth certificate be issued for the child were designed to protect the child from the stigma of illegitimacy, as well as to make sure that the adoptive family was protected from "interference" by the birth family.'

The Horsburgh Report (1937, p. 17) endorses this practice of replacing one birth identity with another: 'The advantages of legal adoption are sufficiently obvious. It secures adopters and child against any interference by the natural parent and gives the relationship a legal status.' What was interesting about this endorsement was how it co-existed with endorsement of other more open practices that far from replacing the child's birth identity sustained and promoted it. Indeed, the same report also constructed 'interference' by the biological family as a response to an adoption society culture that overly excluded them. Whilst in the pre-war era a sealed adoption archive was inaugurated, alongside this were practices that kept that archive open. One such practice was the provision of information about the child from its adoption file. The Horsburgh Report (1937, p. 20) suggested that adoption societies should 'always be ready to answer from properly kept records any reasonable inquires by the mother'. Indeed, the report linked the absence of proper records with the biological parents' 'interference' into adoptive family life: '... we have been told that the parents are often very anxious to learn where their children have been placed and to receive information as to their progress' (ibid., p. 18). The recommendation to provide information from records, made by the Horsburgh Report in 1937, would not emerge into practice until the mid-1980s.

Birth parents contributing to their child's adoption/upkeep

This practice emerged in 1926 and expected relinquishing parents to pay towards the costs of having their child adopted. In some instances financial support continued after the adoption order was made. The poor law antecedents of this practice are clearly illustrated by the Horsburgh Report (1937, pp. 35–40): 'it may be desirable that she [the mother] should be reminded of her responsibilities and that the impression should not be cultivated that adoption societies exist for the cheap and expeditious disposal of illegitimate children.'

Kornizter (1952, p. 63) comments on the corruptions arising from this pre-war practice: 'There were parents ready to give a child away with a sum of money to anybody who would take it and other people willing to adopt for the sake of the capital the child brought into the family.' The corruptions that Kornitzer identifies with this practice were precisely those that legal adoption was meant to eradicate. The adoption societies had campaigned for the introduction of adoption to prevent the kinds of unscrupulous exploitation associated with the baby farming scandal of the nineteenth century, where infants were exchanged for money. Given this, one might have expected a vociferous opposition to the emergence of a practice of financial exchange in adoption. However, the adoption societies' opposition was surprisingly muted, in part because their work was funded by contributions from adoptive parents and birth parents.

It is important to consider what this practice signified about the position of parenting and child rearing in the pre-war era. Clearly, this practice belonged to a culture where parents' responsibilities for their children were considered economically binding, within a system of minimal welfare support. Within the contemporary era of state-sponsored welfare services it is easy to read this practice as exploitative, rather than understanding it as a reflection of a culture that positioned parental responsibility very differently. The biological family's economic responsibility for their child was not transferred with the adoption order, thus preserving and sustaining a parental involvement. It was this dimension of the practice that most troubled the post-war legislators. I will quote the objections to this practice from the Gamon Report of 1947, as it highlights a very stark difference in conceptions of adoptive parenting pre and post war:

> It is inconsistent with the *true relationship* that should be established between the adopters and their adopted child, that the adopters should continue to receive payments for the child's maintenance from a putative father ... such payments would be a constant reminder that the child was the illegitimate child of the putative father and tend *to thwart the development of real family feeling* between the adopters and the child. (ibid., p. 18, my emphasis)

In the post-war era the provision of economic support to a child sustained a parental involvement that would interfere with the establishment of a new family life. This newly emerging conception of adoption was already beginning to have effects in the late 1930s. In the 1939 Adoption Act some regulation was introduced by having the courts supervise financial payments. The practice was removed by the 1949 Act, but continued to have some kind of place within direct and third-party adoptions.

Birth parents' court attendance

This practice emerged in 1926 and required the biological parents to attend the adoption hearing both to ensure their consent to the adoption and to make certain of the child's identity and date of birth. The Horsburgh Report (1937, p. 21) saw this as a very important practice and one fundamental in securing the birth identity of the adopted child. Unless a biological parent was actually present in court to verify the child's identity and his or her date of birth, then the latter could be inaccurate and there would be the risk of a different child being substituted (ibid., p. 21).

This is a practice that was concerned with origins and having those origins secured and verified. This emphasis worked to sustain the biological parent in a position of centrality, as only they were assumed to have the foundational knowledge about their child's genealogy. As I discussed in Chapter 2, the nineteenth century witnessed the consolidation of a new technology of self, a self rooted in an originating childhood history, which is both formative and determining of the subject. In the pre-war era, there were practices such as this that represented the child's origins through the actual physical presence and involvement of his or her biological family. In court the biological parent was a guarantor for the child's origins, their presence securing the child's past. I emphasise this because in the post-war era there will be a redefining of who secured the child's history and how that securing was achieved. The family of origin would be replaced by a team of professionals who would guarantee the child's history through medical reports and social work assessments, removing the necessity for any direct involvement from the biological family. The importance of the child's origins would remain, but the practices through which they were sustained would be radically different.

Teague (1989, p. 71) points out that the Horsburgh Report linked the practice of court attendance with parental rights and parental welfare:

> The committee was concerned for the rights of natural parents, and took some courts to task for not requiring their presence before

them. They saw such attendance as vital so that they might satisfy themselves as to the well-being of the child, and also such attendance would bring home to them that they were 'sundering' all their parental rights and duties.

What is emphasised here was the importance of the relinquishing parent being satisfied with the placement; her consent to the adoption order was implicitly linked with the welfare of her child in his or her new home. In this period parents could withdraw their consent right up until the last moment before the order was granted, allowing them a position of considerable power and centrality. This was the major reason that societies contested the practice of court attendance, as it permitted the potential for consent to be withdrawn at the eleventh hour. In commenting on this opposition, the Horsburgh Report (1937, p. 21) states: 'Serious hardship may be caused to the child where, as not infrequently happens, the adoption society loses touch with the mother or does not co-operate in bringing her to the court.'

The report made a connection between the parent's court attendance and the child's welfare. Here adopted children's welfare was secured in two ways: by a biological parent being in touch with the society and by a biological parent being in court to ensure that the placement of her child was a good one. In this pre-war era there was still in circulation a discourse that understood the adopted child's welfare in terms of his or her past family life. In this construction the adopted child's welfare was linked to his or her family of origin's continuing involvement in its new life. There was already a competing discourse of child welfare represented by the adoption societies where the adopted child's welfare was secured by an exclusion of his or her prior family. The focus was on the future home and not the previous history. Whilst this formulation would acquire more force in the post-war era through new forms of closed practice, the biological family's involvement would be sustained through new forms of open practice.

Kornitzer (1968, p. 33) illustrates how adoption societies evaded the exercise of this practice: 'For this reason they often recommended their applicants to apply for an order through the county courts, where the mother's consent could be given by affidavit and where therefore her presence was often not required.' This is another instance of a practice with legal sanction being directly challenged and opposed by the disciplinary power of the adoption societies. By the mid-1930s, the practice of court attendance was already being eroded; under the previously cited 1936 rules the court could rule to dispense with the personal attendance of parents at adoption hearings.

Third-party and direct adoptions

Third-party and direct adoptions were the terms used to describe adoptive placements made outside of the official adoption societies. Third-party adoptions were those made with the assistance of a third party, usually a professional such as a doctor or midwife who acted as a negotiator between the adopters and the birth family. Direct adoptions were those made by the parent directly with the adoptive family.

These two forms of adoption emerged in 1926 alongside the more professionally mediated form offered by the adoption societies. I have included them here as a radical instance of participatory disclosure since biological parents had an active involvement in their operation. In one way it was not surprising that these kinds of adoption emerged, given that in the 1920s open practices directly involving birth parents were in circulation. However, as I have discussed above, these practices were contested by the societies to the point where their deployment was both stifled and suppressed. Yet, third-party and direct adoptions continued to have a largely uncontested life outside of the professionally managed adoption services. There were persistent calls for these forms of adoption to be banned, but pre- and post-war legislation simply introduced some regulation into their operation. For example, the 1939 Adoption Act made local authorities responsible for the supervision of third-party and direct placements.

Kornitzer (1952) captures something of the contradictory discourses that were at play in the debates about these forms of adoption. She argues that these adoptions bypassed the important element of assessment of adopters and child, leading to unsuitable families taking in unsuitable children of 'low habits' (1952, p. 36). Yet, she also understands direct adoptions as an exercise of parental rights, uninterrupted by the state, acknowledging the reluctance to interfere with such rights in Britain (ibid., p. 38).

A tension between privacy and intervention certainly shaped how early adoption practices emerged. In the pre-war era there was a growing welfare discourse that saw the family in need of all kinds of regulatory support by professional experts, but there was a counter-discourse that saw the family as an autonomous and self-regulating institution. Third-party and direct adoptions sustain a direct and unmediated involvement for the biological family at a time when welfare regulation of the family was assuming a bigger role in adoption work. The persisting presence of these forms of adoption became even more marked in the post-war era.

Conclusion

In this discussion of open practices before the war, I have traced the emergence of two discourses in continuous conflict: a discourse of consensual and contractual practice, in which birth parents were involved and consulted, and a discourse of secrecy, intervention and social work imposition, in which birth parents were excluded and marginalised. Towards the end of this period, discourses of secrecy and confidentiality began to emerge more forcefully to regulate the field, making marginal the more inclusionary practices that had circulated previously. The post-war period would continue this momentum for greater secrecy as adoption is reconfigured following the 1949 Adoption Act. However, this discursive conflict would continue to operate, consolidating adoption's paradoxical mode of intervention.

4
Differences Denied: The Normalisation of Adoption

> His natural love belongs to his natural parents and the more positive and strong a child's character, the more torn he will be in serving two loves. Legal adoption is provided for the express purpose of cutting the natural link. (Kornitzer, 1952, pp. 164–5)
>
> The success of disciplinary power derives no doubt from the use of simple instruments; hierarchical observation, normalising judgement and their combination in a procedure that is specific to it, the examination. (Foucault, 1977, p. 170)

I have prefaced this chapter with two quotations that encapsulate two key ways that post-war adoption was transformed. Kornitzer captures the paradoxical situation of the post-war adopted child. This is a subject both attached to and therefore affected by separation from his or her first parents, yet simultaneously able to bond and attach to new substitute parents. In a culture that was increasingly placing a singular developmental importance on early bonding and nurture, adoption's dual heritage would be constructed as a confused and split genealogical experience. Foucault is describing the covert way that contemporary power regimes operate through the installation of certain disciplinary procedures. Subjects are regulated through an instrumental power that conceals the subjugating force of its operation. Adoption in the post-war period was transformed in two important ways: it became a newly disciplined form of substitute family life and it acquired a new technology of the adopted subject.

This chapter will explore the problematic normalisation of adoption between 1945 and 1970. My analysis will consider how the emergence of a post-war discourse of child psychology and mothering gave impetus not only to the production of a split and torn adopted subject, but also to new disciplinary interventions into the field of adoption. I will discuss how the disciplinary practices of normalising judgement, hierarchal observation and examination operate in the post-war era to initiate new forms of open practice, whilst sustaining in different ways existing forms (Foucault, 1977, pp. 170–94).

As Kornitzer describes above, legal adoption emerged in the 1950s as a complete replacement family to militate against the development of confused and divided loyalties in the adopted child. However, such was the foundational importance attached to the kinship tie that this replacement was only ever partial. This period was characterised by the emergence of an ever increasing social work concern about the legacy for the adopted child of a dual genealogical heritage. As I will go on to discuss, whereas in the pre-war era, the adopted child sustained in both law and practice some kinds of links and ties to his or her biological family, the post-war era problematically severed those ties and then sought to reinstate them in a different form.

Whilst it would appear that in the post-war era secrecy, confidentiality and birth family exclusion dominated the adoption field, I will be arguing that the discursive conflict of the pre-war era continued in a different and less manifest form, centred around practices of verbal disclosure. These transformations to adoption need to be situated in the wider cultural field. My analysis will, therefore, begin by outlining the post-war cultural conditions through which the family emerged as a central resource for welfare work with children.

The familiarisation of post-war culture

> The diffusion of new norms brought about an intensification of family life. Concentrated on itself, the family became an avid consumer of everything that might help it to 'realise itself.' (Donzelot, 1979, p. 224)

Donzelot is describing the accelerated importance and centrality that the family as a social unit came to occupy in the post-war era. As Chapter 2 traced, from the late nineteenth-century onwards there had been a growing move to establish a particular version of childhood and family life for bourgeois society, centred around the foundational importance of the mother–baby relationship. However, it was in the post-war period that the family was to receive a whole proliferation of welfare and psychological services to support its development as the privileged space for the production and regulation of citizens. After the dislocations and separations of the war years, the family was established as the 'natural' centre of society, returning women to their primary role as mothers within a newly emerging field of infant and child psychology. This was the era when government through the family was more completely accomplished, a governance achieved through 'the unifying concept of maladjustment' (Donzelot, 1979, p. 148). The family was increasingly situated as an emotional and psychological space, a locus of illness or health, with parents responsible for the production of children as socially adjusted subjects.

> This therapeutic familialism was one element in a web of programmes and arguments that enmeshed conjugal, domestic and parental arrangements in the post war period...each entailed the revalorisation of the child centred family as a site for the emotional investment and self realisation of citizens. (Rose, 1989, p. 161)

This focus on the internal life of the family was supported by a new theorisation of early nurture and maternal attachment (Burlingham and Freud, 1942; Winnicott, 1984; Bowlby, 1990). The primacy given to the formative events of earliest infancy – both real and psychic – made separation from biological parents a potentially traumatic event (Rose, 1989, p. 168). This emergence of separation as a key psychological experience not only confined middle-class mothers to their households in a position of continuous nurture, but redefined the kind of care that a problem working-class child should receive when removed from its parents. For the first time two distinctive concerns entered child welfare policy: a concern with the effects of separation on a child and a concern to provide a form of care that could best mitigate these effects. Within this new discourse of maternal attachment, it would follow that children separated from their mothers through illegitimacy, neglect or ill-treatment would require new mothering in a better family environment. This privileging of the family gave rise to a number of quite paradoxical developments in terms of public child welfare policy, which were central in shaping post-war adoption practices.

First, there was a new emphasis on keeping families together, even families who were failing in their parenting tasks. By the early 1950s the newly established childcare officers were charged with the responsibility of supporting families in trouble through a range of therapeutic and educational interventions (Packman, 1975, p. 53). This kind of intervention into the life of the family was a distinctively new emergence. The family had become a site of intervention by the end of the last century, but up until the Second World War intervention was aimed at rescuing and removing children, rather than providing support to their strug-gling parents.[1] The failing family was now helped to achieve the proper standards of normalisation, through a family intervention that had a more supportive policing purpose. As I will discuss below, this kind of family intervention became a key way that the post-war adoptive family was regulated for the first time.

Second, family care emerged as a preference to institutional care, making the biological family a model for substitute care. Children in need of such care were to be placed with another family to sustain the 'normal' trajectory of maternal attachment. This marked a quite sub-stantial shift from pre-war childcare policy, where boarding out with a family was far less common than institutional care (Heywood, 1968; Parker, 1990). The 1948 Children's Act marked this change by enshrin-ing the family as a fundamental unit for ideal development, and pro-moting it as the best form of substitute care for children deprived of their biological parents. The Curtis Report of 1946 that had preceded the 1948 legislation had foregrounded the advantages of the family as a resource for the deprived child: 'The methods which should be available may be treated under three main heads of adoption, board-ing out and residence in the communities. We have placed these in the order in which, they seem to us, to serve the welfare and happiness of the child' (Curtis Report, para 447). Whereas before the war the fam-ily was *one* possible site for the regulation of children, after the war it became *the* privileged place, with the permanency of adoption the most prioritised.

Third, the effects of separation on the child in care would be mini-mised by fostering contact with its family of origin. Whereas before the war, a child's welfare could be secured by its removal from a corrupting or neglectful home environment, after the war this kind of interven-tion would contradict the new way that children's attachments were understood to work. Mitigating the loss of a primary parental figure emerged as a key concern for post-war social work and keeping up links with the child's birth family was the advocated practice.[2] The new ideas on attachment and separation certainty informed how post-war adop-tion was shaped and much of this chapter will relate how practices of openness emerged within the very specific new psychology of infancy that was in circulation.

Finally, and following on from above, attachment to a maternal fig-ure was understood to happen in the first few months of life, making the placing of children permanently elsewhere something that should happen very quickly. This marked quite a break with how children's attachments were understood in the pre-war period. As the preceding chapter discussed, at that time older children were often preferred for adoption because parents would already have a sense of how the child would develop. There was not the idea that this would be problematic or traumatic because of an existing and binding attachment to a former family, which would be disturbing or difficult to break. The post-war redefining of attachment centrally changed the way that children were adopted. Infants should be placed for adoption as early and as quickly as possible to prevent any bond with its biological mother becoming established and to facilitate the growth of such a bond with its new mother.

It is clear from the above four areas of child welfare policy that the family had undergone some very important changes in the post-war era. As Chapter 2 elaborated, the family had been transformed by the late nineteenth century into a parenting space dependent on outside intervention in order to fully function. These interventions took different regulatory forms for the working-class family and the middle-class family. The working-class family had its integrity as family undermined or destroyed by social work intervention, for example, children were removed and parents lost their parental responsibilities, whereas the middle-class family had its integrity supported or embellished by educational or psychotherapeutic interventions, for example, children were adjusted and parenting skills were enhanced. In the post-war era, for the first time, the working-class family emerged as a space that could also be regulated by sustaining its integrity as family. This was the era when the working classes were most fully penetrated by this new familial discourse, transforming its 'autarchic' spirit of organisation with governance by professionals of the new psychological sciences (Donzelot, 1979, p. 79). As Donzelot elaborates, the problem working-class child was transformed from a product of a corrupt and degenerate environment to a product of emotionally troubled and damaged parents. This transformation enabled intervention into working-class life in a new way and would eventually become consequential for adoption work in the early 1970s.

These changes signify how the family was acquiring a more stabilised presence in society, a site that could be improved, a space that could be replicated. The figures of excess that were productive of family life – the illegitimate infant, the delinquent youth or the abused child – could be re-normalised, reabsorbed or reallocated to an alternative familial space. Post-war adoption emerged in a changed form within these transformations to the family.

Normalising the adoptive family

Adoption was originally inaugurated to address the 'social problem' of illegitimacy after the First World War and in the post-war period it primarily remained a service for the illegitimate child.[3] However, what changes in this period is the emergence of infertility as an additional social concern that adoption could address. This change in adoption could be understood as a response to a certain crisis in the heterosexual family after the war. The need to re-establish and reconstruct family life in this period meant there was an increasing move to make marginal or pathological forms of experience that fell outside of its normalising sway. Illegitimacy, infertility and sexual immorality acquired a higher profile as social problems within post-war concerns with a falling birth rate and a need to rebuild a 'healthy' population. Commentators of this period (Weeks, 1981; Riley, 1983; Rose, 1989) have emphasised the importance of pronatalism in the reconstruction of the post-war family: 'What was sought was a means of encouraging citizens themselves to make a decision in favour of children, and one that would encourage the best endowed to reproduce, rather than the feckless and irresponsible individuals who made up the social problem group' (Rose, 1989, p. 162).

Adoption emerged as a response to both the infertile parent, incapable of contributing to the pronatalism campaign, and the unmarried mother, producing children but under the wrong moral conditions. These two social concerns could be absorbed and so obliterated within adoption; the couple's infertility would be disguised and concealed by the presence of an adopted infant and the unmarried mother would have the sign of her immorality permanently removed and could pass as a moral woman again. The infant's illegitimacy would be reworked into a new legitimate status by adoption and so would be recuperated as part of the push to build a new 'healthy' population.

For adoption to reassign and rework these social concerns it would need to become a more exclusive intervention and this was the period when adoption emerged as a complete replacement for the biological family. As Chapter 3 discussed, there was already in the pre-war period a move from the adoption societies to regulate against consensual and contractual practices. Immediately after the war these campaigns gathered momentum and there was an upsurge of agitation for adoption reform from the societies, centred on excluding the birth family from both the adoption process and adoptive family life. The proposed reforms went in two distinct directions: the societies wanted to make the functioning of the adoptive family as like the biological family as possible and they wanted to protect and conceal any differences between the two family forms through practices of secrecy and confidentiality. A judgement from 1956 captures the spirit of this reforming impulse in how it understands the effects of an adoption order: '[an adoption order provides] a veil between the past and the present lives of adopted persons and makes it an opaque and impenetrable as possible: like the veil which god has placed between the living and the dead' (Lawson V. Registrar General, 106 LJ 204, 1956, quoted in Howe et al., 1992, p. 99).

Clearly, to achieve such an absolute break with the adopted child's prior family, the pre-war position regarding inheritance and consanguinity would need reforming. Before the war, the adopted child still sustained its blood tie to its first family through both inheritance and the operations of incest. The 1949 Adoption Act introduced legislation specifically aimed at shifting the adopted child from out of this kinship tie. By allowing the adopted child succession rights in its new family and prohibiting marriage between adopted child and parent, this act established a framework through which the adoptive family is more exactly modelled on the pattern of the post-war biological family. This was the period when adoption became an increasingly popular middle-class form of parenting, transforming its more marginal and working-class identity of the 1930s.

The adoption reform committee, the Gammon Committee (1947, p. 5), described how a complete substitution of the biological family was integral to the success of adoption:

And it has become recognized that for complete success an adoption desiderates the establishment of as close a relationship between the adopters and the adopted child *as is ordinarily found subsisting between natural parents and their children*... the problem... is no longer to find a home of sorts for an unwanted child, but to find a *real home with a real father and mother* for a much wanted child. (my emphasis)

In this post-war formulation, the 'otherness' of the adopted child would be completely assimilated within a new adoptive family who would mimic in every possible respect the biological tie between parents and children in 'natural' families. This was reflected in new practices for the recruitment of adopters, who had to 'pass' as biological parents. The practice of 'matching' adopters to a child emerged in this era and was aimed at achieving a far-reaching substitution; 'matching' will produce adoptive families so like the biological family that there was no discernible difference. Adoption agencies sought to match the religion, social background, physical characteristics and even the temperament of child to adopter (Goodacre, 1966, p. 60), so that the child would be as close as possible to a child conceived naturally (Tizard, 1977, p. 7). Concern with matching extended beyond the individual child to incorporate a concern to match the adoptive family's life style with that of the post-war family. As Kornitzer (1952, p. 24) makes clear, this meant that the adoptive mother would need to be a committed housewife, at home dedicated to the task of child-rearing: 'An adoption society will always enquire if the wife is working and will not place a baby with her unless she promises to give up her job.'

What began to emerge in the post-war period was a tension between achieving a complete substitution of one family for another and having a service to facilitate such a transfer. Any form of adoption service would disrupt or unsettle the substitute model for adoptive family life in that it would involve the mediations of a professional worker undertaking assessments, home visits or reports and thus exposing the very substitution that adoption sought to conceal. Given that adoption was meant to simulate the biological family, then intervention through a placement service would be too exposing of a constitutive difference that the field wanted to conceal or deny. In the pre-war era there was a growing welfare discourse that saw the family in need of all kinds of regulatory support by professional experts, but there was a counter-discourse that saw the family as an autonomous and self-regulating institution. In the post-war era, whilst there was a continuing conflict about the degree of family intervention,[4] the adoptive family more clearly emerged as a client of the state, needing or deserving a social work service. This marked an important change in the way adoption was constructed.

It might be useful in this context to think about the distinction Donzelot (1979) makes between the system of tutelage and the system of contract. The former is the system instituted for those usually working-class families who are failing and who need state intervention in order to perform adequately. The latter is the system for those largely middle-class families who are successfully fulfilling their social functions and who therefore enjoy privacy and 'accelerated liberalisation' (1979, p. xxi). The children of these respective systems enjoyed contrasting social trajectories; the tutelary system produced children of 'supervised freedom', whereas the contract system produced children of 'protected liberation' (1979, p. 47). Donzelot's distinction is helpful when considering the ways that the adoptive family became a site for regulation in the post-war era. The construction of the infertile couple as a failure requiring social intervention situated adopters within the system of tutelage, whereas in all other respects they belonged to the system of contract, successfully fulfilling their social functions and enjoying the privacy and freedom of that success. What emerged, then, was an adoptive family caught between the two systems. The adoptive family would enjoy the liberal privacies of the contract system, after they have adopted, but would have to endure the interventions usually associated with the tutelary system whilst they went through the adoption process.

Of course, it wasn't that the contract system was free of the operations of power, but it regulated subjects differently from the tutelary system. Put simply, in middle-class family life power worked to produce a self-governing subject, whilst working-class family life was more governed by outside interventions. Foucault (1977, p. 170) understands this tension between governance and self-governance as being an effect of how disciplinary power works: 'Discipline "makes" individuals; it is the specific technique of a power that regards individuals both as objects and as instruments of its exercise.'

In turning to an analysis of the regulation of the adoptive family in this period, this tension between power as instrumental and power as objectifying is useful. What becomes clear below is how the conflict between governance and self-governance in adoption was always a conflict between disclosing or concealing the substitutive status of this form of family life. Regulation in this era moved between an intervening power that exposed the artifice of adoption against an instrumental power that supported adopters in making themselves into 'natural parents'. Through using the disciplinary techniques that Foucault identified in *Discipline and Punish* (1977), hierarchal observation, normalising judgement and examination, I want to analyse how regulation worked in this dual way to produce adoption as both a governed and self-governing form of family life.

The disciplining of the adoptive family

Hierarchal observation

The 1949 and 1958 Adoption Acts introduced legislation and practices to stabilise the field of adoption through a hierarchy of both professional and parent observation. A whole network of supervisory obligations was installed: local authorities now supervised the societies' placements; adopters were supervised during a 'probationary' period of three months; the child was supervised by the adopters under new rulings that made its removal by its parents more difficult.[5] Foucault (1977, p. 177) is illuminating on the surveillance effects of such supervision: 'By its very principle it leaves no zone of shade and constantly supervises the very individual who are entrusted with the task of supervision.' These supervisory interventions exposed the adoptive family's difference from the biological family in that it implied they could not be left to develop 'normally'. However, by making the adopters themselves assume supervisory responsibilities, the adoptive family could develop into a self-governing family, not needing outside social work support.

Normalising judgement

There was very specific legislation introduced by the 1949 Act to 'normalise' the adoptive family and make its functioning more like that of the biological family. Foucault (1977, p. 183) is again very clear on how normalising interventions work: 'The perpetual penalty that traverses all points and supervises every instant in the disciplinary institutions compares, differentiates hierarchies, homogenises, excludes. In short, it normalises.' The normalisation of adoption was achieved through measures that excluded the biological family through a radical curtailment of the open practices that the pre-war era had permitted. Such exclusion worked to homogenise the differences that adoption would otherwise signify, but also worked to differentiate the adoptive family from the unmarried mother through a comparison of the adopter's marital superiority.

The Gamon Report (1947, pp. 15–16) had been unequivocal about removing practices that had formerly involved birth parents in their children's adoption, linking such involvement with a destabilising of their new family life: 'In a substantial number of cases where the mother has known the name and address of the adopters she has subsequently insisted on making contact with them and the child, and thereby causing the adopters much distress.' The committee wanted actively to prevent such 'interference' by concealing all information about the adopters and the 1949 legislation reflected this concern very closely. Birth parents were no longer required to attend court and consent to adoption could now be given without knowledge of the adopter's identity. The Act also introduced the practice of serial numbers as a substitution for adopters' names. This legislation, by ending the requirement for informed consent, had radical implications for how adoption subsequently developed. By eradicating the original emphasis on 'the need for a parent to take a personal decision about the adopter's suitability', the law opened up the possibility of consent being given before a child was even placed (Cretney, 1998, p. 192). Furthermore, both the 1949 and 1958 Adoption Acts extended the grounds on which dispensing with a parent's consent to adoption could be based.[6] In other words, there was now much more emphasis on the exclusion of parents, rather than their involvement, a change that spoke to a major shift in the position of the natural parent. Within a time span of 30 years the natural parent's status had been legally transformed from a person with a paramount right to decide about the future of her child, based on full information, to a person whose involvement may be detrimental to that child's future placement, and who may have their consent dispensed with on legal grounds.

This removal of the biological parents' involvements 'normalised' the adopted child more securely within its new adoptive home. The family of origin no longer participated in the adoption of their child, but were replaced by professional social workers who took charge of the placement and the transmission of the child's history. By the 1950s there was a growing consolidation of the view that adopted children's welfare was linked to the exclusion of their birth family from their lives. It was the exclusion of the *physical* presence of the biological parent that was most critical here. Interference was understood to signify an unwanted physical intrusion that would unsettle the adopted child. The implication was that adopted children would not be unsettled by more indirect or less overt forms of intrusion, such as the disclosure of their adoption, as will be discussed later.

Examination

In the post-war period, adoption first became a measurable, comparative system of social work through instituting different procedures for examination. Foucault (1977) identifies three elements in the technique of the examination: first, there is the principle of 'compulsory visibility' (Foucault, 1977, p. 188). Through social work visits, court reports and assessments the adoptive family and the adopted child acquired a new kind of visibility at a time when there was a move for their social assimilation. Goodacre in her 1966 study reports how far both social worker and adopter resisted the supervisory relationship because it pointed up too starkly the substitute nature of adoption (1966, pp. 83–4). The issues that childcare staff should be raising on their probationary visits – exploration of infertility, views on illegitimacy, talking about adoption – paradoxically made visible the adopter as a substitute parent within a system that was attempting to elide that difference. Consequently, social workers did not want to exercise the 'inspection' element of their role and adopters experienced supervision visits as threatening and an 'obstacle' to be endured in order to get the child (Goodacre, 1966, p. 89). This was an instance where the move to govern the adoptive family from the outside broke down and the family itself asserted its own form of self-governing. As I will discuss more fully later, adopters in this period commonly resisted the forms of identity through which social workers wished to understand them. Adopters in Goodacre's study recognised themselves as 'natural parents' and resisted any views of themselves that unsettled this.

Second, there is a 'system of intense registration and of documentary accumulation' (Foucault, 1977, p. 189) which works to create both the adoption participants as describable and analysable objects and a comparative system through which those individuals could be measured (ibid., p. 190). The post-war era marked the emergence of a much more systemised approach to both the keeping of adoption records and the keeping of adoption archives.

Third, and following on from the above point, there is the making of the individual as a 'case': 'It is the individual as he may be described, judged, measured, compared with others, in his very individuality and it is also the individual who has to be trained or corrected, classified, normalised, excluded' (Foucault, 1977, p. 191). This period marked the emergence of the 'professionalisation' of adoption, where it assumed the status of an area of social work needing research to both account for its performance and produce it as a serious science of child placement. From the early 1950s onwards, there was an increasing proliferation of research studies, commonly measuring adoptive family life against 'normal' family life and aimed at proving how successfully adoption had become fully normalised. By the 1960s adoption was considered a more 'complex' experience requiring adoptive parents to have more training, more preparation and more support (Smith and Logan, 2004, pp. 9–10). The adoptive parent began to emerge in this period as a subject in need of special education because of the specific problems arising from their substitute parent status. There were also studies on the unmarried mother, 'her 'pathological personality' and research to secure the superiority of married life to single parenthood in terms of child development (Yelloly, 1965; Roberts, 1966).

In short this was the era when adoption participants acquired a biography, with attributes and elements that stabilised their performance within the field of adoption. Deviations from these officially circumscribed narratives signified pathology, failure or deviance. This emergence of distinctive adoption biographies, with distinctive trajectories of normal and pathological development began to signal a change by the end of the 1960s. Governance by the outside professional expert would become an increasingly common intervention into adoptive family life within an adoption culture that was slowly articulating its difference from biological parentage.

Adoption as unmourned loss

This account has so far emphasised the dominance of exclusionary practices in the post-war era. However, adoption never completely achieved its aim of re-writing out of existence those histories of infertility and immorality despite the legal and practice imperatives that worked to exclude the birth family. Paradoxically, adoption in this era is constructed through the effects of these excluded narratives and its commentaries and studies are dominated by concerns with the unmarried birth mother, the illegitimate child and the infertile adoptive parents. One might argue that this was the period when adoption was most actively constituted through the unmourned loss of its participants, most centrally the unmarried mother and the infertile adopter.

It has been well documented how in this period there was an intensification of the positioning of the unmarried mother as unfit to parent, with adoption the best alternative for both themselves and their illegitimate infant (Shawyer, 1979; Inglis, 1984; Reich, 1988a; Howe et al., 1992; Wells, 1993). Their unfitness was an effect of their unmarried status, a status that made maternal attachment an impossibility: 'There is just this stupid assumption that a baby for adoption is a baby not cared about' (Inglis, 1984, p. 116).

This positioning of the natural parent as not wanting their child was an important ground for their exclusion from that child's life. The paradox here, of course, was that the adoption societies wanted to base the adoptive family unit on the biological family unit, where parents want and cherish their children. This 'real' model of family life is clearly unsettled when 'real' mothers give their children away. These mothers, then, must be re-categorised as unreal, in spite of their biological connection to the child, and situated as either unnatural or pathological. 'Shocked, bruised, guilt-ridden, most did as their parents and society expected of them, and tried to put it all behind them and carry on with their lives as if nothing had happened' (Howe et al., 1992, p. 111). This cultural disavowal of the unmarried mother's experience led Howe et al. (1992, p. 104) to see them as a group without an identity: 'As a group they have failed to gain an identity; as individuals they have escaped notice... it is as if the birth mothers' dilemma confused those who wish to think clearly and consistently about women and their relationships to children and motherhood.'

Whilst I think the above authors are right to draw attention to the absence of any visible social identity for unmarried mothers at this time, clearly they had a very specific identity within adoption work. Indeed, the 1940s and 1950s saw the emergence of research studies aimed at explaining the unmarried mothers 'pathological personality' (Young, 1954; Rall, 1961; Roberts, 1966). Butler (1997a, p. 2) is instructive on the possibilities provided by even a negative identity position: 'By being called a name, one is also paradoxically given a certain possibility for social existence... If to be addressed is to be interpellated, then the offensive call runs the risk of inaugurating a subject in speech.'

By the 1960s and 1970s the unmarried mother's narrative had been recuperated and there was an emergent social movement aimed at recognition for her experiences. I will return to this in Chapter 6 when I discuss the 1985–1990 period. What seems important to emphasise here is that the apparent exclusion of the unmarried mother paradoxically included the ground for her inclusion by providing an identity position from which she would eventually speak. Furthermore, within the adoptive family, there was increasing social worker incitement to talk about the child's original birth heritage, allowing the unmarried mother a strange kind of visibility and participation.

As I have already discussed, in the post-war period, infertile married couples were constructed as the ideal kind of adoptive parents. Indeed, some commentators (Goodacre, 1966; Tizard, 1977) understood infertility as a necessary condition for adoption in this period. Goodacre (1966, p. 30) saw infertility in adopters as important, as it would mean no subsequent birth children would be born to unsettle the adopted child. Tizard (1977, p. 7) sees the importance of infertility being proven because the arrival of birth children would lead to the rejection of any adopted child in the family. Clearly, both these commentators were reflecting an adoption culture that worked to conceal infertility in order to make the acquisition of adopted children as close to biological reproduction as possible. Goodacre's study (1966, pp. 88–9) reported how far adopters saw themselves as biological parents: 'Once adopters had received their child they were intent on identifying with "ordinary" parents. They were inclined to reject the differences between biological and adoptive parenthood.'

However, adopter infertility was not just concealed in this period; it also acquired a visibility in terms of assessment of adopter's suitability to parent. As I will discuss more fully later, social workers viewed adopters' capacity to 'talk' about adoption to their adopted child as a reflection of how resolved they were about their infertility (Goodacre, 1966, pp. 88–9). In the post-war construction of adoption, then, infertility was a condition simultaneously concealed and disclosed; it was an issue for discussion and an issue to be denied.

There was in this period a disenfranchising of certain experiences that, with no public discourse in which they could be named and mourned, were forced to occupy a life in the unarticulated margins of society. Butler (1997b, p. 139) is again instructive on the effects of a culturally prohibited mourning: 'When certain kinds of losses are compelled by a set of culturally prevalent prohibition, one might expect a culturally prevalent form of melancholia ... one which signals the internalisation of the ungrieved and ungrievable.'

A cultural disavowal of experiences such as infertility and illegitimacy induced a shame that was then shrouded in the secrecy of post-war adoption practices. Shame worked to foreclose the active acknowledgement of loss; the adoptive mother and father could not mourn the birth child they longed to have and the birth mother could not mourn the birth child she had to relinquish. This drive to pass off the adopted child as the biological child may well speak to a certain difficulty or impossibility with grieving. The foreclosure on mourning would sustain both the birth parents and the never conceived birth child as disavowed identifications, attachments to that which have been lost, but which sustained a ghostly and enduring presence within the adoptive family (Butler 1997b, pp. 141–3).

This construction of adoption as an experience of loss reflected the effects of the new discourse of maternal attachment and infancy, which gave such a foundational place to the original bond of birth. Whilst the need to provide the illegitimate infant with a new mothering experience made problematic the involvement of the infant's biological family, that family's importance remained irreducible and was sustained in the post-war period by various open practices, such as talking about adoption. The emergence of the discourse of maternal attachment and infancy into adoption work had, then, two quite paradoxical effects: it excluded the family of origin and the adopter's infertility from the new adoptive family, yet, simultaneously brought them back in through practices of disclosure. However, whilst illegitimacy and infertility were brought into the heart of the adoptive family, in the wider culture they remained hidden and denied sources of shame. This created a paralysing field of deployment, where secrecy and disclosure worked together to produce adoption as a paradoxical form of substitute care. This will become clearer as I turn to an analysis of post-war open practices.

Open practices

Provision of information to adopted persons

This was the practice of providing information to adopted adults about their birth records. Since the 1926 Adoption Act such information was in a sealed archive, only accessible by a court order. Whilst post-war legislation did not amend or change the pre-war position, what did change was the status that the issue of information about kinship origin occupied. Throughout this period, it emerged as an increasingly forceful adoption issue, with a growing movement for the birth records archive to be made open.

The Hurst Report (1954) had a specific focus on the question of open access to birth records for adopted adults.[7] The report cited the legislation in Scotland where an adopted person had an automatic right to information at 17 and goes on to suggest something similar in England:

> A number of witnesses in England thought that the adopted person has a right to information and expressed the view that it is not in the interest of adopted children to be permanently precluded from satisfying their natural curiosity ... We therefore recommend that the statue should enable an adopted person on reaching the age of 21 to apply to that court for a full copy of the adoption order, which would give as much information as the Register general would be able to supply from his records. (ibid., p. 201)

The report mentions the possibility that on receipt of such information, the adopted adult could then trace their birth family, but disregards this possibility: 'We believe however that most adopted persons would be content with knowledge of their natural parentage, and would take no steps to make contact with their natural family ... so that the risk would be slight' (ibid., p. 202). This proposal was not enacted in the 1958 legislation and birth records remained closed until the 1976 Adoption Act.

Kornitzer's 1968 study cites the story of an adopted adult who did access her birth records through the courts and who eventually traced her biological mother with the information she gained. She quoted the following extract from the adopted woman:

> I think the adopted child has an absolute right ... to know who the natural parents are ... There is an absolute need to know about your natural inheritance. Complete cutting off [from the natural family] is good for childhood but makes difficulties when you are growing up ... If I had seen a photograph or had known more I would not have tried to see my mother. But in desperation I went to the magistrate's court.' (Kornitzer, 1968, p. 189)

This brief vignette captures a very distinctive discourse of kinship origins and the self as incomplete without knowledge of those origins. The adopted woman linked the absence of such knowledge with her search for her actual mother. This was a familiar theme in this era: the provision of information in the form of dialogue about adoption would circumvent the desperate search that characterised this woman's later life. In this period the archive was only to be partially opened, the site for information, but not for further connection. Kornitzer clarified this with the adopted woman: 'It was possible to discuss with her at some length the value of right telling and of the place of *continuity of knowledge of background*, as opposed to *continuity of contact*, for the mental health of the adopted person' (ibid., p. 189, author's emphasis). For Kornitzer the adopted adult's desire for knowledge from the archive was a reflection of an inadequately performed practice of telling. The 'health' of adopted children was secured through the verbal dissemination of information abut their background that worked to satisfy curiosity and militate against the need for a greater contact with the family of origin.

Provision of information to adopters

This practice was linked to the practice of telling a child about their adoption, as the process of telling would depend on the gaining of information first about the child's background. This practice largely operated as a form of verbal disclosure, although social workers would sometimes give written information to adopters. However, it was not until the 1970s and 1980s that written information in the form of life story books and later life letters really entered adoption work. There is something ephemeral about the transmission of information through speech that is not so through the written word. The documentary form stabilises the information transmitted and it can be more easily referenced and returned to. As I will discuss below, this verbal transmission of information to adopters reflected the status that the information occupied – fleeting and transitory.

Practices bound up with the transmission of information became a central part of adoption work from the post-war era onwards. Information was always mediated through a social work service and there was rarely a direct transmission from parent to parent. This reflected the construction of adoption as a secretive and confidential practice, with identities being concealed, histories being mediated and safeguarded. This practice emerged as a way of helping adoptive parents make a decision about a particular child. Both Rowe (1966) in her manual for adoption workers and Goodacre (1966) in her research study identified this as the primary function that the practice served. Goodacre (1966, p. 68) understands the provision of information to help 'adopters feel satisfied about the offer of a particular child'. Similarly, for Rowe (1966, p. 217) it was to enable adopters 'to decide whether they wish to make the child a member of their family'.

Clearly, this reflected the emergence of adoption in this era as a service structured around the needs of infertile adopters: 'Because of the emphasis on meeting the needs of the parents, children with any visible imperfections or whose family history contained evidence of any abnormality were not considered suitable for adoption' (Tizard, 1977, p. 8).

It would follow that medical information about the child would be the most important information for adopters to acquire. It is striking that a practice which was clearly aimed at providing a full-replacement healthy baby opened up the whole question of the adopted child's heritage and what of that heritage should be communicated to adopters and to the adopted child.

Rowe (1966) and Goodacre (1966) identified two further purposes for the transmission of information to adopters: to help adopters better parent and to help answer the child's questions about its antecedents. To undertake these tasks adopters would need information about the child's own life experiences and its social and family background. What was immediately apparent was that these reasons for information were linked with managing the child's difference. Adoptive parenting emerged here as a specifically different kind of activity, requiring knowledge about a child's other heritage. Rowe (1966, p. 220) elaborated this difference:

> Wherever possible mementoes of a child's early life should be preserved ... adoptive children can feel chopped up and with pieces missing. Scrap books and pictures help to integrate their past and their present to see themselves and their lives as a coherent whole.

Rowe anticipated here the forms of documentary disclosure that would emerge in the 1970s – later life letters and life story books. I will return to these later forms in Chapter 5, but for the present note how by the 1960s there was emerging a well-articulated biography for the adopted child. This was a subject who was incomplete, whose life line had been chopped about by the severance of its first kinship tie. Information about that first bond could fill in the gaps and complete the otherwise interrupted biography. In this formulation a life was akin to a jigsaw puzzle where the adopted child has crucial pieces missing. The provision of information about this child would provide the adopters with its absent links and make his or her biography more like the full and complete narrative of the unadopted child.

The commentaries and research studies in this period had a contradictory relationship to the issue of information. On the one side, there was a continual recognition of an adopted child's incomplete nature, and a need for the truth about its origins to be transmitted to adopters. However, on the other side, there was an often repeated view that distorting or concealing background information, particularly if it was 'bad' or 'damaging', was a perfectly acceptable social work approach (Kornitzer, 1952; Rowe, 1959, 1966; Goodacre, 1966). Burdening adopters with too much negative or upsetting history created unnecessary anxiety (Goodacre, 1966, p. 69) and might prevent them from identifying with the child (Rowe, 1966, p. 222). The impression from these commentators is that a sanitisation and/or distortion of the child's history enables adopters to develop empathy for the child they would be adopting.

There was a tension within this practice of providing information that would allow an adopted child to be appropriated or absorbed into its adoptive family against providing information that sustained the child's other heritage. Clearly, this tension emerged from a discourse that gave a foundational importance to the adopted child's original kinship tie. Adoptive parents had to struggle with this formative event within the dynamics of their own family set up. Kornitzer

(1968, p. 216) was clear that women's desire to identify with a child encouraged self-deception about their 'true' status as adoptive mothers: 'Self-deception was encouraged by the general current idea that adoption is or ought to be just the same as having a family of one's own.' Similarly, Goodacre (1966) reported from her study how adopters went to great pains to convince themselves that the child had similar physical and temperamental qualities as themselves. Often adopters rewrote difficult information into information that made the child's background more like their own. There was a real sense of a child's otherness being appropriated and rewritten, particularly if the background facts did not fit in with the family life the child had joined.

The problematic incorporation of illegitimacy into adoptive family life was a theme from adoption's legal inauguration. Whilst adoption could rewrite and reassign illegitimacy through legally transplanting the child into a new legitimate heritage, there was this continuing concern with the contaminating transmission of an immoral sexuality in the child. Kornitzer (1968, p. 214) notes: 'They [adopters] had brought themselves to adoption still uneasy about taking into their homes children of unknown, and as they felt, dangerous antecedents.' Given this was still a prevalent attitude amongst adopters, Kornitzer found that the adoption societies were reluctant to disseminate information about the child's background, particularly if it contained immoral information. Some societies actively encouraged lying about the background, suggesting that adopters tell the child his or her parents were dead. Clearly, adopters in the range of research studies I have sampled refused to recognise themselves as substitute parents through a refusal to take on the information that installed the adopted child as 'other' to themselves.

Telling the adopted child about adoption

The practice of telling involved the adoptive family informing their adopted child that he or she had been adopted and was not therefore biologically tied to them. It emerged into adoption work most prominently after the Second World War, although some commentators trace it back earlier (Triseliotis, 1973, p. 3). Certainly, in the postwar period, the practice kept open a place for the biological family's involvement, when in law that place had been substantially reduced. One of the increasing features of this era was the sustaining of two quite distinct positions regarding the adopted child's birth family: the child should make a complete break with their original family and yet, he or she should be 'told' of their adoptive status. Once the confidential status of adoptive family life had been secured through legislation, the question of birth family involvement entered the terrain in a different form.

The Hurst Report (1954) made some very strong recommendations about telling, which anticipated the increasing place it occupied in debate and practice through the 1950s and 1960s, a latency that always unsettled the manifestly closed character of adoption of this period. The report was concerned that adopted children were not being told about their adoptions. 'They [adopters] should understand clearly that they may seriously jeopardize the child's emotional development and future happiness by withholding this knowledge from him' (ibid., p. 22) and it went on to recommend that adoption is disclosed as early as possible to the adopted child: 'An adopted child must be told that he is adopted or "chosen" and it was generally agreed that it is best not to wait until he is of an age to comprehend fully what that means, but to tell him so early that he can never remember a time when he did not know it' (ibid., p. 150).

The above quotations touch upon a number of themes around the practice of telling that increasingly dominated social work debate: that telling was not a one-off event, but should be returned to and reinforced throughout childhood; that withholding this information led to emotional disturbance in adopted children; that telling always involved a confrontation with the whole issue of sex and reproduction, and telling about adoption always brought up telling about the biological family.

The paradoxes built into the whole issue of telling were well captured in Kornitzer's early study (1952, pp. 175–6). The author cited a contemporary 'expert' on the key considerations when undertaking the process of telling with an adoptive child, which included the duty to protect the natural mother's secret, not to blacken the natural mother's name, not to give reasons for the child's adoption that would make them insecure with adopters and to ensure that the child felt adopters were like natural parents to him or her. The expert concluded from this contradictory list that it might be best if the child was told the mother is dead, as this would mean the child would not fantasise either about her return or about finding her later in life.

What seems crucial here is that the child's new family life was not troubled or disturbed by 'telling' about his or her birth history. This priority justifies the transmission of distortions, omissions or outright lies. This approach to the practice of telling was corroborated by Rowe in her 1959 guide for adopters.

In her later 1968 survey of adoption, Kornitzer (1968, p. 200) describes how telling operated as a simple communication of fact for adopters in her study sample:

> Many adopters were schooled to the now accepted idea that a child must be told he is adopted and nerved themselves to a simple telling, but the emotional atmosphere they engendered and their reluctance to answer later questions put a more or less complete stop to a child's enquiries.

Kornitzer confirms what the previous discussion on the practice of information elaborated about adopters in this era; they were commonly resistant to having much information about the child's birth heritage, so 'telling' was often restricted to the 'simple' communication of the fact of adoption.

The Hurst Committee wanted verbal disclosure about adoption to be in legislation to force adopters to undertake the task.[8] Neither the 1958 Adoption Act nor subsequent legislation ever included such enforcements. It is interesting both that the Hurst Committee should have wanted such a legal intervention and that it has always been refused. The idea that adopters could be forced to talk to their adopted children about their adoption would be a very big incursion into the privacy of family life, an incursion which would require the kind of policing that would keep adopters permanently tied to a tutelary position, governed rather than self-governing. Whilst telling never became a legal directive, the force with which it became an underpinning psychological necessity for the adopted child, made it seem as if it had acquired such a status. By the 1960s there was an enormous literature on the subject:

> There was a ... growing debate among academics, researchers and clinicians about the nature and significance of identity issues for adopted children. This promoted a recognition that telling children about their adoptive status required sensitivity, continuity of discussion and attention to 'timing' in terms of the child's maturity and degree of understanding. (Smith and Logan, 2004, p. 10)

What the above authors draw attention to was the emergence of a new technology of the adopted child, where the development of its divided nature required particular therapeutic and parenting interventions. Two concepts that emerged in the same year of 1964 captured the way that the adopted subject was now being constructed.

'Genealogical bewilderment' (Sants 1964) and 'Shared fate' (Kirk 1964) were two concepts that described the dual identity of the adopted subject. 'Genealogical bewilderment' is a concept predicated on the idea that genealogical clarity is an effect of being raised by biological kin. The adopted subject is bewildered by a dual genealogical heritage and 'needs' information about his or her prior birth history to clarify its place in its new family. Shared fate again is a concept that problematises the adopted subject's dual background. In order to really claim the adopted child as theirs, adoptive parents needed to be able to identify with the child and their background. They needed to align their 'fate' with that of the child's through talking to the child about his or her history, thus creating a 'shared fate'. Both these concepts are based on a technology of the subject that only makes belonging possible if difference is obliterated or recuperated. Within this technology, the practice of telling paradoxically works to both minimise and promote the adopted child's difference.

Third-party and direct adoptions

The sole form of participatory disclosure that continued in the post-war era was third-party and direct adoptions. Given the exclusionary practices that entered adoption in this era, it is somewhat paradoxical to find these unmediated and open forms of adoption still operative. There was reported opposition to this form of 'virtually unrestricted' practice by the Gamon Committee (Gamon Report, 1947, p. 5), but there seemed to be a reluctance to legislate for their removal in both the preceding Adoption Acts. There were various legal directives aimed at further regulation of these forms of adoption; for example, the 1949 Adoption Act gave local authorities the power to inspect such placements and the 1958 Adoption Act tightened up some of the existing controls.

The Hurst Report of 1954 dwelt at some length on the controversial issue of third-party and direct placements. The committee had clearly received many appeals for such placements to be banned, a step which the report described as too great an 'interference with individual liberty'. Given that such adoptions accounted for a third of all orders made, their continuing popularity was clearly difficult to oppose and the report was concerned that 'any restrictions on third party and direct placing will and would be evaded and that such placings would continue but adoption orders would not be applied for in those cases. Prohibition of such placings would increase de facto adoptions' (Hurst Report, 1954, p. 46).

The report also noted that that there was insufficient evidence that these adoptions were any worse than official placements. In an era when legislation had made more marginal the natural parent's involvement, these more informal placements sustained that involvement in some cases and even permitted a certain degree of contact following the order. In Goodacre's 1966 study, she focused on the informality of the relationship between adopter and natural parent in these adoptions and the contact that the parent often continued to have with the child. She reported a lengthy case study where the 'disadvantages' of such placements seemed to come down to the far higher levels of openness that everyone experienced. Clearly, the involved professionals opposed the adoption because they feared the child would have divided loyalties; they described the relationship between the adopters and the birth mother as 'unusual' (Goodacre, 1966, pp. 125–30). This continuing practice speaks to an underpinning tension in the field between the family as governed by a fully professional and managed social work service and the family as self-governing, directly managing its own adoption process.

Conclusion

In this chapter I have traced how adoption emerged in a changed form after the Second World War, working to regulate the adoptive family as complete replacement parents. However, whilst certain open practices from the pre-war era disappeared, others emerged or were sustained to consolidate adoption's paradoxical mode of operation. The practice of telling increasingly emerged into adoption work, complicating adoptive parenting with a discursive impetus for full acknowledgement of original kinship, a marking out of adoption's difference. This discursive trend would become a more forceful presence in adoption of the 1970s, as the constituency of children for adoption undergoes a radical transformation. The fields of public childcare and adoption converged in this period within a strategy of exclusionary practices around the involvement of unfit families. Both fields of substitute care were transformed by this encounter.

5
Differences and Identities: The Making of Contemporary Adoption

Children have no psychological conception of relationship by blood tie until quite late in their development ... What registers in their minds are the day to day interchanges with the adults who take care of them and who, on the strength of these, become the parent figure to whom they are attached. (Goldstein et al., 1973, pp. 11–13)

A compulsive, repetitive, and nostalgic desire for the archive, an irresponsible desire to return to the origin, a homesickness, a nostalgia for the return to the most archaic place of absolute commencement. (Derrida, 1996, p. 91)

I have placed together two very different quotations to introduce my account of this period of adoption. The first quotation from the early 1970s signals the emergence of the concept 'psychological parenting' to designate a new theorisation of how children were attached to families. The continuous and consistent attention of a person in a parental position would facilitate attachment, whether or not that person was linked to the child through biological kinship. The securing of the child's attachment to a psychological parent was dependent on the severing of other, prior attachments; in order to belong, the foundational place of the child's blood tie must be loosened or extinguished.

In the second quotation Derrida is describing the contemporary passion for archiving, for returning to our earliest origins and beginnings. He is suggesting that the beginning still operates as a compelling and nostalgic force in how contemporary subjects think about and fashion themselves.

By placing these two contrasting quotations together I want to underline how adoption in the 1970s pulled in two quite different directions. On the one hand, adoption became a 'permanent' solution for the older child, providing a new set of attachments and making a clean break with the damaging failures of past parenting. On the other hand, adoption moved more actively towards an acknowledgment of the past, reinstating the importance of original kinship through a range of practices – the opening up of birth records for adopted adults, life story books and later life letters.

There were two competing discourses at play here in terms of how an adopted child's welfare was understood. First, that adopted children needed protection from their early histories and, second, that adopted children needed to have those early histories preserved. These competing discourses reflect some major transformations in how childhood – and more specifically the child in substitute care – was reconceptualised in this era. Chris Jenks, a contemporary writer on childhood, argues that children had acquired a new centrality in response to the conditions of late or post-modernity; that in a culture now characterised by change, fragmentation and discontinuity, there was a desire to preserve, watch over and guard children. In his book, *Childhood* (1996, p. 106), he writes: 'Late-modern society has re-adopted the child. The child ... has become the site or the relocation of discourses concerning stability, integration and the social bond. The child is now envisioned as a form of nostalgia, a longing for times past.'

The quotation above captures the dual, paradoxical discourses that circulated in the 1970s and 1980s around the figure of the child. The child, and what the child represented – lost innocence, a cohesive social order, a secure family for life – was to be protected and its history preserved, even as those very values it represented were in the process of being questioned and overturned.

As previous chapters have elaborated, the idea of an interior childhood history has been an important element in the formation of the contemporary technology of the self, making both the time of childhood and the inner child of adult life foundational sources of knowledge and truth. Jenks (1996, p. 109) described how this technology acquired a dominant force in a time of increasingly destabilised and disintegrating social bonds. This can be seen most clearly in how adoption emerged during this period. In a childcare culture characterised by discourses of risk, protection and stability, adoption emerged as a form of substitute care, protecting damaged children from their histories as well as preserving those histories of early damage. Of course, a central claim that this study has made is that adoption has always operated as a paradoxical field of practice. However, between 1970 and 1985, this constitutive paradox became more marked and contested, anticipating the eventual introduction of 'open adoption' at the end of the period.

This chapter will explore how adoption emerged in a changed form in the 1970s and how the two central concepts that structured its practices – permanency planning and psychological parenting – operated to both facilitate and contest the different open practices that were introduced in this period. My analysis will pay particular attention to the way that adoption participants – adoptive parents, birth parents and adopted child – were differently constituted in this era.

The reconfiguring of adoption

Up until the 1970s the discourses of adoption and child protection had sustained quite discrete social work trajectories, addressing different populations of welfare subjects and operating within a different notion of the law. Put simply, child protection work, even when it was 'preventive', was a largely coercive discourse, whereas adoption had always operated as consensual. In the 1970s these two distinctively different interventions into family life coalesced, transforming how adoption participants were produced and understood.

Until the 1970s, the unfit parent of child protection work had very little encounter with adoption.[1] Whilst fostering was often a permanent home for children in care, it was not a form of permanency that extinguished parents' status as parents. Most commonly, this constituency of failing parent would lose her child to institutional or foster care, but would not lose her fundamental parental tie to them. There was a great legislative reluctance to adopt children against the wishes of a mother, however unfit that mother's parenting was judged to be.

For much of the twentieth century, decision-making about substitute care, whether a child was adopted or fostered, revolved around the issue of breaking kinship ties. As Chapters 3 and 4 explored in some detail, the natural family's consent to adoption occupied a central place in the making of such placements and dispensation with that consent has only relatively recently become an active practice. Professionals rooted their decisions about substitute care in whether a parent consented or not to the breaking of the child's kinship ties and if consent was not given then the child would not be adopted. Whilst in the post-war era other differentiating factors emerged to shape fostering and adoption more distinctively, health and age of the infant, for example, the issue of consent continued to operate as central in choosing the form of substitute care. However, in the 1970s, this consensual discourse began to lose some of its operative force, while a more adversarial and interventionist discourse entered adoption work. This discursive transformation was impelled by the changing constituency of adoption. Up until the early 1970s adoption had been a service for infertile adopters, wishing for a perfect baby to parent as if their own biological child, but from the mid-1970s onwards, adoption became a service for troubled children from care in need of specialist alternative parenting. This convergence of child protection subjects and adoption worked to transform adoption practices in two quite paradoxical ways: a discourse of compulsion reworked the previously consensual basis to adoption, making consent both irrelevant and marginal to its operation, and a discourse of partnership and involvement with unfit families challenged the more closed practices and led to the contested introduction of open adoption by the late 1980s.

It is one of the most surprising elements to this study that adoption practices were more closed when it was most consensual and more open when it became more adversarial. This section will now trace in more detail these transformations in the culture of adoption.

Commentators (Howe et al., 1992; Triseliotis et al., 1997; Parker, 1999; Bridge and Swindells, 2003) have identified the huge social and legislative changes that occurred at the end of the 1960s as central to this transformation in adoption. Weeks (1985, p. 33–4) understands the early 1970s as a period where contradictory discourses were at play in the emergence of the family as an institution in crisis. Discourses of liberatory politics worked alongside more conservative discourses to create a culture pulling in two directions: a questioning of traditional social institutions such as the family and a reinstating of the values associated with those institutions. Social movements emerged to organise, protest and demonstrate for the reform agenda, at the same time as that agenda was being opposed and contested. For example, Weeks (1985, p. 30) notes that prosecutions for homosexual acts increased following the 1967 legislation that decriminalised homosexuality.

Certainly, the form of family life that adoption had promoted and provided became part of this wider crisis in the family. A number of legislative reforms put into question the traditional heterosexual marital unit as the basis for family life and signified a shift in the way that family life would be regulated: in particular, the legalisation of homosexuality; the introduction of the contraceptive pill and the liberalising of sexual relationships outside of marriage; the 1967 Abortion Act, which extended the grounds for abortion, and led to a doubling of abortions in the first five years after the act; the 1969 Divorce Law reform, which relaxed grounds for divorce, making lone mothers a more common form of family.

These changes not only transformed the position of the unmarried mother of post-war adoption, but in the process reconfigured the moralising framework through which adoption had operated. Parker (1999, p. 1) comments: 'The new terminology of "one parent families" marked the increasing incorporation of unmarried motherhood into this all-embracing category. The issue of illegitimacy and its attendant stigma were fast disappearing.' One of the most immediate effects was a dramatic decrease in the number of adoption orders. From a peak period of 27,500 orders in 1968, the numbers of adoptions consistently fell throughout the next decade. However, whilst the numbers of babies for adoption rapidly fell as an effect of this redefining of practices of mothering, the numbers of couples still wishing to adopt remained constant. In the 1970s the demand for adoption continued at a time when the social pressures to relinquish a baby for adoption were relaxing. This installed the necessity for a redefining of the nature of adoption by changing both its moral framework and those who would be its participants. This would involve a transformation in notions of unfit mothering and how the unfit mother would be engaged with by the law. This crisis in adoption intersected with a reconfiguring of child protection work, making a productive convergence that fitted together the child at risk in need of protection with adopters in need of a child. Both these different forms of substitute childcare were transformed by this encounter.

The making of a new kind of permanent family

As Chapter 4 explored, after the Second World War adoption emerged as a complete replacement family for illegitimate infants and operated as a full substitute for the family of origin. Whilst open practices unsettled and put into question adoption's replacement status, the discursive force of such practices was kept in check by an insistent discourse of adoption as a fully naturalised and normalised substitution.

By the end of the 1960s this picture was beginning to be unsettled by a growing move to psychologise the adopted child's difference. The acknowledgement of difference discourse in adoption immediately challenged any model of adoptive parenting that identified with so-called biological parenting. There emerged a move to make adoptive parenting a particular and discrete task and role, separate and different from birth parenting and potentially requiring professional intervention and support. This discursive trend within adoption work had always made possible the adoption of children whose differences were manifest and clear. If being adopted was always an experience that marked the subject as different to that of biologically raised subjects, then it would follow that any child, not just a healthy infant, could be adoptable. Furthermore, as the welfare of adopted children became tied to an acknowledgment of a difference regime of parenting, the tradition of passing off the adopted child as one's own began to be more consistently questioned. Both Kellmer Pringle (1967, pp. 25–6) and Seglow et al. (1972, pp. 126–7) in their different studies understood adoption as a specific and different form of parenting, acknowledgment of which was imperative to prevent psychological damage to the adopted child.

In this same period there was already interest from some voluntary agencies in making adoption available for older children in care, whose differences would be evident. Reich (1988b) and James (1980) both discuss the emergence in the mid-1960s of two projects – British Adoption Project and Independent Adoption Society – specialising in the adoption of black and mixed-race children from institutional care by white families. These transracial placements made the child's difference a very evident and exposed part of its everyday family life, but, in spite of this, were deemed to be successful adoptions (see Gill and Jackson 1983). This is not the place to debate the contested status of transracial adoptions in the 1980s, Gaber and Aldridge (1994) and Tizard and Phoenix (2002) go into this history in detail. What I do wish to emphasise here is how transracial placements marked the emergence of adoption as a form of care where the child's difference could be acknowledged, managed and assimilated.

What I have hoped to illustrate is how by the late 1960s there were already the discursive possibilities for adoption transforming itself into a very different kind of permanent care. This transformation would be accelerated in the 1970s with what has come to be known as the permanency movement. It emerged at a time of falling numbers of babies for adoption and when discourses of risk and prevention were structuring more interventionist approaches in public childcare work. Commentators (Packman, 1975; Thoburn et al., 1986; Triseliotis et al., 1997; Triseliotis, 1998b) have identified a number of elements that converged in this period to produce this movement. First, the fostering studies from the 1960s showed a 50 per cent disruption rate, and brought fostering into disrepute. Second, the death of Maria Colwell following her return home raised questions about the policy of rehabilitation with birth families. Finally, the *Children Who Wait* study (1973) revealed a national picture of high numbers of children in the care system, and showed the failure of post-war preventive work.

It is important to interrogate why these events, events that had certainly occurred in other, earlier periods, came to such prominence in the early 1970s. In focusing on the present circumstances of their emergence, I am arguing against more causal and developmental accounts of this history. Foucault offers an important critique of this kind of historical analysis: 'These developments may appear as a culmination, but they are merely the current episodes in a series of subjugations' (Foucault, 1998a, p. 376).

Clearly, in this era these events were signifying or representing a number of concerns that were newly emerging into public childcare: the plight of vulnerable children in insecure and impermanent fostering placements; and the biological family as both resistant to change and dangerous. These concerns centred on the child at risk, a figure who was becoming increasingly pivotal to both childcare policy and the wider culture. This child, living either in dangerous circumstances at home or in insecure circumstances in care, emerged in this period as a welfare subject in need of both protection and permanent family life. With fostering situated as an inadequate substitute care and the policy of returning children home in question, adoption entered the public childcare field as a more permanent, safe and secure alternative. Rowe et al.'s (1984, p. 226) study of long-term fostering reflected the period's view of adoption's superiority: 'The inescapable conclusion of our findings is that many long-term foster children would be better off if they were adopted ... not because fostering is so bad, but because it is not good enough.'

The association of adoption with permanency seems key to understanding its emergence as a new form of public childcare. Only adoption as this enduring and 'forever' form of family could address the risks and insecurities of the child in care's life. This belief in the curative potential of adoption had been endorsed by American adoption projects that had successfully placed older 'special needs' children in adoptive families, demonstrating that trauma was reversible with the right kind of re-parenting.[2] By the mid-1970s, adoption as a form of 'treatment' (Triseliotis, 1998b, pp. 14–15) forcefully emerged into British childcare, inspiring various pioneering projects such as Parents for Children (established 1976). The quotation below is from the founder of this project and captures the philosophy of this new approach to adoption: '[The] beginning of a recognition that every parentless child could potentially be adopted and the greater his handicap perhaps the greater his need for adoption' (Sawbridge, 1980, p. 163). We have clearly moved a considerable distance from the post-war adoption of healthy white infants passing as the adopter's birth children.[3] Here the difference of adoption was embraced as precisely the key to its successful treatment of maltreated or disabled children in public care.

There were three important elements in the reconfiguring of adoption as a new form of permanency for older, troubled children, signifying a considerable shift in the technology of the adopted subject. These elements reflect the new importance given to 'permanency for children' as not only a childcare policy, but a new psychological discourse. I want to briefly outline the main elements in the emergence of the psychological discourse of permanency.

First, there was a new centrality placed on the child: 'From parent's rights being paramount to children's interests being of prime importance' (Sawbridge, 1980, p. 163). Within this discourse the blood tie no longer operated as a significant psychological bond in terms of the child's welfare. The child's welfare could be assessed and secured as a separate issue to its family of origin. The starkest example of this discursive emergence was the advertising of children that controversially became an aspect of practice in this era (ibid., pp. 170–1). Ryburn (1992a) makes the point that the local and national advertising of a child for a new family dramatically separated that child from its family of origin, presenting him or her as an orphaned child.

Second, there was a new emphasis on brief, focused planning in order to make fast and focused decisions about children's futures. This became a central tenet of the permanency philosophy. The psychological underpinning for this approach to child placement derived from an influential publication: *Beyond the Best Interests of the Child* (Goldstein et al., 1973). The authors argued that children are 'incomplete beings' (ibid., p. 9), living in a different sense of time to adults (ibid., p. 11): 'Unlike adults, who have learned to anticipate the future and thus to manage delay ... [the child] is not sufficiently matured to enable him to use thinking to hold onto the past he has lost.' The child's inability to manage separation made fast decision-making about its future a psychological necessity (Goldstein et al., 1973, p. 42). The authors recommended that placement decisions must be treated as an 'emergency' (ibid., p. 42), otherwise 'irreparable psychological injury' would be done to the child having to wait in uncertainty (ibid., p. 40). This led to a policy and practice to remove children from unfit parents as quickly as possible to mitigate psychological damage to the child.

Finally, there was the emergence of the concept of psychological parenting. Bowlby's work on attachment had been used in the 1950s to theorise separation as a pivotal psychological task in substitute care.

His theory argued the necessity for a continuous maternal bond in early infancy, with any interruption potentially causative of trauma. Consequently, the dynamics of separation from a primary maternal figure became central to diverse childcare policies in the post-war era – rehabilitation, access with biological family and the rapid placing of infants for adoption. Rutter's 1972 study, *Maternal Deprivation Reassessed*, whilst still drawing on Bowlby's work, challenged the formative place of separation and privileged deprivation as key to the emergence of childhood trauma. Rutter claimed that children can cope with disruption to their attachments, but deprivation of care would be emotionally damaging (ibid., p. 49). He argued that it is not the breaking of bonds that causes damage, but the failure to make bonds in the first place that is the root issue: 'It is bond formation which matters and that is of less consequence than to whom the attachment is formed' (ibid., p. 106).

Rutter's reworking of attachment theory was reflected by the authors cited earlier, Goldstein et al. (1973), whose key distinction between 'biological' and 'psychological' parenting assumed an enormous importance in the reconfiguring of adoption of this period. Put simply, the authors (1973, p. 13) understood attachment as residing in the 'day to day interchanges' between parent and child, and not in the kinship tie. Bonds were built not biologically given and were achieved through children having 'emotional constancy' (ibid., p. 25) within a continuous parental relationship (ibid., p. 31).

The significance of the concept of psychological parenting is, then, threefold: First, there was a new emphasis on the quality of the parental bond, and a move away from an innate valuation of the original kinship tie, which is now deemed of less developmental importance. Second, there is no longer a role for contact in mitigating the effects of separation within a discourse that privileged the enduring effects of unfit parenting. Indeed, achieving a speedy separation was a psychological necessity for a child with dysfunctional attachments. Third, reparative re-parenting with a substitute carer acquired a central role in helping children recover from the troubled attachment patterns of unfit parenting.

A number of practices immediately followed from the emergence of this new psychological discourse of permanency, which Adcock et al. (1983, p. 44) neatly summarised: 'The use of the permanence philosophy could lead to the assumption of parental rights at an early stage, termination of access and placement for adoption against the wishes of natural parents.'

For unfit families, then, the consequences of this new adversarial discourse was transformative: loss of parental rights, loss of child to adoption and loss of any contact with that child. The new discursive conditions of permanency reworked adoption into an aggressively interventionist set of practices, which I will discuss in more detail below. First I want to consider how adoptive parenting was transfigured within this new permanency discourse. One might think that for the adoptive parent this discourse would structure them as complete replacement parents, sustaining their identity with that of the post-war infertile adopters. However, it is interesting to discover how alongside this role, adopters were also regulated as clearly defined substitutes, with their difference requiring support, education and recognition. It is to this analysis that I will now turn.

The regulation of difference: the adoptive family redefined

It was the 1976 Adoption Act that established adoption as a central part of public childcare provision, making it a statutory duty for local authorities to provide a comprehensive service for adoption for children in its care (Lowe et al., 1999, pp. 30–3). Adoption became 'professionalised' and completely regulated as part of its integration into childcare work (Bridge and Swindells, 2003, p. 9). Of course, as Chapters 3 and 4 made clear, adoption had always been regulated but in this era there was a change in how regulation worked. In Chapter 4, drawing on Foucault's analysis in *Discipline and Punish* (1977), I showed how the post-war adoptive family was regulated by both an intervening power that exposed the artifice of adoption and an instrumental power that supported adopters in making themselves into 'natural parents'. What emerged in the 1970s was the normalisation of intervention; the adoptive family's difference was no longer concealed, but was normalised through different interventionist regimes, assessment, therapeutic help and economic support. The 1976 legislation and the 1983 Agency regulations introduced a range of interventionist measures that reshaped the technology of the adoptive parent. I have selected three examples as illustration.

First, the assessment of adopters as a more rigorous and protracted undertaking. Adopters had to prove their suitability to adopt through an assessment procedure that included being approved by an agency, being screened by an adoption panel and then examined as to whether a particular child should be placed in their care (Bridge and Swindells, 2003, p. 9). Second, the provision of post-placement and post-adoption support to adoptive families. Such provision was a growing intervention throughout the 1970s and 1980s, receiving endorsement through the 1983 legislative requirement for adoption agencies to provide counselling to all parties to adoption (Lowe et al., 1999, p. 33). Finally, the payment of adoption allowances. Adoptive families were now financially supported in their parenting role (Lowe et al., 1999, pp. 26–7).

These measures all worked to produce the adoptive family as a unit requiring special help to function as a family. Clearly, becoming an adoptive family was now only possible through the mediations of an adoption agency. This was the era when independent adoptions, that is, those made outside of the professional services, were banned by the 1976 Adoption Act.

These forms of help worked to sustain the adoptive family's difference from the biological family and made any move towards an assimilation of the two problematic. Reich (1988b, p. 3) makes a comparison between the adoptive family in this period and the post-war era: '... if they [adopters] were seeking a close replacement for the baby they might have had, they would not be able to cope with the reality of bringing up some one else's child and the task of explaining adoption.' The key difference for Reich was that adoption now involved the raising of someone else's child, a difference that could not be concealed in the way that seemed possible with a post-war infant. Furthermore, it was no longer possible or beneficial for adoptive parents to model their family life on that of biological parents; adoption in the 1970s was about parenting a child's difference.

This was the era when adoptive families began to also seek support from each other, marking a kind of 'coming out' for adoptive parents. A national network of support through self-help, Parent to Parent Information and Adoption Service (PPIAS), was established in 1971, becoming an organisation that highlighted the complexities and issues facing adoptive families in the 1970s. This public emergence of adoptive parenting as both challenging and different to biological parenting stood in marked contrast to the post-war culture of assimilation and concealment.

This normalising of intervention made the adoptive family permanently governed by what Donzelot has called the tutelary system, where governance is by outside agency. This system has historically been used to govern working-class family life, but in the 1970s middle-class adopters began to be subjects of a tutelary form of social work. In this era instrumental power worked to support adopters into making themselves into specialist parents, where outside support was an integral aspect to their functioning as a family. The self-governing adopters of the post-war era, resisting the intrusions of social workers, were redefined by new discursive conditions governing adoption in the 1970s. The limits of privacy for adoptive family life had been radically re-drawn.

However, this era was not simply about the difference of adoptive parenting. As the preceding section discussed, the psychological discourse of permanency constructed adopters as full-replacement parents, with superior attachment patterns with which to parent the damaged older child. Whilst on the one hand the child's difference was emphasised, there was simultaneously a move to elide that difference through providing the child with new affectional bonds as a full replacement for their original dysfunctional family. Tizard (1977, p. 9) captures the paradoxical nature of the adopter's position: 'Their task is not to regard the child exactly as if he were their own...instead they must rear the child with the same commitment as the natural parent, while at the same time everyone concerned remains very clear that this is not "their" child.'

From consent to compulsion

The momentous transformation of adoption from a consensual to an adversarial set of practices has been well documented by historians and commentators of adoption (see particularly Thoburn, 1990; Triseliotis et al., 1997; Cretney, 1998; Lowe et al., 1999). In a field historically characterised by voluntarily relinquished responsibilities, the emergence of a discourse of compulsion and coercion has been a significant and contested change, simultaneously supported and resisted.

As earlier chapters in this study have discussed, adoption had always operated as a consensual transaction since its legal inception in 1926. Whilst consent had lost some of its more participatory force by the post-war era (see Chapter 4), it was still foundational to the granting of an adoption order. I am not suggesting that coercion and compulsion did not operate in these earlier eras – there is a substantial literature detailing the pressures that moralising discourses exerted on unwed mothers in the 1950s and 1960s (see Chapter 4) – but I am suggesting that up until the 1970s there was not an adoption culture where social workers or the courts would aggressively intervene to remove and place a child against a mother's wishes.[4] However, from the 1970s onwards it became an increasing pattern for adoption orders to be granted in opposition to and so without parental consent.[5]

This emergence of adversarialism in adoption work can in part be understood by its convergence with public childcare at a point when it was becoming more aggressively interventionist. The 1970s was the era when the child at risk began to assume a more structuring importance in work with unfit families. Discourses of compulsion began to dominate child protection work, with a dramatic increase in children removed under emergency measures. This group of children had previously been subjects of 'preventive' or 'rehabilitative' work, or subjects for foster care, but in this period they slowly began to emerge as subjects for adoption. These children of unfit parentage now acquired biographies that demanded they were given a new permanent start in life with better adoptive families. They would be 'freed' for adoption by new legislation, removing the need for consent from families who were judged to be undeserving of any kind of consultative process. Freeing is an interesting term, evocative of a state of liberation, a child freed from circumstances of confinement to a better life elsewhere, reflecting the permanency philosophy of adoption of this period.

This transformation to the consensual basis to adoption was slow in acquiring an operative force, in part because professionals in the field resisted implementing adoption work as an aggressively coercive practice. A number of research studies during the 1970s and 1980s reported amongst social work professionals an abiding association of adoption with consent, and a corroborating reluctance to place a child for adoption unless a parent was in agreement.[6] This was a period, then, of two distinctively contrasting discourses: the traditional consensual discourse where parents agreed the adoption order and a newly emerging coercive and contested discourse where children were adopted against the wishes of their parents, and where parental opposition was dispensed with by a new legislative intervention, freeing orders. I want to briefly analyse the emergence of freeing legislation as it encompasses the dual discursive conditions governing the way that adoption operated in this period.

Paradoxically, a genealogy of freeing reveals that it was not introduced as a draconian measure but to facilitate the adoption of relinquished infants. By installing a procedure that would expedite the mother's permission, the mother would be removed from a continuing painful involvement in the adoption of her child (Thoburn, 1990; Lambert, 1994; Bridge and Swindells, 2003). Freeing legislation 'released' a child for adoption by transferring parental responsibilities from parent to local authority. The purpose was to clarify and secure a child's legal position in advance of adoption proceedings, thus easing anxieties of both relinquishing and prospective parents. It was anticipated that this would be an uncontested process within a consensual adoption culture. However, as Lambert (1994, p. 79) elaborates below, by the time of its eventual emergence in 1984 the cultural terrain had changed:

> Instead of being used mainly as a shorter route in *uncontested* proceedings, freeing has become synonymous with contested adoption in people's minds. This is because the other factor for which freeing was proposed has become the dominant factor ... the sanctioning of adoptions in care without parental consent. (author's emphasis)

Lambert describes very well the two distinctively different adoption discourses that converged to shape the emergence of freeing. The more adversarial and coercive discourse – the 'other factor' – certainly was already shaping a very different kind of adoption work. Indeed, Lambert (1973) was one of the researchers, alongside Tizard (1977), whose work had influenced the introduction of the freeing legislation. Both their studies highlighted the 'plight' of children in the care system, whose need for a permanent home was compromised by their parent's refusal to consent to their adoption. The new legislation would secure such children a future in a new adoptive family by removing their parent's involvement from their lives.

This was really the legislative moment when discourses of child protection and adoption converge. Here we have an instance of two distinctively different discourses coming together and working together to sustain adoption as an exclusionary practice. 'The main thrust of this law was to give priority to the long-term welfare of the child even if this entailed overriding the wishes of parents' (Rowe, 1991, p. 11). Here Rowe linked the more adversarial dimensions of the 1976 Adoption Act with a changing notion of child welfare. As I have already discussed, within the psychological discourse of permanency, a child's welfare could be assessed independently of its parents; the paramount concern was the child at risk and in danger. This marked a considerable reworking of the post-war notion of welfare, where a biological parent's consent to adoption was understood to be linked to the welfare of the child. This unhinging of the child from its biological origin would make possible all kinds of exclusionary practices where the family of origin had no involvement. Freeing legislation was one such example, where parents' involvement was dispensed with even before the adoption order had been made. Through the 1970s and 1980s parental agreement and its dispensation became inextricably linked to the paramount welfare of the child (Bridge and Swindells, 2003). In other words, a child's welfare depends upon its safe removal for adoption from unfit parents, whose resistance to that plan is detrimental to the child's future well-being.

Within such an adversarial culture, where the biological family's involvement was both actively terminated and pathologised, the sustaining of open practices with that family would appear to have little discursive possibility of emergence. However, this was the era when different open practices did emerge, extending the possibilities that the post-war period had circumscribed. As I have already said, it is one of the more paradoxical findings of this study that adoption became more open when its mode of operation became more adversarial, eventually leading to what has come to be known as 'open adoption'. The following section will trace the emergence of open practices within the cultural context of permanency.

Permanence and open practices

> This [permanency] ... was linked to the idea that it would not be possible to recruit adopters for these older children unless they were given a 'clear run' unimpeded by reminders of the child's first family and earlier attachments. (Thoburn, 1996, p. 131)

In the paper from which the above quotation was taken, Thoburn directly linked the discourse of permanency with what she understood as more closed adoption practices, where adopters could parent without the intrusions of the child's family of origin (ibid., p. 136). As I have discussed earlier, the discourse of permanency certainly operated to curtail the place of the family of origin, working to limit more active forms of involvement. However, this was also the era when open practices that incorporated the child's first history began to emerge in ways that were not operative previously.

As Chapter 4 discussed, post-war adoption rarely encompassed contact of any kind between adopted children and their families of origin either through letters or by visits. Open practices in that era were mostly bound up with the transmission of information about the child's adoptive status and it was only within so-called private adoptions, outside of adoption agencies, that more direct forms of contact happened. The long history of public childcare followed a similar trajectory around open practices to that followed by adoption, with one exception: from the post-war period onwards, public childcare endorsed the open practice of visiting, but over two decades of its endorsement the practice was resisted and contested. In the 1970s within a culture of compulsion and aggressive intervention, this practice of passive discouragement was superseded by one of active prohibition regarding children's contact with their families. Adcock (1980, p. 17) elaborated the standard position of the era: 'When the child is unlikely to leave care, a decision about continuing or terminating contact should depend on how far continuing the parent–child relationship hinders the establishment of the child in a permanent home.' She goes on to write: 'Contact does not need to be maintained simply to avoid disrupting attachments to a parent who is not fulfilling other functions of the parental role.'

Adcock is making a number of points that would be central to how open practices emerged in the 1970s: first, contact in this period emerged as a practice linked to parenting; it was seen as an activity that would sustain a child's relationship to his or her absent parent at a time when it was making a new family connection. Second, sustaining such past attachments would prevent a child from making new attachments with a new family and, finally, if an absent parent was never going to be a fully involved parent again, then contact with that parent became irrelevant.

In this period in public childcare there was a now a link between severing contact with the birth family and securing a new family for the child. This prohibition on contact was central to the emergence of adoption as a substitute family for children from care. Adoption in terms of its post-war practices had already minimised the degree to which it included the family of origin, making the adoption of children from care without contact an unproblematic continuity with its recent traditions. The more exclusionary discourse of adoption was given an additional momentum by freeing legislation, which, as commentators have noted, did not only free a child for adoption, but also achieved the termination of its contact with its biological parents (Adcock, 1980; Lambert, 1994; Ryan, 1994). As no access clause could be attached to a freeing order, the possibility of continuing contact for a child freed for adoption was effectively ruled out by this legal procedure (Thoburn, 1990, p. 94).

In one sense, then, it not surprising that when public childcare became dominated by discourses of compulsion and exclusionary practices in the 1970s, that adoption emerged as its ideal form of substitute care. However, this critical convergence of adoption and public childcare did not just work to exclude unfit parents from their children's lives. In fact, this convergence worked to destabilise the way that adopted children had historically been understood to belong to adoptive families. In the 1970s and 1980s, practices that included the birth family began to emerge into adoption work, as did debates about adopted children having access to their first families within the context of adoption hearings. It had always been historically possible for conditions to be added to an adoption order and the 1976 Adoption Act sustained this tradition with section 12 (6), which states: 'An adoption order may contain such terms and conditions as the court thinks fit.' It was usually the case in this period that the courts deemed adoption and contact irreconcilable; if contact was desirable, then adoption was the wrong placement choice. White (1993, p. 93) cites an adoption case from 1986:

> It would be difficult to imagine a greater interference with the rights of adopters ... to grant access to someone who, by reason of the adoption order, has become in law a stranger. That is the reason why an order for adoption with a condition of access should only be granted in very exceptional cases.

However, Bridge and Swindells (2003, p. 17) report that section 12 (6) was mobilised to incorporate access in some adoptions during this period, although this was always undertaken with 'hesitancy' and only granted on the grounds that there was prior agreement by the prospective adopters. In a similar vein, Fratter (1996, p. 35) cited an adoption case from 1976 which held that the autonomy of adoptive parents should not be affected by any condition imposed: 'Clearly no condition should be imposed which would be regarded as detracting from the rights and duties of the adoptive parents.'

What seems important to emphasise here is that a connection between adoption and contact had entered public discourse and whilst it was mainly contested and refuted, there were now the discursive possibilities for this connection to be made. This is a very good example of how a reverse discourse produces the opposite effects of that which it manifestly intends. By upholding the integrity of the adoptive family unit, the above cases implicitly call that integrity into question by raising it as an issue that needs both defending and protecting. Chapter 6 will explore in more detail how open adoption as a set of practices that actively encouraged indirect and direct contact emerged most forcefully as a paradoxical effect of their prohibition in this period. Now, I will conclude this chapter with an overview of the open practices that emerged into adoption work during the 1970s.

Open practices

Opening up of birth records

> We take the view that on reaching the age of majority an adopted
> person should not be denied access to his original birth records. We
> therefore recommend that all adopted adults, whenever adopted,
> should in future be permitted to obtain a copy of their original birth
> entry. (Houghton Committee, 1972, p. 85)

Access to birth records became law in section 51 of the 1976 Adoption
Act. For the first time, adopted people, but not birth parents, were enabled to access their original birth and adoption records. People adopted
prior to the date of this legislation in November 1976 were required
to have one session of compulsory counselling prior to accessing their
records. The rationale for this was a concern about the motivation of
the person wanting information and a wish to prevent vengeful acts
towards the adoptee's biological family (Triseliotis et al., 2005, pp. 7–8).
Additionally, the 1989 Children Act retrospectively inserted into the
1976 Adoption Act a provision for an adoption contact register, whereby
both adopted adults and birth relatives could record their names, signifying that they wished to be contacted. This gave birth parents' position some legislative recognition for the first time, although without
any legal access to information, their position to locate an adopted
child remained as limited as previously.

One of the key individual influences driving this legislative change
was the work of John Triseliotis, published in 1973 as *In Search of
Origins*. This study of open access to birth records in Scotland, introduced since the legal inception of adoption there in 1929, had been
commissioned by the Houghton Committee and its findings led to the
introduction of similar procedures for England and Wales. Triseliotis's
work had identified a number of issues with post-war adoption: that
adopted children were not always informed about their adopted status; that a late disclosure felt particularly traumatic; that even when
informed, many adoptees reported that there was little further corroborating information about their family history. The linking of
this secrecy in adoption with life-long insecurity in adopted people was a compelling part of the book's findings (Triseliotis, 1980a,
pp. 226–7):

> All adopted people want to learn about their parents of origin and to
> establish continuity between past and present. A tiny minority may

also wish to meet their birth parents. Adoptees need to trace their roots, establish their identity and generally place themselves in relation to their present self and past heritage.

The technology of the adopted subject that Triseliotis describes above was to emerge forcefully into the adoption culture of the 1970s and 1980s, a culture now marked by a very different population of adopted subjects. At a time when children from care were being placed for adoption and all contact with their unfit families terminated, this counter-discourse emerged, emphasising the foundational importance of origins and the risks attendant on ignoring the adopted person's need for both knowledge of and connection with their first histories. Of course, the legislation was addressing a very different group of adoption subjects, but paradoxically, worked to impact upon the contemporary adoption culture in two ways: The practice of providing background information about the child to adoptive parents began to emerge as a practice imperative through the 1970s and the practice of archiving became more thorough and organised with the advent of the open archive.

As Part II of this study will elaborate, once records are open to the scrutiny of adopted people, the requirement for reliable record keeping becomes more urgent. An official information leaflet for adopted adults, issued by the General Registrar's Office, gives a glimpse of how adoption archives operated before the 1976 Adoption Act:

> There can be no certainty that any additional information about your adoption or your background exists. Before 1984, adoption agencies were only required to keep their records for twenty five years... they may have been lost or destroyed... old records are often brief, so that information you may want to have may not be included. (GRO ACR 100, p. 5)

The above reflects one of the dominant technologies of the adopted subject, that adoption confers a new replacement identity, thus removing the operative force of an originating birth identity. Within such a technology, records of a previous life or history become irrelevant or redundant, making their safekeeping in an archive unnecessary. Of course, alongside this technology there has always been another co-existing, where original kinship is an enduring, structuring foundation to identity, a technology that was gathering regulatory momentum with the opening up of birth records.

Provision of information to adopters

As Chapter 4 discussed, post-war adoption had already installed this practice of providing information, mostly as a support to the practice of telling. The information was often of a rudimentary nature from records that were inadequately kept; it was often verbally communicated in a dismissive and circumspect fashion to adopters who were resistant to their child having another history elsewhere. In the 1970s the provision of information became a 'professionalised' practice, with legislative endorsement. There were a number of different kinds of information, which I will discuss in turn: general information to adopters, life story books and later life letters.

Providing general information was laid down as a regulatory requirement, where adoption agencies should provide written information to adopters about the child being placed: '[they] .shall provide the prospective adopter with written information about the child, his personal history and background including his religious and cultural background, his health history' (Adoption Agencies regs, 1983, p. 12). Clearly, the archive was now operative and open. Rowe reflects this in her 1982 revised guide for adopters where she stressed the role of the placing agency in having records and information as a resource for adopters if they cannot answer their child's questions. 'If you cannot satisfy your youngster's curiosity, go back with him to the adoption agency and ask for more information' (Rowe, 1982, p. 182).

Tizard's (1977, p. 141) study of adoption from institutional care noted a 'standard content of communication recommended by most social workers' on the subject of the adopted child's family of origin and institutional history. Clearly, there was an emerging sense that certain kinds of information should be standard and available to adopters and that this information is 'essential for the child's healthy development'. This new emphasis on the provision of information from well-kept records was partly an effect of the opening up of birth records legislation. Rowe (1982, p. 182) linked the practice of giving contemporary adopters information about their child to the documented need for information from adopted adults:

> Every major piece of research into the outcome of adoption has shown that adopted people regard those who brought them up as their real parents, but that they want to know something of their natural family background and that they feel it is their adoptive parents' responsibility to give them this information.

The undertaking of life story work and the making of life story books became related adoption practices in this era. James (1980, p. 185) summarised the purpose of a life story book: 'A life story book is often used as a way of piecing together the past and providing a pictorial memory for the child which can accompany him into his new family and to which he can refer and add to in the future.' Triseliotis (1997, pp. 125–8) further elaborates the link between a life story book and direct work with children about their histories. He understands a life story book as a chronological account of an adopted child's life up to its placement in its adoptive family. It could lead to or be part of 'direct work' with the child, where forms of therapy were used to help the child work through difficult emotional issues arising from the legacies of their life story. Triseliotis et al. (1997) saw these documents increasingly entering adoption work by the early 1980s, partly as an effect of the older children being placed for adoption.

Life story books were predicated on the importance of the recovery and reconstruction of lost histories as an important regime of truth about the adopted person. As I have already discussed, the 1970s was the era when discourses of original kinship began to more forcefully operate in adoption work. The necessity to acknowledge the adopted child's different heritage was an increasingly important condition for adopting and life story books were a tool in helping adopters to both recognise and assimilate this difference. These books operated to reduce and domesticate complexity in order to make it manageable for the new adoptive family. On this theme, Cohen (1995, p. 2) comments on how the 'official' version of his adopted son's life story book was at a considerable distance from the complexities of the boy's own version of his history:

> It quickly became apparent that this was not how he read his life ... if the life story book was meant to serve as a kind of passport for him into the foreign country which was his new family, it was a total failure. He made it clear that he did not recognise himself in the 'official' version of his identity.

What Cohen captures was how official adoption narratives worked to exclude and to make marginal the other stories that they simultaneously generated. Whilst life story books appeared to be an inclusionary form of practice for birth parents, they actually worked to exclude through imposing a sanitised or edited version of the birth family's life. Atherton (1986a, p. 15) saw life story books as a way of removing the child's first family from its life: 'This work itself is sometimes used as an argument against continuing access and this has led to a charge of life story books being used as a "ritualistic burial" of natural families.' Thoburn (1996, p. 130) made a similar point and understood the role of life story books in the 1970s as a facilitator of grief work. Children were supported to work through the loss of their first families in order to detach and disinvest from those relationships.

Later life letters also emerged in the 1970s as an effect of concerns about the place of original kinship histories. These letters were written either by a social worker or by a birth parent and were intended to be read by the adopted child at some later more mature point. As with life story books, they contained an account of the child's life up until the adoption order, but differed in being a more adult account of that history. Unlike the life story book, they were put together for the future and were given to adopters to safeguard. As Part II of this study will discuss the practice of later life letters continued into the contemporary era and operated alongside indirect contact, the practice of sending letters every year. Interestingly, whilst a letter for later was placing the adopted child's history at some distance from his or her contemporary life, there was also a sense of inviting in that history for later. A letter for later, particularly if it was from a birth parent, powerfully signified an enduring love, a statement of commitment to the adopted child that will persist through time. Paradoxically, then, these letters work to install an importance that their original 'for later' status had worked to minimise.

These letters also represented an emerging theme in adoption work of this era, the idea that the historical legacy of adoption was something that required management and maturity; letters were for later rather than for now. There was a sense that adopted subjects needed more time to mature than biologically raised subjects; that the 'additional' task of adoption delayed or postponed the acquisition of developmental milestones, keeping the adopted adult in a state of protracted immaturity. It is one of the paradoxes so characteristic of adoption that it installs a place for original kinship through a range of practices, then compromises or disables the full deployment of those practices.

Provision of information to birth parents/relatives

This was the practice of passing on information to a birth parent either about their adopted child or about their adopted child now adult. Whilst opening the archive to provide adopters with information entered practice uncontentiously, it was a different matter with respect to birth relatives. However, once disclosure of information began to actively enter adoption work, limiting the forms that this disclosure took began to become more difficult. Once the archive was opened for adoptive parents and adopted adults, it became more difficult to keep it closed for birth parents.

White (1993, p. 92) discusses the impact of regulation 15 (Adoption Agency regs 1983), which allowed an adoption agency considerable discretion in disclosing information to adoption parties, including birth relatives. He cites a guidance circular of 1984, which gave two examples where an agency could disclose information – to a birth parent about a child's progress and to an adopted adult about his or her background. Triseliotis et al. (2005, pp. 11–12) argue that this guidance was an effect of pressures for birth parents to have reciprocal access to records, immediately installing concerns about confidentiality; any information imparted to a birth relative had to be 'non-identifying' to preserve the confidential identities of the adoptive family.

This was the period when a number of studies emerged documenting the enduring psychological effects of relinquishment upon mothers from adoptions made in the 1950s and 1960s (e.g., Winkler and Van Keppel, 1984; Reich, 1988a; Bouchier et al., 1991). These studies described the pathological consequences of a disenfranchised grief in birth mothers and contributed to pressures upon legislators and practitioners to make the adoption archive more accessible for this group. However, this is another example of how a change aimed at historic adoptions worked to transform contemporary practices. Whilst the archive remained closed for birth mothers who had relinquished infants many years earlier, it was slowly becoming opened for contemporary parents whose need for information was registered in practice guidance. This anticipated the open adoption practice of indirect contact.

Explaining adoption

This practice was a reworking of the post-war practice of 'telling', a semantic shift that signified a transition between these two periods of adoption. What might this transition from telling to explaining signify? Clearly, to explain adoption requires corroborating background information, whereas telling might operate as a one-off transmission of a disclosure – you are adopted. As Chapter 4 discussed the practice of telling was intended to be a complex and reiterated process, but was often a more limited exercise, if it happened at all. In the 1970s and 1980s the increasing centrality of kinship origins in forming adoptive identity worked to transform this practice, with a growth in books and manuals exploring and explaining this identity (see particularly Brodinsky, 1984; Brodinsky and Schecter, 1990; Burnell, 1990). This change is well captured by comparing two chapters in the two editions of Jane Rowe's guide for adopters, *Yours by Choice*. The 1959 edition referred to telling, but by 1982 the chapter had been re-titled and reworked to explaining. I will briefly discuss the differences.

First, the birth family were more actively included with the practice of explaining. This was well illustrated by Rowe when she discussed how adopters should talk about adoption to their child. In the 1959 edition the emphasis was on the child being chosen by adopters because of his or her specialness – a narrative that effectively rewrote any prior history from the adoption story. In the 1982 edition Rowe advocated a very different approach: 'You may like to explain that the adoption agency chose you to be his "forever parents" because they knew he would be happy with you and that you could provide the sort of home that his birth mother wanted him to have' (1982, p. 174). So here there were a number of changes: the agency not the parents did the choosing and the birth parents were involved in the process, endorsing the child's new family.

Second, the practice of explaining required biographical information and Rowe elaborates how life story books and later life letters helped with 'explanations', a 'substantial task' for adopters (1982, pp. 175–6). In the first edition, Rowe counsels against too much information about the child's background, constructing this as an interference in the child settling into its new home.

Third, the practice of explaining was predicated on honesty and openness in marked contrast to the practice of telling where Rowe supported distortions, omissions and untruths about the child's background. This approach was now in question: 'Even painful truths will be more bearable than doubts and uncertainty' (1982, p. 178).

Finally, there was a much more proactive role for adopters in the practice of explaining, whereas with the earlier practice of telling there was a more reactive role – responding rather than initiating. There was a sense in the 1982 chapter that adopters should actively promote a positive picture of the child's first family:

If you have achieved a sympathetic understanding of your child's birth parents and the reasons they placed him for adoption, then you will be able to convey this to him. It will, of course, be a help if you have met them and can give some first-hand impressions, but in any case you can pass on what you learned about them from your social worker. (1982, p. 179)

This comparative exercise has demonstrated that two competing technologies of adoption were operative in regulating different practices in different historical periods. The emergence of the practice of explaining reflects a technology where original kinship is understood to operate as a continuing and important foundation in securing the adopted child's identity. Clearly, the post-war practice of telling, whilst emerging from similar concerns, operated to curtail the place that original kinship could potentially occupy, such was the era's emphasis on the assimilation of the adopted child's differences. By 1982, the child's difference became an issue requiring explanation within a technology where the child's health depended on sustaining a link with the original kinship tie.

Search and reunion

The practice of search and reunion with the family of origin was a direct effect of the opening up of birth records. Once adopted people could access their records, it became possible to trace family relations from their past.

Much has been documented about the motivation to trace and meet birth relatives (see particularly Triseliotis, 1973; Haimes and Timms, 1985; Howe and Feast, 2000; Triseliotis et al., 2005). Researchers have been keen to discover what an adopted person is wanting from a search and how far there is a link between accessing information and wanting a reunion. Studies have sought to understand whether an inadequately performed practice of explaining adoption leads to an enduring wish to find a birth parent (see Howe and Feast, 2000). These research interests and questions speak to the challenge that this practice poses to adoption as a full-replacement family experience. This technology of adoption makes curiosity and a desire for knowledge acceptable motivations but make unacceptable the desire to rejoin in some form the original family. Rowe in her 1982 guide wanted to convince her adoptive parent readership that having information and wanting a reunion are not necessarily consequential events and most searchers were after information, not contact. She goes on to make the following point about reunions: 'When such reunions have proved possible, they seem to have been generally successful in putting minds at rest on both sides, but they have seldom led to long-term relationships' (Rowe, 1982, p. 180).

Reunions dramatically reconfigured the place of the family of origin, bringing them back from the margins and into a particular kind of involvement. In the above quotation Rowe hoped to consign such figures to a momentary engagement whose function is to relieve worry, but not to become a sustained presence. Reunions are an interesting emergence in an era when the technology of attachment was dominating the way that adoption was understood. Within such a technology there was only room for one singular attachment and Rowe underlined how reunions did not challenge that dominant attachment model. However, this practice actively opened up the possibility of former attachments being reformed, rekindled or reawakened in ways that put into question the 1970s attachment technology.

In spite of the challenge that this practice represented, it has continued to proliferate, producing support services and advocacy groups to promote its development. The 1980s saw the emergence of National Organisation for Counselling Adoptees and Parents (NORCAP) in 1982, a campaigning organisation for adopted adults and birth relatives and Natural Parents Support Group (NPSG) in 1987 (later to become Natural Parents' Network (NPN), an organisation for parents who had lost a child to adoption. Much of the focus of these self-help groups was to pressure for support services with search and reunion work and to equalise legislation so that birth parents could have the same right of access to information as adopted adults.

Chapter 6 will explore in more detail how the practice of search and reunion contributed to the emergence of the open adoption practice of direct contact. Triseliotis et al. (2005, pp. 379–80) emphasise how the narratives of loss that researchers had documented from adopted adults and relinquishing birth mothers contributed to the opening up of this form of open adoption. These narratives of course became more available for transcription with the opening up of the adoption archive bringing into visibility figures that had been formerly excluded. Furthermore, narratives of reunions worked to reconfigure the happy ever after adoption story that had been such a dominant discourse in the post-war era. I emphasise this because it is another example of how adoption's paradoxical constitution was always productive of practices that were in manifest conflict with its replacement status.

Conclusion

Thoburn (1996, p. 136) captures something of the way that the open practices discussed above worked together in this era:

> Workers will talk about the importance of 'grief' work with the first family and the child, helping each come to terms with their loss as they...break the attachments so that the child can attach to the new family. They ask the birth parents to write 'letters for later' and prepare the adopters for how they will talk to the child about his or her first family...Requests made by the child for a reunion with the birth parents are usually resisted and the young person is told that this will be possible when they reach the age of eighteen.

This chapter has documented the considerable transformations to adoption in the period of the 1970s and early 1980s. However, what Thoburn wants to underline is how these transformations have not reworked the more exclusionary adoption discourses from the post-war era. She describes how the open practices that were installed to include the family of origin still worked to exclude or sustain them as marginal figures.

Such an account understands the history of adoption as one where closed and open practices operate in an oppositional way. This study has emphasised the simultaneous presence of both open and closed practices throughout adoption history, operating together to create a strangely paradoxical field of deployment. In the 1970s this tension between open and closed practices was productive of some paradoxical effects. For example, life story books enshrine and sanitise the past, but also work to bring that past into the adopted child's present life. Whilst the adoption archive remained closed for birth mothers of historic adoptions, it was being slowly opened for contemporary parents through the provision of information.

What I am arguing is that considerable discursive complexity is at play in this period of adoption, as adoption work starts to converge with other discursive regimes, most centrally that of public childcare (Butler, 1997, pp. 92–3). Chapter 6 will trace how this discursive complexity increasingly produced practices that worked to both contest and promote open adoption practices by the end of the 1980s. It is to an analysis of this contested emergence that I will now turn.

6
Contested Attachments: The Controversial Emergence of 'Open Adoption'

> Agencies which have experience of open adoption were much more likely to explore this as an option ... However, this issue is one where strong and contradictory views are very much in evidence. (Fratter, 1991a, p. 79)
>
> Contact between older adopted children and members of the birth family was one of the most contentious practice issues which the study explored. (Lowe et al., 1999, p. 278)
>
> One specialist social worker who was interviewed for this study and highly committed to the concept of contact expressed concern about how ideologies are translated into day-to-day practice: 'As far as contact is concerned I sometimes feel as if things are spiralling out of control'. (Macaskill, 2002, p. 5)

I have begun this chapter with three short quotations from three different research accounts of adoption work. I have quite deliberately elided the very different cultural conditions of their production in order to highlight a stark continuity, from the mid-1980s to early 1990s open adoption appears to have been both an implemented, yet contested set of practices. In all the above accounts, open adoption practices were being actively introduced, but simultaneously challenged. The studies from which the quotations are taken were undertaken at very different times; Fratter et al.'s research was pursued between 1980 and 1984; Lowe et al.'s between 1994 and 1998 and Macaskill's in 1999. What was curious about this lengthy and continuing trajectory of contestation was the profession's impervious or resistant relationship to the by now many well-documented research accounts of open adoption's benefits.

Indeed, the research itself has become part of this contested field, with the findings of numerous studies being challenged or disputed as inadequate guides to justify the continuing practices of open adoption.[1] One might consider that such contested findings would bring the practices of open adoption into wider and more agreed disrepute. Yet, conversely, the profession persists in implementing these practices and has done so for at least the last 15 to 20 years. Smith and Logan (2004, p. 20) capture something of this paradoxical situation in their own study of direct contact: 'So, on the one hand we seem to have practice increasingly geared towards arranging indirect and direct contact following adoption and, on the other; we are confronted by uncertainty about whether contact is demonstrably in children's best interest.'

One might have thought that time alone would have provided some confidence in what some researchers have deemed 'the social experiment' of open adoption (Quinton et al., 1997). Smith and Logan (2004, p. 51) identify two issues that they consider central to the continuing lack of confidence in this area of adoption work: first, they argued, if the research findings are continuously contested, then policy and the law would continue to have no confidence in the promotion of such practices. Second, an adoption order constructed new families with full 'ownership' and 'control' of children, a set-up which was inimical to the more open-endedness that open adoption practices installed.

The authors identify the constitutive paradox at the heart of adoption as a form of substitute care, a paradox that this study has set out to trace and explore. As preceding chapters have elaborated, adoption has sustained both open and closed practices since its legal inception in 1926. This trajectory, which achieves a far-reaching replacement of one family for another, whilst simultaneously disclosing that very substitution, has produced an enduring terrain of controversy and contestation throughout adoption's history. However, in the era of so-called 'open adoption' this contestation has become more marked, more controversial and more public.

In this chapter I will be exploring the advent of open adoption, tracing its emergence and analysing its continuing contested reception into the public domain of adoption social work. I will be arguing that open adoption practices are both a continuity and a discontinuity with previous traditions. As Chapters 3, 4 and 5 elaborated, open practices have always circulated within adoption work and 'open adoption' as a set of practices certainty sustains continuity with those earlier traditions. The break with previous histories lies within the more publicly contested status that has operated to regulate the appearance of these practices.

My argument, drawing upon both Foucault and Butler, will explore three interrelated issues: first, the move to open adoption as a paradoxical effect of the more 'closed' practices of the permanency era; second, the contestation of open adoption practices as a sustaining of their presence in the field, but also a circumscribing of the scope of that presence and, finally, the arguments to support open adoption as drawing their resources from the same arguments used to oppose it.

Moving towards open adoption

> In the early and mid-1980s many authorities had rigid policies regarding child placement – for example that all children within a certain age range, say under 12 or under 14, should be placed for adoption, and that all contact with birth relatives should be severed as a prerequisite. There now tends to be much more flexibility ... and children may be referred ... for adoption with continued contact with members of the birth family. (Fratter, 1991b, p. 106)

In the above quotation Fratter identifies a break in adoption practices. At some point in the mid-1980s the nature of being adopted underwent a transformation, moving from discourses of rigidity, here associated with severing a child's ties, to discourses of flexibility, where biological ties were sustained. Fratter seems clear, and the research in her study confirmed[2] that the 1980s was a period when open practices began to evolve to more actively incorporate the unfit families of older adopted children. What was happening in this decade that could have produced such a shift? It is to this analysis that I will now turn.

> It also made possible the formation of a 'reverse' discourse: homosexuality began to speak in its own behalf, to demand that its legitimacy or 'naturality' be acknowledged, often in the same vocabulary, using the same categories by which it was medically disqualified. (Foucault 1978, p. 101)

In the above quotation Foucault describes how the prohibition and pathologisation of homosexuality in the nineteenth century gave rise to a reverse discourse, one where the homosexual acquired a certain visibility and social identity through a reworking of the very discourse that had achieved its disqualification. In this section I will be undertaking a similar analysis regarding the emergence of contact in public childcare in the 1980s by arguing the following points: first, that the introduction of access legislation in 1983 to address the *termination* of contact paradoxically provided the basis for its *recognition* by the end of the decade with the 1989 Children Act and, second, that the arguments used to promote and defend contact, drew their resources from the same arguments that were used to oppose it.

The 1980s was the decade when the convergence of adoption with public childcare became more consolidated, with rising numbers of children being adopted from the care system. This meant therefore that debates about the welfare needs of children in public care would inevitably effect and impact upon the way that adoption practices responded to those children. The issue of contact most dramatically illustrated this complex play of influences as it forcefully emerged in the 1980s as a social work concern for children in care. As the following section will analyse, this emergence was to have far-reaching effects on the contested emergence of open adoption practices towards the end of the decade.

In defence of the natural family: the discursive turn towards contact as a 'right'

The 1980s was a period where manifestly opposing discourses circulated around the family as a site of intervention. It was a decade where certain childcare cases emerged as high-profile signifiers of different discursive positions around the degree of permissible public intrusion into family life. In mid-decade a series of child deaths came to represent the more adversarial and interventionist discourse, while in the late 1980s the investigation into sexual abuse in Cleveland came to represent both liberal and conservative discourses around the family's right to privacy and self-determination. At the beginning and end of the decade, legislation was passed endorsing and promoting practices of contact for children in care with their absent families, the first time that such practices had achieved legislative recognition. Whilst this apparently signalled a move towards more inclusionary policies towards unfit families, this emergence was taking place within a childcare culture where adversarial discourses continued to structure intervention into family life. Before considering this legislation in more detail, I want to first analyse the contradictory discursive conditions through which it emerged.

Parton (1991, p. 204) understands this era as one where child protection discourses were consolidated, with the broadening and extension of child abuse categories and a growing prominence within social work and wider society of the dangers of child sexual abuse.[3] He sees the

1980s as a period where the concept of dangerousness – the dangerous individual and the dangerous family – began to more actively structure child protection work (Parton, 1991, pp. 142–3). Towards the end of this decade, the sex offender as dangerous individual began to emerge forcefully into public childcare work, reinforcing an impetus towards detection and diagnosis. As Parton et al. (1997, pp. 189–90) elaborated, sexual abuse underlay the 'hidden nature' of all child abuse, compelling the increasing use of diagnostic intervention and assessments in all areas of child protection practices. Within such a culture of detection and surveillance, contact with unfit families would be constructed as a risk and a danger to be avoided.

However, this adversarial and exclusionary discourse circulated alongside a more inclusionary and family rights discourse, which emphasised more co-operative and less punitive practices towards unfit families. What Parton identifies as the 'family rights lobby' had been a growing and insistent discourse in childcare work from the late 1970s onwards. There were two central concerns that structured this discourse through the eighties: a concern about an increasing use of compulsory powers in childcare work, in particular about the overuse of both emergency measures and parental rights resolutions, and a concern about the increasing numbers of children in long-term care with no contact with their families of origin. The issue of compulsion and the issue of contact were linked together within this discourse – when children were removed under compulsory powers, contact with their absent family was often terminated.

These concerns captured the government's attention in this period, leading to a series of research studies undertaken between 1978 and 1982. These focused on a range of issues including the trend towards compulsion in decision-making processes and contact for separated children (Vernon and Fruin, 1986; Milham et al., 1986; Packman et al., 1986). The Short Report and the DHSS review (1985) marked a reassertion of a less interventionist and more preventive discourse. As Milham et al. state below, the 1980s was the decade when contact for unfit families emerged as a high-profile issue in public childcare culture: 'In the 1980s, links between children in care and their families remains a contentious issue and the cause of many families have been taken up by pressure groups such as Family Rights Group (FRG), Children's Legal Centre and Justice for Children' (Milham et al., 1986, p. 10).

The 1980s was an interesting decade in terms of an increase in consumer agitation for change, particularly around the inherent rights associated with the blood tie of birth. As well as campaigns in public childcare for the rights of the family of origin for access, there were also pressures from adoption groups, such as NPSG and NORCAP, pushing for a similar agenda from a very different position. Representing the interests of historic birth parents and adult adoptees, these groups campaigned for greater openness, more support services and greater equality for people whose lives had been affected by the severance of post-war adoption, experiences brought into greater prominence following the access to birth records legislation in the 1976 Adoption Act. Parton encapsulates the concerns that operated to structure both these very different campaigning initiatives:

> Pervading such concerns were more fundamental values and issues related to the relationship between state and family; the importance of the natural family, the blood tie and psychological parenting and how far the law should intervene to mediate and transfer parental rights. (Parton, 1991, p. 26)

Both the campaign for contact for children in care and the campaign for greater openness for adult adoptees and historic birth parents converged within adoption practices of the 1980s. Whilst representing different interests and different subjects, these two discursive trends worked together towards the production of open adoption practices by the end of the decade. What both these social movements shared was the promotion of a particular technology of the adopted subject, one governed by self-knowledge rooted in original biography and early life, a knowledge that the separation of adoption had rendered problematic. The different narratives generated by these very different adopted subjects united within an agreement that separation from knowledge of beginnings was traumatic and difficult. These concerns with the rights of the 'natural' family and the place of original kinship emerged most forcefully in the 1980s as an effect of their progressive marginalisation in the 1970s. Judith Butler, reworking Foucault, is instructive on this process:

> In Foucault the possibility of subversion or resistance appears a) in the course of a subjectivation that exceeds the normalising aims by which it is mobilised, for example, in 'reverse discourse', or b) through convergence with other discursive regimes, whereby inadvertently produced discursive complexity undermines the teleological aims of normalisation. (Butler, 1997b, pp. 92–3)

We can see both these processes in operation in terms of the issue of contact in this period. First, the regime against contact in the 1970s 'exceeded' its own normative aim and actually worked to produce contact as an issue in the 1980s. Working as a reverse discourse, the arguments used to terminate contact became a resource in its promotion. Second, the issue of contact converged with other tangential or related issues such as the rights of the family to privacy, the role of substitute parenting, the role of the state in regulating the family, the rights of the child as independent subject, creating what Butler has termed 'discursive complexity'. This matrix of complexity worked to defeat the univocal aims of normalisation.

In this era adoption was reworked by this discursive complexity, with numerous discursive regimes structuring its operation and transforming its more narrowly normalising trajectory of the 1970s. There are two legislative events in the 1980s that whilst not directly aimed at adoption became part of what I have termed the 'discursive complexity' that structured its regulation in this era – the 1983 Health & Social Services & Social Security Adjudication Act (HASSASSA), including a code of practice and the 1989 Children Act. I will analyse their emergence in turn.

The HASSASSA legislation was the first occasion that contact for the family of origin became the subject of legal intervention. Prior to this, contact had always been a practice entirely at the discretion of individual social workers (Ryan, 1986, p. 33; Milham et al., 1989, p. 5). This legislation now meant that social workers had to notify parents formally if their access to their child in care was going to be terminated. Parents then had a right to apply to the courts for an access order to have their access reinstated.

What is interesting about the emergence of this legislation was its reactive impetus – the legislation only addressed cases where contact had been terminated or refused, placing a great deal of responsibility on the parent in challenging these decisions. The legislation did not deal with cases where a parent's access was insufficient or had been changed. However, in spite of the compromises and limitations in its operation, it granted a space for the first time for birth families to challenge local authority's plans around contact. More importantly, the legislation also reflected a change in how unfit families were regulated, initiating a regulatory process that worked through involving rather than completely excluding unfit families. This discursive shift would evolve through the decade giving rise to more co-operative notions of social work with unfit families that worked to conceal the more compulsory techniques that were still operative. As I will go on to explore, this became a dominant way that regulation operated through the 1980s and 1990s with the legal emergence of the concept of partnership with the 1989 Children Act. This notion of partnership will be key to the gradual introduction of open adoption.

The HASSASSA legislation was accompanied by a DHSS code of practice which was a first government-led attempt to address how to keep children in care in touch with their absent families. The code worked to encourage better practices for local authorities in promoting children's links with their families of origin, although in previous eras, such endorsement had negligible effects on changing this area of practice. It was the view of Milham et al. (1989, p. 1) (a group of researchers studying the workings of HASSASSA) that without legislation the issue of access would have received little 'prominence in social work thinking and planning'. One might argue here that this view represented a rather naive faith in the law as a vehicle for disciplining the practices of social work and enforcing a change that the profession resists. The interface between the law and disciplinary power was central to how practices of contact have been introduced and contested and I will return to this in more detail below. For the present, I want to emphasise a striking disjuncture between the code and the legislation – the code promoted proactive work with contact, whilst the legislation only addressed situations where contact has already been terminated. Whilst the emergence of the code did signal a change to a more recognised role for contact, this role was very circumscribed and limited.

An overriding message from the code was the irreconcilability of contact with two categories of children: those placed permanently elsewhere, adopted, and those on a care order who had been injured or abused (1983, p. 4). Of course, these two categories of children were often convergent – abused children were usually those who would be permanently removed for adoption. The code was a paradoxical document in that it both encouraged and promoted contact, whilst restricting and limiting its scope, reflecting a childcare strategy that worked to exclude, even whilst it was apparently introducing inclusionary practices with the family of origin. Furthermore, whilst the code was specifically *not* directed at adopted children, Fratter reports in both her studies that social workers were using it to facilitate open adoption arrangements (1991a, p. 63, p. 74; 1996, p. 52). This is particularly surprising, given that the code only identified a function for contact in terms of return home, whether it was for the long-stay adolescent who will eventually return home or the foster child in short-term foster care who will be rehabilitated. The HASSASSA legislation achieved very little for the constituency of children to whom it was aimed (Milham et al., 1989), but did impact upon the constituency of children for adoption, who as this decade unfolded began to be placed in what would be termed 'open adoptions'. This is a good example of how the manifest 'use' of a piece of legislation was compromised or subverted through a convergence with an entirely other discourse. The code of practice was for children in foster care returning home, but it was taken up to address adopted children permanently separated from their families. It shows how discursive complexity operated in this era, pulling into relationship issues and practices that had been historically kept separate.

The code defined two practices of contact – access, which designated 'personal meetings', which were 'the most satisfactory way of maintaining relationships', and contact, which designated letters, telephone calls and exchange of photographs (1983, p. 5). These two forms of contact would emerge as the two central open adoption practices by the beginning of the 1990s and would sustain the definitions as described above, except for a change in terminology introduced by the 1989 Children Act, where 'access' became 'contact'.

It is clear that the purpose of these two practices was the 'maintenance of relationships with an absent family'. As the expressed purpose of contact was to assist children returning home, it was defined in terms of maintaining a singular familial attachment, a technology of the self that had been dominant in public childcare since the Second World War. The following quotation illustrates this:

> In the case of older children, settling in a substitute family does not mean the inevitable cessation of every contact with natural parents or other relatives, including siblings, with whom *a relationship has developed*. Such links can *keep alive for a child a sense of his origins* and may keep open the options for *family relationships in later life*. (1983, p. 5, my emphasis)

The two purposes for contact the code cited – keeping a sense of origins alive and maintaining 'developed' relationships – implicitly suggested that keeping origins alive keeps relationships alive and developing. Furthermore, the code also suggested that keeping history alive in present time facilitated those relationships being returned to in later life. I am arguing that the code was marking out very new terrain in social work, which would imply a role for contact in permanent placements where return home was either a considerable time ahead or never expected to happen. We are entering the territory of adoption.

There was a strong endorsement for birth family involvement in the code, with a whole range of inclusionary practices listed that promoted the birth family's ongoing role in a proactive way. These practices would eventually acquire legal endorsement in the 1989 Children Act, where the notion of partnership operated to regulate unfit families in a new way. One could argue that practices such as involving parents in planning (1983, p. 8), advocating for visits from the beginning of placement (ibid., p. 6), funding for visits (ibid., p. 19) and written agreements (ibid., p. 9) were all indicative of a move towards more inclusionary work, bringing parents into decision-making and supporting their involvement with their children. However, as I will briefly outline, the HASSASSA legislation and the accompanying code of practice did actually very little to improve children's links with their absent families.

> This picture of isolation and withering links between parent and child is maintained ... Not only have links with home scarcely changed in the last 6 years, but these findings offer little encouragement to those who hoped that the HASSASSA legislation would have a swift and beneficial impact upon the access between children absent in care and their parents. (Milham et al., 1989, p. 85)

The above quotation was taken from the Dartington research team's study of the workings of the HASSASSA legislation, published in 1989. Their study was important in highlighting a number of themes that continued to structure both debate and practice on contact. I want to briefly look at their findings through the distinction Foucault makes in *Discipline and Punish* (1977) between the law and disciplinary power. This distinction is central to the way that contact as a practice has been deployed, resisted and contested and I will therefore quote the lengthy section in full:

> The disciplines should be regarded as a sort of counter law ... First, because discipline creates between individuals a 'private link', which is a relation of constraints entirely different from contractual obligation ... the way it is imposed, the mechanisms it brings into play, the non-reversible subordination of one group of people by another ... all these distinguish the disciplinary link from the contractual link,

and make it possible to distort the contractual link systematically from the moment it has as its content a mechanism of discipline. (Foucault, 1977, p. 222)

What Foucault helps to clarify is the way that disciplinary power creates a relation of constraints between social worker and unfit family, which works to 'distort' how the law regulates. What Milham et al. discovered was that the disciplinary relations between their study families and the social workers had sufficient subordinating force to nullify or neutralise the workings of both the HASSASSA legislation and the code of practice accompanying it. The authors identified a number of ways that this disciplinary relationship prevented contact from happening: first, 'non-specific' restrictions to access, such as 'difficulties inherent in placement, hostility, distance and inaccessibility', were identified in two-thirds of the study sample. In other words, there was operative a disciplinary technique of resisting parents' access, even when that access had been manifestly agreed and permitted (Milham et al., 1989, p. 3). Second, the researchers identified a pattern that would be central to my later analysis of open adoption practices in Chapters 8 and 9. When contact had been resisted and neglected by a local authority, its resumption would be refused on the grounds of the passing of time – to reintroduce a parent again would unsettle the child (ibid., p. 55). Here we have an instance where a passive resistance to contact then becomes a resource in a more overt refusal of it. Finally, 'in practice, access legislation (was) often subsumed and sublimated to other negotiations, some of which may have priority, such as the need for permanency planning outside the natural family and the stability of placement generally' (ibid., p. 35). Here other mechanisms were brought into play and operated to distort the contractual requirement for access.

This last point immediately installs a very specific technology of the self, which, as I have discussed, had been operative in childcare work since the 1970s. The need for a new permanent home was synonymous with the need for a new singular attachment, making problematic the sustaining of ties with the earlier family of origin. This technology was powerfully at play in the reasons social workers listed for the termination of children's contact. These included contact placed the child at emotional risk; contact hindered the child's educational progress; termination of contact facilitated the establishment of new placement and contact would disrupt the present placement (Milham et al., 1989, p. 32). These reasons were in service to a form of attachment that was unsettled and compromised by earlier attachments being sustained.

This technology would shape a forceful anti-contact discourse within adoption work as it began to incorporate indirect and direct contact in the late 1980s.

Clearly, then, as contact began to acquire some legislative and practice recognition, there was simultaneously a move to oppose and resist its implementation. Contact in the 1980s was both contested and marginalised by the disciplinary operations of social work power. Foucault (1977, p. 219) points out how disciplinary power works to neutralise the potentially productive counter-discourses that are always an effect of dominant regimes of normalisation:

> Discipline fixes; it arrests or regulates movements; it clears up confusion ... It must also master all the forces that are formed from the very constitution of an organised multiplicity; it must neutralise the effects of counter power that spring from them and which form a resistance to the power that wishes to dominate it.

Here we can see how the counter-discourse of contact for previously excluded families was defeated even before it became an active discursive presence. However, the operations of disciplinary power are always in excess of their manifest aim; power, as Foucault often states, is endlessly proliferative. In the mid-1980s the case for children having contact had been sufficiently registered to install the conditions for an insistent support and campaign around its achievement. This was an interesting moment, as the momentum for contact began to assume considerable discursive complexity, with discourses operating to both support and oppose different forms of contact for different kinds of children.

First, there was a dominant discourse that was vocal in wanting contact as a support for children returning home. In this period, contact began to emerge as an acceptable practice when linked to the child's eventual rehabilitation. This discursive pressure, justified and represented by the research of Milham et al. (1986 and 1989), would eventually impact upon the 1989 Children Act and its introduction of the statutory requirement that children in care have contact with absent families.

Second, a less dominant discourse emerged, arguing for contact for children permanently living away from their families of origin. This discourse had already been glimpsed in the HASSASSA code of practice, but began to occupy a space of greater visibility in the contentious and controversial debates about contact. It was this discourse that was important in terms of open adoption practices. Its claim is that contact, far from de-stabilising placements, worked to help children settle and attach to new carers. Within such a discourse the termination of contact, rather than securing a child's welfare, placed that welfare at risk. The reasons habitually for ending contact were here mobilised as resources in arguments to support it. The FRG emerged in the mid-1980s as a major campaigning organisation that articulated this counter-discourse in their work representing unfit families in their relations with social services.[4]

Part of the discursive complexity here was how supporters of contact in terms of rehabilitation were often vehemently opposed to contact for children who were not returning home. This distinction was central to how these discourses operated within adoption work. Given that by the end of this decade, children from care were an increasingly large part of adoptions constituency, adoption work would be inevitably transformed by this conflictual discursive shift towards contact in public childcare.

These two contrasting discourse on contact were already in circulation in adoption work by the mid- to late 1980s. Fratter (1991a, p. 70) cites these two discursive positions when ascertaining social worker perspectives on open practices in adoption:

> The views of Goldstein and colleagues were cited as representing the 'exclusive' concept of permanence, in which contact with birth relatives should be severed... The inclusive end of the continuum was informed by the advocates, such as the Family Rights Group... of a form of permanence which would encompass a child's links with birth relatives.

Fratter (1991a, p. 58) clarifies how she defines the practices emerging from these two discursive positions in terms of adoption work. The 'exclusive' position or what she terms the 'more closed model of adoption' had limited opportunities' for adopters and birth family to participate directly. Fratter saw the agency 'controlling' the amount of information that it was possible to share and there was no contact between the parties. This was a familiar and established adoption set-up that emerged in the 1970s.

The 'inclusive' position or 'more open model' of adoption had more direct involvement for the adoption parties. They may meet, they may agree to exchange letters or telephone calls (indirect contact) or they even agree to have visits (direct contact). In terms of her study of 22 agencies, Fratter concluded that there was a 'strong impression' of 'a trend towards more openness in adoption' (1991a, p. 74). Certainty her research sample represented practices that embraced direct contact and indirect contact between adopted children and their first families (see pp. 71–2 and Chapter 5 in particular). Conversely, she also cited agencies where the issue of contact was 'rarely considered in connection with adoption' (ibid., p. 68). Fratter is staking out the terms of a debate which would acquire a central place in adoption work by the 1990s. Put simply, the debate centred on a pro-attachment or a pro-contact position. Atherton (1986b, pp. 98–9) anticipates what would become one of the central issues to this discursive conflict:

> Much of the debate about continuing access to the natural family ... centres on notions of attachment, about the need to attach with a new family, and about the difficulty or ease of having close relationships with more than one set of adults. Some parents have had their access terminated because they were assessed as being too little attached ... other parents have had their access terminated because they are considered to have had too much attachment with their children in care.

Part II of this study will illustrate how this technology of attachment continued to have a contested and paralysing place within decision-making about contact for adopted children. For the moment I am marking out how the terms of the contested status of open adoption practices first emerged into the cultural field in the mid-1980s. Towards the end of the decade this pro-contact lobby began to more actively enter debates within adoption. Murray Ryburn was a key proponent of open practices in adoption, drawing on the more open traditions of his native New Zealand, traditions which he brought to inform his campaign for greater openness in UK adoption (see Rockel and Ryburn, 1988; Ryburn, 1992b). An important, if underemphasised, element in the pro-contact movement was the same race placement lobby that had entered social work vigorously in the early 1980s. This lobby had emerged in opposition to transracial placements, emphasising the importance of black identities and traditions for black children in care. Commentators central to this movement (Dutt and Sanyal, 1998; Barn, 2000) criticised the 'European concept of family' and its legalistic and exclusive notion of adoption in comparison with the more informal, inclusive and open models of substitute care from African and Caribbean cultures (Dutt and Sanyal, 1998, pp. 175–6). This discourse articulated two specific purposes for contact for black adopted children. First, it was important for their identity formation within their individual kinship origins and, second, it was a link to their 'roots within a collective ancestry' (Cohen, 1994, p. 59).

Such pro-contact campaigning emerged at the same time as the 1989 Children Act, which was introduced partly as an effect of the earlier HASSASSA legislation. In spite of the contested nature of that legislation and the little it manifestly achieved regarding the sustaining of children's previous ties, it did paradoxically impact upon the 1989 Children Act. Whilst I have problematised the role of the law in enforcing the practice of contact within the operations of disciplinary power, the 1989 Children Act did mark the emergence of a more rigorous regulatory framework for the securing of contact for children. It also gave a more indirect impetus to the continuing emergence of open adoption practices.

> Access was a parental right controlled by the local authority ... contact is endorsed as a child's right which local authorities are duty bound to promote for all children who are looked after. (Newman, 1995, p. 52)

In the quotation above, the author is capturing what he understood to be the impact of the Children Act on contact for children in care. From a practice 'controlled' by the local authority to a 'right' secured by the courts, Newman (1995, p. 52) saw the legislation transforming children's experiences of care through a maintenance of their links with their families of origin. Whilst undoubtedly the Children Act marked a significant moment in the long history of public care contact, I contest this author's view that this law defeated the more diffuse operations of the disciplinary power of statutory social work. I will be arguing that this power continued to operate around, within and against the legal framework established by the legislation.

As I have previously discussed, the 1980s was a decade characterised by contradictory discourses around unfit families and their children in care. On the one hand, there was an increasing move to further police such families and to diagnose their relations with their absent children through assessments of risk. On the other hand, there were far-ranging concerns about the privacy of the family, the grounds for intrusion and the place of original kinship for children separated in care. The 1989 Children Act reflected both these discursive trends and was an attempt to balance the need to intervene into abusing families to protect children, with a need to respect the privacy of family life to protect parents. Parton et al. (1997, p. 28) understood the Cleveland case of 1987[5] to have contributed to the discourse of family privacy that was so central to this legislation: 'The rights of parents and the rights of children to be left at home, free of state intervention and removal, were placed on political and professional agendas.' This discourse positioned the welfare professional as abusively intrusive, a discursive trend which certainty contributed to the legislative move to make social workers far more accountable to the courts and to their clients.

The 'failed' or 'abusing' family occupied a position on the threshold between the right to privacy and the need for intervention. As this study has discussed, the problematics of intervention into the life of the family has had a long and conflictual history. The 1989 Children Act marked out a new disciplinary intervention to resolve the conflict between privacy and protection for children. The act recognised that even unfit families had a right to have their family life respected and this respect was achieved through the problematic notion of partnership between families and the local authority. Under the act, local authorities had a statutory obligation to work in partnership with those families whose children were in state care. This partnership should promote the sustaining of contact between birth parents and their children in foster care; the integrity of the private family unit would be recognised by keeping parents in touch with their separated children.

This Act is commonly cited as one of the most influential interventions in the introduction of open adoption practices. However, Jordan (1994, pp. 10–11), in commenting on this legislation, places in opposition public childcare and adoption work. He understands adoption as belonging to the 'old orthodoxies' of adversarial compulsory interventions at a time when the Children Act had introduced more partnership approaches to childcare work. I would argue that this supposed polarity overlooks the way that adoption had been reworked by these discourses of partnership and co-operation. It is clear from my discussion in the preceding section that the emergence of open adoption practices bears witness to the influences of what Jordan describes as 'partnership approaches' that were emerging in the 1980s within a range of discourses representing the place of the biological family. The government review of adoption (1993) clearly, if critically, cites the influence of the 1989 legislation: 'There is also some feeling that planning for a child who needs a permanent new family can be more difficult because of the emphasis in the Act of maintaining contact with birth families' (HMSO, 1993: 3.16).

As far as the above authors are concerned, the Children Act's presumption of contact had unsettled and begun to rework the way adoption was planned for children in care. The Act, then, had a number of effects on adoption in the 1990s: first, adoption workers were now increasingly placing children for adoption who would be sustaining contact with their families of origin under the Children Act; second, the notion of working with rather than excluding birth parents was now a counter to the more aggressively exclusionary discourse of adoption freeing legislation; and, finally, section 8 contact orders under the Act could be attached to an adoption order, thus making it possible for adoption with contact to be legally enforced.

The 1990s, then, would be an era characterised by a convergence of a number of competing adoption discourses that circulated around the family as a site for intervention. There was a coercive adoption discourse, where children were 'freed' for adoption against their parents' wishes. There was the continuing discourse of voluntary co-operation and support, where children were relinquished with consent. And then finally there was the strangely hybrid discourse that kept unfit families in contact with their adopted children through a set of practices that re-engaged the very family that the adoption order had excluded. This discourse was structured through a paradoxical relationship to the birth family, encompassing notions of partnership and co-operation, as well as notions of risk, assessment and protection.

However, I am not suggesting that these discourses are operating oppositionally, in spite of their oppositional force. In fact, they are part of one strategy where both adversarial and partnership interventions work together to simultaneously produce and contest birth family involvement. Adoption, then, was paradoxically situated within a culture where unfit families are both irreducibly important, but also potentially irreducibly dangerous. This discursive field was central in shaping how open practices emerged in a contested form in the 1990s.

Towards discursive complexity: open adoption practices in the 1990s

'It feels like someone keeps moving the goalposts' was how an experienced adoption practitioner...described working in the field of adoption currently. Adoption practice has changed and continues to change in response to moves towards a more 'open' approach. (DOH, 1995: foreword)

It is plain that the institution of adoption has undergone profound changes...Many more adoptions are now contested...more children continue to have some form of contact with their birth families and the need for adoptive parents and their children to be offered support. (Parker, 1999, p. 5)

I have prefaced my discussion with two quotations from official government publications that emerged in the mid- to late 1990s. Both quotations encapsulate an adoption field in a process of ongoing transformation generated through the emergence of open adoption practices. 'Moving the goalposts' was an interesting metaphor, suggestive of an adoption culture that once had a stable field of play, but where that stability had now been disrupted and the rules of operation were no longer clear. Yet, in spite of these documented confusions and conflicts, the profession continued to endorse and promote open adoption practices throughout the 1990s.

The contested status of open practices was debated in many different places through the decade – government review bodies, the courts, research studies, academic institutions. Such debates kept open an insistent, if unsettled space for open adoption, sustaining the profession in a place of productive doubt. This 'doubt' produced numerous research projects, some to promote and some to question the benefits of openness. These studies in turn became a source of contestation, with their findings challenged and questioned, without any conclusive outcome regarding open practices. More longitudinal studies, better sampling, better control groups – it seemed that the profession could never adequately address its insecurities and questions about open adoption practices. I want to briefly outline the two discursive positions around open practices that worked to produce a contested field of operation through the 1990s.

Contestation

As preceding chapters have explored, the adopted child's birth heritage has haunted the adoptive family since adoption's legal inception. If the truth of one's being was culturally defined through the foundational origin of birth and early life, then separation from those origins would produce an enduring 'need' or 'wish' to recover that identity. Open practices had variously emerged to address this 'need', but up until the 1980s this original history was 'dead' history and quite split off from the adopted child's lived present life. However, in the 1980s the discursive momentum for recognition of the place of the natural family began to rework this consigning of history to the past. As I have already discussed this came from two quite different directions. First, the access to birth records legislation made more public how previous histories were still operative in the lives of adopted adults and birth parents. Testimonies bore witness to the enduring claim that original kinship exercised on adoption subjects. Narratives of search and reunion suggested that some adopted adults benefited from resuming contact with their first families (see particularly Howe and Feast, 2000). Second, older children being placed for adoption brought with them histories that clearly and visibly informed adoptive family life in the present. These histories were present through the figure of the contesting birth parent, the child's prior life in his or her life story book and the child's challenging and difficult behaviours in the adoptive home.

As it became increasingly difficult to consign histories to the dead past, adoption work began to be troubled and divided by the question of the place such history could have in adoptive family life. What centrally concerned adoption workers was whether keeping an original birth identity alive for a child would unsettle the new identity and attachment of the child in its adoptive family? Can open adoption practices limit the degree of involvement they invite? Such questions, of course, were generated from the technology of attachment that had been a dominant force in adoption work since the 1970s, with its emphasis on the securing of a new singular attachment and the relinquishing of former 'poor' attachments. Some forms of contact posed more of a challenge to this operative technology than others. Indirect contact, where an information exchange was set up between adopters and birth family, either reciprocally or one way, did not overly challenge or disrupt this technology of attachment. This form of contact was often understood as an extension of the 1970s practices of life story books and later life letters and although these letters were being sent in present time, they were understood to be a supplement to the adopted child's sense of its 'past' history that could be unproblematically absorbed into its new adoptive identity. Direct contact, in contrast, had always occupied a much more controversial and contested place, representing an actual lived incursion into the life of the adopted child. The practice of visiting siblings or other relatives has been less contested than visits with a former parent.

The opposition to the implementation of direct contact remained consistently articulated within the technology of attachment, where the emphasis was on securing new attachments and breaking those former unhealthy links associated with unfit parenting. This opposition was given a particular impetus in the 1990s with the emergence of a range of 'attachment disorders' increasingly diagnosed as a growing pathology amongst adoptive children, and requiring specialist interventions for their adoptive families (see Quinton and Rutter, 1988; Fearnley, 1996; Howe et al., 1999). This discourse has proliferated a vast and growing literature with ever complex diagnostic models for identifying pathologies in attachment behaviour. One of the central paradoxes at the heart of this discourse was the position of the 'well-attached family'. The belief in the curative potential of the well-attached adoptive family began to be compromised when the placement of attachment disordered children disturbed the normalising regimes of that family life. The dominant response in the 1990s has been a move to resource the adoptive family with both therapeutic work and parenting techniques. Increasingly sophisticated models for assessing and then matching attachment styles emerged as a further support in the placing of troubled older children, where certain kinds of attachment behaviour in adopters was assessed as better able to respond to certain disordered attachments in adopted children (see Beek and Schofield, 2006). It would seem that the technology of attachment generated more and more practices to secure a normativity of adoptive parenting, a normativity that consistently eludes any form of stabilisation. Alongside the emergence of open adoption practices then, there was a parallel emergence of both statutory and independent support services for attachment disordered children, and their new families.[6] Open practices and attachment services have often operated in an exclusive way in the field – where a child has attachment difficulties, contact is deemed unadvisable. However, there was an increasing move to rework this technology of attachment in the service of more open practices, using that more exclusionary discourse as a resource in the promotion of more inclusionary practices. In the 1990s, then, two discourses around contact in adoption emerged simultaneously, both drawing upon the technology of attachment. I want to briefly look at these two discursive positions.

Thoburn (1996, p. 134), contributing to a book on attachment and loss in child and family social work, articulates the pro-contact position very well:

> Research studies and the work of practitioners who have had to pick up the pieces when placements have broken down ... have shown that the child's and the new parents' need for a sense of permanence has to be met without doing harm to the child's sense of identity and self-concept.

In the above quotation Thoburn implicitly suggests that the psychological discourse of permanence had done 'harm' to the adopted child's sense of identity by not allowing its previous history sufficient place in its new life. She brought together both researches on the benefits of contact with the high breakdown rates of older child adoptions, suggesting that the one will mitigate the other:

> Some child placement workers have moved away from the total severance model of placement. They attempt to offer the benefit of good quality parenting, stability and security...with the added benefit of having a clear sense of identity reinforced by continued contact with the first family. (1996, p. 134)

Here Thoburn correlates the possession of a clear identity with continuing contact with the adopted child's first family. The important word in this sentence is continuing. In the 1970s, as Chapter 5 elaborated, there was an increasing concern with adopted children having knowledge about their origins to enhance and complete their sense of identity. This was achieved through life story books and life story work, practices which worked with history as past events. Thoburn is suggesting that these approaches associated with the 'total severance' model of adoption were not adequate and that adopted children required a more ongoing or continuing sense of their family of origin. This required different and more birth family-involved forms of contact. Thoburn is careful to reconcile security and permanence with contact. Drawing on attachment theory, she referred to 'dual or multiple psychological parenting', suggesting that children could sustain more than one attachment and that therefore earlier attachments did not need to be 'broken' in order to allow a child to settle. This discourse promoted all forms of contact, both indirect and direct, understanding that the adopted child would need different ways of keeping in touch with former family, at different point in his or her childhood.

The counter-discursive position was well captured by a recent publication from British Association of Adoption & Fostering (BAAF), *Good Practice Guide – Contact in Permanent Placement* (1999). The central part of this publication outlined the key factors in reaching decisions about contact for permanently placed children. This guidance document was clearly written within the permanency discourse, still operative in adoption work. This situated the family of origin as formative of bad attachments and contact with them as a traumatic repetition of that bad attachment history:

> Whether children with early damaged attachments are helped by continuing contact...will depend very much on the nature of that

relationship and whether it helps to reinforce the new attachment rather than undermine the new carers. In some circumstances ongoing contact may inhibit healing, recovery and the development of alternative, healthier ways of relating especially following severe trauma and/or abuse. (1999, p. 11)

This discourse based assessments about an adopted child's contact on whether it helped secure a new attachment. It is clear that contact was here associated with undermining or inhibiting the child's new family life. This was not a discourse that understood child welfare in terms of continuity with people from the past. Indeed, in this guide previous parents are associated with damaging parenting behaviour:

Bonding – or the capacity of the parent to nurture – is a further important consideration in planning contact... research (Gibbons et al., 1995) does indicate that parenting which is characterised by low warmth/high criticism is particularly damaging to children's well-being. (1999, p. 12)

In the above, parenting and contact are elided and no distinction is made between birth family as parents and birth family as participants in a child's life. It was assumed that contact visits would reproduce the 'bad' attachment patterns of former family life and the birth parent would be incapable of making any other kind of contribution. This discourse was more likely to promote forms of indirect contact, understanding the need for the adopted child to have information about its kinship origins, but wanting to keep those origins at a safe and removed distance. As I have already discussed, in this discourse indirect contact is understood as a continuity with the 1970s tradition of life story books and explaining, a tradition that keeps the past 'past'.

However, whilst I have underlined certain differences between the positions above, I now also want to emphasise certain similarities through showing how both these discourses draw upon the same technology of attachment.

First, both these positions draw upon research to support their arguments. Thoburn is drawing upon research into contact for adopted children, both in the United Kingdom and in New Zealand and the United States. The BAAF guide was drawing on the growing body of research on the use of attachment theory to work with damaged children in new families. Both use the 'evidence base' of empirical research to attack or undermine the opposing position.

Second, both discourses understand attachment to be a central organising concept although it is mobilised very differently. Put simply, attachment either was compromised/unsettled *by* contact or was prevented/reduced *without* contact.

Third, both these positions located the family of origin as central in the formation of a child's sense of being, but that importance was very differently constructed in the two discursive positions. One situated the family of origin as a resource to adopted children; the other as the cause of trauma and damage.

Finally, and following on from above, both constructed the past as central to the adopted child's identity. Whether this past is one of abuse within dysfunctional attachments or a past of significant family ties, it remained of irreducible psychological importance in terms of the adopted child. The two discourses understand the past as operative in the present and therefore requiring recognition. The pro-contact discourse worked with the past by bringing people from that past into the present life of the child, through letters, photographs or visits. The pro-attachment discourse took a more therapeutic approach, providing therapy for the child and its new family to help work through the legacies of traumatic earlier history. In the former discourse there was a sense of the past continuing to be present through contact, but with the latter discourse there was an emphasis on the past being disinvested of emotional affects by a programme of therapy. One discourse therefore worked to sustain the family of origin, whilst the other worked to progressively remove them as active presences. Both these discourses circulated together through the 1990s, creating a field of contested implementation.

Implementation

In this decade, then, the previously irreconcilable terms, adoption and contact, assumed an increasing contested correlation in commentaries, research studies and practice guidance. The idea of placing children with either indirect or direct contact was no longer constructed as a contradiction of what adoption signified. The two discursive positions that I outlined above worked together through the 1990s to both implement and contest adoption open practices.

This decade was marked by an ongoing campaign for adoption reform, beginning after the 1989 Children Act (Fratter, 1996, pp. 41–8; Parker, 1999, p. 5; Smith and Logan, 2004, pp. 41–4). Open adoption was a key area of the reform agenda throughout the decade, beginning with the Review of Adoption law (1993), a government White Paper (1993), a stalled Adoption bill (1996) and a resurgence of reform with the new labour government at the end of the decade (Prime Ministers Review of Adoption, 2000). The adoption law reform group kept up pressure through the 1990s for a clearer policy on open adoption contact, campaigning for a framework and legislative enforcement for open adoption practices (Smith and Logan, 2004, p. 41). This was a markedly controversial aspect of the adoption reform agenda and Fratter (1996, p. 20) describes considerable public opposition to adoption with contact at the time of the 1993 review, opposition that attracted national media attention.

As the decade progressed debates and conflicts about open practices increasingly emerged, with opposition to open adoption centred on the practice of direct contact. As I have already discussed, the discourse against open adoption was essentially against this practice, a practice that too prominently sustained for the adopted child the unfit family and their history of poor attachments. Furthermore, opponents of this form of open adoption were concerned that it was being implemented without any known outcomes, subjecting children to a form of social experiment (Fratter 1996, p. 20). An influential group of childcare researchers at the Maudsley Hospital and Bristol University represented this position in a paper reviewing the research on contact: 'The issue we take up in this article is...whether contact has been demonstrated to have the beneficial effects that are claimed for it in circumstances where stable nurturing relationships with birth parents have usually *not* been part of the child's experience' (Quinton et al., 1997, p. 294, author's emphasis). The article initiated a heated debate that encapsulated the two discursive positions that structured the contested place of open adoption practices. Four subsequent papers were published, two by Murray Ryburn staking out the pro-contact position and two further by the original authors in response.[7] The articles were widely circulated amongst social workers, in spite of the relative obscurity of the journals in which they were published. Ryburn, as already stated, was a central figure in articulating the pro-contact position (see particularly Ryburn, 1992, 1994, 1995, 1996). Quinton et al. were a group of researchers associated with adoption research of older children from backgrounds of considerable adversity, where that history of dysfunctional attachments produced a cautious and/or negative position on contact (see in particular Quinton et al. 1998).

The discursive conflict waged in this series of articles assumed two particular foci: first, a question about whether an unfit parent's direct involvement makes a positive or negative contribution to their child's life post adoption and, second, a dispute as to whether the research in the field was sufficiently substantive to justify the continuing practice of direct contact. Interestingly, both opponents and supporters of contact placed great reliance on the field of empirical research, whilst arguing over what the research findings actually 'proved' about open practices. What was essentially in dispute between the two discursive positions was not the status of research in the social sciences, but whether the research delivered accurate findings. Both sets of authors evoked the 'evidence' base of good research, with an implicit confidence that evidence could be accomplished. For Ryburn (1998, p. 62) the research was already in place. For Quinton et al. the research was still 'unresolved' particularly on the issues of adopted children's 'psychosocial development and identity' (1998, p. 13). Both discursive positions drew upon the technology of attachment, a technology governed by self-knowledge rooted in original biography and early life. Neither discourse opened up for exploration the forms of family life that open adoption practices unsettle and destabilise. Part II of this study will return to this.

So, within this culture of contestation, open practices emerged. Indeed, it is more accurate to state that they emerged as an effect of their contested status, the contestation both permitting their circulation and simultaneously operating to curtail it. I want to conclude by analysing how open practices were established.

Partnership within adversarialism: working with open practices

It is clear from both research studies and large-scale government surveys (see particularly DOH, 1995; Lowe et al., 1999) that open adoption practices were an increasingly large part of adoption work through the 1990s. Both the 1995 and 1999 surveys just cited quote statistics of nearly 50 per cent of their sample families having letterbox contact. Direct contact was a markedly less occurring practice, but Lowe still reported a third of his study families having this form of arrangement in place. Triseliotis et al. (2005, p. 18) cited the influence of some small-scale studies of direct contact as an influence in promoting it in adoption work. Clearly, the contested field was a productive site for the continuing emergence of open practices. I want to now consider how open practices were paradoxically deployed in an adoption culture which had birth parent involvement severed by law.

In her review of adoption research, Thoburn (1990, p. 90) comments on the presence of both adversarial and co-operative discourses that structure the regulation of open practices:

> Thus although much literature on legal aspects of adoption reflects the 'clean break' approach, and assumes that there is resistance to continued contact after adoption, it appears that such orders are being made. The explanation may be that very few orders are made where an access clause is included in the order... and it would be difficult to know how many orders for adoption were made *where contact is expected to continue as a result of informal agreement.* (my emphasis)

Thoburn draws attention to the way that a coercive adversarial adoption discourse where a child was severed from its family worked alongside a more partnership discourse where families made 'informal agreements' to remain in some form of touch after adoption. Foucault (1977, pp. 222–3) captures very well the insidiously coercive way that disciplinary power operates when it installs these apparently equal and partnership-based notions of working, such as adopters and birth families agreeing about contact: 'They have the precise role of introducing insuperable asymmetries and excluding reciprocities... "the surplus" power that is always fixed on the same side, the inequality of position of the different partners in relation to the common regulation.'

What Foucault underlines was how a constitutive inequality installed by the regulation of adoption could not be transcended by moves to include birth family after the adoption order. However, it is important to underline how the interface between Children Act legislation and adoption had created a complex regulatory situation where both juridical and disciplinary power worked together to both promote and contest open practices.

Whilst in the 1990s the fields of public childcare and adoption increasingly shared the same constituency of children, the way that open practices were regulated were markedly different. Following the Children Act, children in public care had a statutory right to have contact with their separated families. However, whilst adoption reform campaigns wanted some similar legal enforcement, contact in adoption remained outside of the law, subject to disciplinary power but with no juridical underpinning. The courts had always demonstrated an entrenched reluctance to legislate against the wishes of adopters and this remained the case in respect to open practices. Triseliotis et al. (1997, pp. 85–6) cite a ruling that captured this ethos: 'A condition prerequisite to open adoption is the consent and co-operation of the adoptive parents. This was absent here and the idea of open adoption had no place here' (Re D1992 FLR 461).

It would seem that whilst the profession began to embrace open practices there was a reluctance to impose such practices on the life of the adoptive family. However, expectations of adopters from the adoption profession to engage with open practices operated to persuade, if not enforce. The use of written 'agreements' or 'contracts' in the setting up of an open practice emerged as a solution to enforcement via the courts (see DOH, 1995, pp. 20–6; Fratter, 1996, pp. 93–4; Macaskill, 2002, pp. 39–45). Many commentators have noted that adoption workers intended such informal contracts to induce compliance from adopters through the installation of conscience or duty as an effect of having made an agreement. Sometimes, the adoption worker's plan for the child would be contact and taking the child became part of a complex process of accepting or re-negotiating that plan (Smith and Logan, 2004, pp. 76–82). These are instances of how disciplinary power operated to indirectly enforce in the absence of a legal directive.[8]

One of the ongoing paradoxes generated by open adoption practices was the position accorded to the birth family. Having had their involvement severed by the adoption order, this involvement was then reinstated by open adoption practices. Who does this previous parent become, if parental status has been lost, but involvement with their child continues precisely because of their former status? This placed birth parents in a paradoxical bind in that they are doubly positioned as parent and not parent within the prevailing way that adoption work constructed them. This dilemma was particularly marked for social workers in situations where adopted children were having direct contact with a former parent (see Lowe et al., 1999, pp. 297–8 for a discussion of this issue).

However, whilst a concept of partnership was now operating within adoption work to include birth family in open practices, it also operated more insidiously to exclude and to terminate the possibility of those practices. Thoburn (1996, p. 136) makes this latter point: 'Some agencies and individuals still adhere to earlier practice theories and, having achieved comfortable contact between parent and child, but decided that adoption will be in the best interests, seek leave of the Court to terminate contact.' What Thoburn explains is how the Children Act was used to terminate contact (section 34 (4) in advance of an adoptive placement. As Chapter 9 will elaborate, in my study local authority there was much evidence of children in foster care having contact with absent families under the Children Act, but this form of partnership became just another means of surveillance around parenting. Many families were having their parenting assessed during contact visits as a way to determine their child's future plans, often with the result that their contact would be terminated in preparation for their child's placement for adoption.

Conclusion

Part I of this study has mapped the establishment of adoption as a paradoxical social intervention through tracing the emergence and deployment of different open practices at different historical periods. I have shown that adoption was inaugurated and sustained in a paradoxical relationship to the family of origin, producing an enduring terrain of controversy and contestation. In this chapter I have traced how open adoption practices mark a continuity with preceding adoption histories in that the involvements they invite were simultaneously introduced and contested. The two discourses that have supported and opposed the implementation of open adoption have both drawn their arguments from the same technology of the adopted subject. This is a subject governed by self-knowledge rooted in original biography, a knowledge that the separation of adoption has rendered problematic. In the contemporary era, different forms of open practices have emerged controversially to address this issue of knowledge, but not to put into question the technology itself. The continuing mobilisation of this technology would continue to produce a paradoxical place for open practices, a place where they were both required and simultaneously put into question. Within this technology original kinship was both irreducibly important, but irreducibly unsettling.

However, whilst I have argued that open adoption is a continuity with earlier traditions, I also now want to suggest that its advent marks the emergence of a break in the field. It is the intensity and controversy generated by open practices, particularly the practice of direct contact, that are indicative of the emergence of something new. Whilst in earlier eras open practices were both resisted and challenged, there was not the level of contention and debate to their implementation that the field has experienced in the 1990s. What have open practices installed to produce such opposition? It is my contention that one can glimpse with the emergence of open adoption practices of the self that resist accommodation to the contemporary technology of self-knowledge through self-discovery. Part II of this study will explore how far open adoption practices imply or indicate a different technology of the adopted subject. In undertaking this genealogical analysis, I will be drawing upon another strand in the work of Foucault, his last project, technologies of the self.

Part II
The Open Archive

7
Introducing the Archive Study

> The local authority archive is in the basement of the building; a dark and ill-lit room, with hardly any natural light and nowhere to sit. The room is vast, in a state of disrepair and unheated. The social worker showed me the adoption archive, housed at the back in a dark recess and comprising files alphabetically ordered under the child's birth name. (Research diary July 2002)
>
> The letterbox system is housed in the adoption team, in two drawers of a filing cabinet, whose designated purpose is post-adoption issues. It is organized under the child's birth name and there was a dual system in place – 'active files' and 'dormant files'. After five years of dormancy the papers should all be returned to the archive and joined up with the child's adoption file. (research diary, July 2002)

I am beginning this account by evoking a contrast between two systems that were operating in the local authority in which my study was based. The first quotation describes a system of archiving, where adoption files, stored alphabetically in a basement, recorded the history of children's adoptions. The second quotation describes a system for exchanging letters, where letterbox files, stored in the local authority office, record the history of mail exchanges between adopters and birth family. The former is a system for the storage of dead history, where events described are past and the latter is a system for the recording of living history, where events described have an ongoing life in the present. This distinction is clearly reflected in the geographical location of these two systems: the letterbox files are housed in the social work office, easily accessible and part of the contemporary life of adoption work, while the adoption files are at the back of a locked basement, difficult to access and part of the past history of adoption work. These two systems clearly reflect two very different notions of what it means to be adopted and it was in order to interrogate the transition they signify that I undertook my local authority study. This chapter will introduce the study and the questions that I wished to address.

The working archive

In common with all adoption agencies, the local authority in which I conducted my research had an extensive archive of all adoptions made under their jurisdiction. The practice of preserving the adopted child's prior history in an archive of adoption files emerged most systematically after the 1976 Adoption Act.[1] As Chapters 5 and 6 elaborated, the opening up of birth records in the 1970s had transformed the adoption archive from a sealed depository to an open reference space. The truth of the child's original history needed to be accommodated somewhere secure and unchanging to await that point when it would be resurrected for the adopted adult seeking his or her origins. This practice of archiving is clearly embedded in the idea of the origin as a source of truth and knowledge for the adopted subject, an idea that had gathered momentum throughout the 1960s with the practice of 'telling' (see Chapter 4) and throughout the 1970s and 1980s with the practices of later life letters and life story work (see Chapter 5). One of the foci of this study is whether the era of open adoption reworks this archiving impulse and Chapters 8 and 9 will consider this question through a close reading of the adoption archive files.[2]

My study focus was adoption placements made in the period 1989–2000, a decade in which 'open adoption' was commonly understood to have emerged as a body of practices in the United Kingdom (see Chapter 6). The research was undertaken between 2002 and 2004.

Collecting the archive sample

My original idea when undertaking this research was to compare adoptions from two particular years within one local authority, 1990, before open adoption had really emerged and 2000 when open adoption practices had entered adoption work. My hope was that the local authority in which I would be working would be able to provide me with a list of adoption orders for these respective years and I would simply access the files in the archive. However, the authority had only very recently begun to keep full records of annual adoption orders and this meant I only had a full list for the year 2000.

This 'setback' was soon transformed into an opportunity to rethink my original approach. I was advised by the Services Manager that I could collect my own sample of adoption orders by working from adoption panel grids, which indicate when adoption was decided for certain children. I would then need to go to the adoption archive to see whether that decision had become an actual adoption. Equipped with panel decisions from 1986 to 1996, I realised that by composing my own sample in this rather laborious way I would be able to trace the emergence of open practices throughout the decade, rather than the more limited comparative exercise that I had originally planned.

I read the files in a chronological order – earliest to latest – and arranged the sample into three groupings that reflected the direction of my reading: 1989–1991; 1992–1998 and 2000. The adoption files recorded information on documentation that was universally used in local authority work during the period of my research (see footnote for further details).[3] It is important to emphasise at this point that my chronological reading was not intending to trace developmental patterns of practice in order to chart 'improvements' through the decade of the files. One of the primary purposes of the study was to trace the emergence and deployment of open adoption practices, so a chronological reading would allow me to mark both the periods when these practices first emerged and the periods in which they were consolidated, changed and more actively deployed. Chapters 8 and 9 will be focusing on the periods 1992–1998 and 2000. I will conclude this chapter by introducing my approach in reading the archive adoption files.

Reading the archive

As Chapter 6 elaborated, the emergence of open adoption practices was a continuity with previous adoption histories, where birth family involvement was both invited and contested, creating a paradoxical field of operation. However, towards the end of that chapter I raised the question of how far open adoption marked a break or a change in the field, given the way that its implementation was so publicly debated and opposed. In this part of the introduction, I want to explore this question further through a close analysis of my study local authority adoption archive, drawing upon Foucault's late work in the lecture series of 1982 *Hermeneutics of the Subject* (2005).

My contention is that we can see with the emergence of open adoption in the late 1980s practices of the subject that resist accommodation to the contemporary technology of self-knowledge through self-discovery. Adoption, as Part I of this study explored, emerged within this modern technology and its techniques of self-formation reflect the same concerns with internal knowledge and self-decipherment. The regimes of truth that govern the kinds of knowledge in which adoption subjects form themselves reflect those that are operative in the wider culture: the foundational importance of the original kinship tie; personal childhood history as a determining and clarifying source of truth; the past of childhood concealed and hidden from the adult subject; knowledge about family origins as fundamental to mental health.

As the preceding chapters have variously demonstrated, this technology lies paradoxically at the heart of open practices in adoption. These practices have functioned to facilitate the discovery of self-knowledge for the adopted subject. What is emphasised is the discovery of a knowledge in which the adopted subject had *already* been truthfully formed, but which had been forgotten or unworked by the incursion of adoption. For Foucault (2005, p. 190) it is this dimension of discovery that is a crucial distinguishing element in contemporary subjectivity – modern subjects come into the world complete and live their lives reclaiming and restoring the knowledge with which they arrived: 'The subject does not have to transform himself. The subject only has to be what he is for him to have access in knowledge to the truth that is open to him through his own structure as subject.' For the adopted subject such a quest is heightened by their separation from one of the primary sources of self-knowledge, their family of origin.

Foucault emphasises that it is not just this relationship between truth and knowledge that distinguishes the modern subject – it is also the way that this knowledge is accessed. This modern subject is shaped through what Foucault termed the hermeneutics of the self, where the subject is formed through an endless self-deciphering based on internal truths that are concealed or repressed. Open practices work to support an adopted subject in undertaking this process of self-scrutiny to arrive at the hidden truths of original kinship.

In turning to Foucault's work in *Hermeneutics of the Subject* (2005) I want to show how this dominant technology of adoption is marked by a very different technology which the emergence of open adoption has produced. Foucault's claim in this lecture series is that contemporary subjectivities still bear the trace of a very different kind of aesthetic, a technology which produces a very different relationship to truth (2005, pp. 16–17, pp. 207–8). He used narratives from different eras of antiquity to trace how the contemporary subject emerged in a complex way from out of earlier traditions: 'How did it come about that we accorded so much privilege, value and intensity to the "know your-self" and omitted, or at least left in the shadow, this notion of care of the self that … framed the principle of "know yourself" from the start' (2005, p. 12).

Foucault is comparing two very different technologies of the subject, with contrasting relationships to the question of truth. Caring for the self in antiquity was not tied to self-knowledge, whereas for the modern western subject this link is fundamental. Furthermore, truth is not an internal property of the subject of antiquity, as Foucault (2005, p. 365) elaborates:

> He must … carry out a subjectivation that begins with listening to the true discourses proposed to him. He must therefore become the subject of truth: he himself must be able to say the truth and he must be able to say it to himself. In no way is it necessary or indispensable that he tell the truth about himself.

This distinction between a technology where truth is rediscovered and a technology where truth is transformative is central to the analysis that Foucault conducts in *Hermeneutics of the Subject*. The relevance to my own study lies in the way that Foucault identifies continuities and discontinuities between these two technologies. This makes his work an invaluable guide in tracing how both letterbox and direct contact are practices that operate within two different regimes of truth – one governed by self-knowledge and one by self-transformation. Before beginning my genealogical exploration of letterbox and direct contact in Chapters 8 and 9, I want to briefly outline the way I will be using Foucault's work on technologies of the self to frame my analysis.

Transforming or discovering the self?

O'Leary (2002, p. 31), in his study of Foucault's late work on ethics, understands the absorption with antiquity as a way of thinking about the present. In turning to the 'culture of the self' that flourished in first and second centuries AD, Foucault wants to evoke both a contrast and continuity with who we are today. The overarching continuity that is implicit in Foucault's whole last project resides in the term he uses to characterise the Greek mode of being: subjectivation – the relation to oneself. This mode of being first emerged in Greek culture and has been central to western forms of subjectivity to the present day (O'Leary 2002, p. 118). Deleuze, in his study of Foucault, beautifully captures the reflexive movement inherent in the concept of subjectivation in its inaugurating emergence: 'They folded force … they made it relate back to itself. Far from ignoring interiority, individuality or subjectivity they invented the subject … they discovered the "aesthetic existence" the doubling or relation with oneself' (Deleuze, 1999, p. 101).

Whilst this taking of oneself as a subject has a long and continuous history in the west, Foucault wants to drew attention to the different ways that subjectivation has operated and the different kinds of subject positions that have been historically possible. Many of the practices of the self that emerged in late antiquity are still operative today in how subjects form and fashion themselves. As I will discuss more fully below, practices such as memorisation of the past, examination of conscience and checking representations structure and inform open adoption practices such as letterbox contact. However, Foucault's point is that in this earlier era these practices were achieving and performing a very different kind of subject. I want to briefly outline these differences whilst drawing attention to the ways that these differences have been sustained in adoption work.

Fashioning the self

> One cannot have access to the truth if one doesn't change one's mode of being. (Foucault, 2005, p. 190)

The subject of antiquity was not understood as possessing an inner truth, installed in one's biography through birth and early life. The truth was something one lacked and that needed to be formed and fashioned; it was not inherent; it was something that was acquired rather than discovered. The self of late antiquity was a self that emerged in action; it had no essential core or root, but came into being in activity. This conception of the subject had three effects: first, the subject needed to work on itself to effect transformations that would make him or her capable of truth; second, the subject's being was malleable, protean and capable of change and finally the subject was not anchored to itself though its biography.

There is a clear and emerging sense in the history of adoption that subjects of adoption need to undertake work on themselves. However, this work was usually in the direction of rediscovering the truth that is based in their original biographies of birth, placing a limit on how far subjects would be transformed. With the advent of open adoption a different kind of personal work begins to emerge into open practices. The ongoing involvement of birth parents in adopted children's lives through the practices of letter writing or visits potentially creates new history rather than restaging past history. This immediately opens up the possibility of a transformative experience that is not reducible to self-discovery through biographical knowledge. I will be exploring how far letters and visits are tools of rediscovery or instruments of self-transformation and if the latter, how such transformation works.

Training

Following on from the above, there was the related idea of life as a continuous form of training, the self as an ongoing and unfinished project. The foucauldian commentator May (2006, p. 101) captures this sense very well: 'Care of the self involves a life long commitment to self-creation, to getting free of who one is so that one can become something else'.

In adoption work by the 1970s, as I have already explored, there was a growing sense of the need for training for adoptive families, training to help them become subjects of adoption. What is interesting about this form of training is that it goes in the opposite direction to other regimes like psychotherapy, which are mostly rooted in narratives of self-discovery. For adopters as a new family, there was nowhere to look back to, although their own biographies were often mobilised as sources of knowledge to draw upon or to work upon in the interests of their new roles. I am interested in tracing how far open practices work to free adoptive families or to re-centre them in forms of old biographical knowledge.

Knowledge

Foucault discusses the very different place that knowledge occupied in terms of subject formation in antiquity. Knowledge was relational, not substantive, by which he means that it was not knowledge of the self, but knowledge to help change the self that was operative: 'Not a knowledge that would take the soul or the self as the real object of knowledge. It is rather, knowledge concerning things, the world, the gods and men, but whose effect and function are to change the subjects being' (Foucault 2005, p. 243). There are two important points that Foucault elaborates: this kind of knowledge was 'useful', to hand and this knowledge did not need deciphering in terms of the subject's internal being.

For the contemporary subject formed through regimes of self-exegesis, this is a very different account. As I have already discussed, letterbox contact is commonly understood to be a support to help adopted children decipher their early lives and so enhance their functioning as subjects. In my reading of the letterbox system, I will be exploring, first, what kinds of knowledge that letterbox communicates and, second, the ways this knowledge is interpreted and used by social workers with adoptive families. Is this solely a hermeneutic practice or is there another technology of self at play? By requesting birth parents to write about their everyday lives, are children being invited to construct narratives, rather than discover them in themselves?

Everyday life

Foucault makes an implicit comparison between biography and everyday life in terms of ways of forming oneself as a subject. He highlights the importance of ordinary life and the ways that one conversed about it in the construction of subjectivity in late antiquity: 'With regard to the self (to the day you have passed, to the work you have done and to your sources of entertainment), you have the attitude, the stance of someone who will give an account of it to someone else' (Foucault 2005, p. 163).

The role of the everyday in terms of how one reflected upon and shaped oneself was not informed by personal biography. Whilst Foucault draws attention to the importance of the domestic sphere in narratives of the self – diet, the running of the household, one's erotic life (ibid., p. 161) – this domestic life was not situated within a psychological biography; it was the events not the self that were the focus. This importance in reflecting and recording of small everyday matters will become inextricably linked to the unfolding of biography by the contemporary era (ibid., p. 362). The modern subject cannot separate their ordinary life from their biography. The emergence of open adoption practices reflects this link between the everyday and the biographical. Letters and visits are aimed at 'building up' the adopted child's biography by transmitting information about the everyday lives of their absent birth family. I will be interrogating this claim and suggesting that these practices actually work to separate the everyday from the biographical, potentially effecting a different kind of subject position.

Making the truth

> It is a set of practices by which one can acquire, assimilate and transform truth into a personal principle of action. (Foucault, 1988, p. 35)

In *Hermeneutics of the Subject* (2005) Foucault devotes a great deal of time to askesis, practices of self on self, tracing the ways that subjects took themselves and made themselves subjects. Askesis has an enduringly long legacy in western cultures and the practices that Foucault identifies are still practices familiar to us in the contemporary era. First, there were practices where the subject acquired and assimilated the truth – listening and speaking to another, reading and writing for oneself in solitude (2005, p. 340 onwards). Then there were exercises through which the subject actively transformed themselves into a subject of truth, abstinence, meditation, examination of conscience (ibid., pp. 416–17).

These practices of the self are still operative in how contemporary subjects form themselves, although of course the technology through which this subjectivation is fashioned has changed. Foucault clarifies that in the Hellenistic period, these practices were 'not taking place within the framework of a rule, but of an art of living' (2005, pp. 423–4).

Clearly, open adoption can be understood as a set of practices of the self, helping adopted subjects form themselves as adopted. These practices are framed by certain rules, tied to certain laws about what it means to be adopted; one cannot fashion oneself without regard to certain rules of truth about adoption. However, as the preceding chapters have explored, being adopted is in one important sense having a made-up life, where one is freed from the cultural confines of identity tied to biography, of implicit truths rooted in origins. I am interested in considering how far open adoption practices enable subjects to acquire and transform themselves in truths that are not reducible to the rules governing the technology of adoption.

In summary I will be undertaking a genealogical analysis of letterbox and direct contact through a reading of adoptions made and recorded between 1989 and 2000 by my study local authority. I have two clear objectives in this undertaking: First, to trace how these open practices first emerged and how they were deployed throughout the period and, second, to trace the ways that these practice were operating within two distinct regimes of truth – one governed by self-knowledge and one by self-transformation.[4] In exploring this I will be drawing upon the questions that I listed in Chapter 1:

Do these practices create new history or restage old history?

Are children's biographies transformed or re-centred in former birth narratives by letter and direct contact?

Are letters and photographs hermeneutical tools or do they operate differently?

Does the transmission of information about birth family 'build up' an adopted child's prior history or construct new history?

And finally how far do open adoption practices break with the dominant technology of adoption and produce a different kind of subject.

8
Knowing or Transforming the Self: Tracing Letterbox Contact

> He has started to ask about where he came from and sometimes looks at the pictures of the birth family. Our desire for K is to be a well grounded, balanced child who knows who he is (Adoption, 2000).
>
> ... on a yearly basis Ms B will receive information on T's progress and developments from adopters. Also Ms B may send information about T's sisters and herself that is by way of photos, letters etc. (Adoption, 1998).

I have introduced this chapter with two examples of letterbox contact from the adoption files from my study local authority. They evoke two contrasting pictures of how this form of open adoption operates, reflecting two distinctly different technologies of the adopted subject. In the first quotation the photographs from the letterbox are understood as hermeneutical tools to help the adopted child access the truth of his kinship origins. The knowledge of family beginnings is linked to the child acquiring a more 'grounded' identity. This technology is rooted in a regime of truth governed by a self-knowledge based on familial origins. In the second quotation the letters and photographs that are exchanged between the adoptive family and the birth family transmit information about the contemporary lives of the adoption participants. These communications are about the present, not the past and potentially work to reconstruct or transform the adopted child's former birth narratives. This technology is rooted in a regime of truth governed by the transformative potential of relationships in present time.

In this chapter I will be arguing that both these technologies are problematically at play in how my study local authority conceptualise and deploy the open practice of letterbox contact. In undertaking this analysis I will be paying particular attention to the way that this form of contact suggests and promotes a technology of the subject that runs counter to the more dominant technology in adoption work.

Introducing letterbox contact

The local authority in which I conducted my research began to introduce letterbox contact in the early 1990s in a spasmodic and unsystematic way. As the decade progressed, a more systematised arrangement emerged in some of the file accounts. It was not until 1999 that a separate system for letterbox contact was established and this was housed in a separate place in the adoption team's office. Prior to this, all accounts of this form of contact were held in the adoption archive files. In common with most local authorities, my study local authority ran two distinct systems of record keeping simultaneously. This dual practice of archiving was not challenged by the emergence of open adoption until quite late in its operation. What I want to emphasise here is how the two systems reflected two different notions of history. With the inauguration of a separate system, letterbox cases are no longer regarded as 'archival'. They are separated out from the 'dead' archive cases and put in a place of current work, indicative of their current, not past status. This, I will be arguing, speaks to a problematic contradiction in how the local authority theorise and practice this form of open adoption.

The files do not contain any clear policy directive about letterbox contact or any definition of the practice until 1999. However, the earlier files contain references to the practice, and the kinds of documents that would be relevant in implementing the practice. The services manager confirmed in an interview that letterbox contact was in operation for at least a decade (1989 onwards) before any formal policy and procedure was introduced. The following discussion will focus on the periods 1992–1998 and 2000.

Middle sample 1992–1998

> She remains very happy about T's placement and she is happy about the telephone contact she has – she also sends money for his birthday and Christmas. She would be happy about T telephoning her also...She is prepared to send photographs to him – she has one of him when 5 years old. She would like to send T a letter explaining why she gave him up as he asked her about this. (Adoption, 1994)

In the above quotation it is clear that the practice of letterbox contact has started to emerge into adoption work by this period of the mid-1990s. The different forms of letterbox contact detailed in this short report – gifts, telephone calls, cards – have clearly been instigated by the local authority. On this home visit the social worker appears to be gathering feedback from the birth mother about how she is experiencing the contact arrangements with her child. The report also highlights a convergence of two quite different open practices – later life letters and letterbox contact. In many of the files from this period, it was quite common for these practices to be simultaneously deployed – the provision of a one-off later life letter and the sending of letters and photographs on a regular basis.

During this period letterbox contact begins to emerge as a systematised practice, acquiring definitions and purposes, which are cited in case files when workers are implementing letterbox arrangements. This form of contact was emerging within a dominantly coercive and contested adoption discourse. The majority of these cases were older children from the care system, whose parents were subject to child protection interventions. As Chapter 6 noted, adoption became most open when it was most adversarial and this is clearly reflected in my study local authority's practices. The status of the adoption – voluntary relinquishment or coercive/contested – did not seem to have an active bearing on whether letterbox was implemented. Across the sample there are relinquished babies and older children from care both placed with and without letterbox contact. There is also a growing sense from the file accounts that this is the acceptable and 'easy' end of open adoption practices, with direct contact increasingly becoming a contested area of practice. In the earliest sample of files (1989–1991), letterbox was a contested area of practice; as this becomes routine, direct contact becomes the new terrain of controversy. However, alongside this growing systematisation, there are simultaneously examples of resistance and refusal towards its implementation. I will be arguing that in this period letterbox contact as a set of practices is simultaneously contested and foreclosed, as well as defined and implemented.

Contested, foreclosed

Some of the cases do not include any details of the implementation of letterbox contact or any mention of it as a recommended practice. One could say that in these instances the practice has been foreclosed. I use this term to evoke the sense of a local authority repudiating the significance of a practice that they are simultaneously in the process of introducing.

There are cases where the local authority are slow and inefficient at putting a letterbox arrangement in place, sometimes taking up to two years after the order has been granted. An adoption from 1995 is a good example of this, where there is still no letter exchange by 1997. The file contains correspondence from the social worker to the birth mother where the protracted nature of the situation is noted and explained, but not ameliorated. The final letter from 1997 is to inform the birth mother that the social worker is leaving the department, but there is nothing else on the file to suggest whether anyone else would be attending to the letterbox contact. This case is interesting in that it provides a chronology of failure and reluctance about the letterbox, addressed to the birth mother, making her a subject who requires explanations about a practice that she should be experiencing. The following quotation from the social workers' final letter combines this dual sense of a service that is simultaneously offered and contested: 'You may be thinking of writing to him via the post box. I know you said you might want some help with this. I am likely to be quite busy, but we may be able to make a time to meet before I go.' Clearly this is the territory where help with letters is offered, but the social workers' time schedule works to neutralise the offer, keeping the birth mother in an excluded position.

There is one striking case where the local authority actively contests letterbox contact, with reasons which reveal a very clear picture of the technology of the adopted subject being mobilised. This adoption from 1993 concerns an older boy, M, from a troubled background, who was adopted from care. The file contains a very lengthy addendum to the Schedule 11 report specifically dealing with the issue of birth family contact. I want to focus on the two sections where the local authority articulate their case against M sustaining letterbox contact. Clearly, as a practice it is now sufficiently in circulation to be the object of opposition. Interestingly, the same arguments used here against letterbox contact will be mobilised to oppose direct contact, as Chapter 9 will elaborate. The terrain of contestation will shift as the decade progresses. So what views are embedded in this document?

First, letters from the birth family are understood as unsettling, undermining and confusing and will prevent M from settling down in his new adoptive home. It is reported that his birth mother has now written to M saying she loves and misses him: 'It was felt that the contents of the letter would have an unsettling effect on M at this important stage in his life.' The letter would 'confuse' M and 'undermine' his new home life. It will be saved 'for future discussion'. Clearly, the view here is that M will only be able to sustain one primary attachment, not two and any letter contact will interfere in M's capacity to make a new bond with his adopters.

Second, letter contact will exacerbate M's tendency to fantasise about his birth father, which will work against him settling down: 'M has a strong tendency to fantasy particularly about his father and I feel that letter contact may feed that fantasy.' There seems to be an idea that fantasy is an effect of proximity, something that is produced by presence, not absence. By keeping M's father absent, fantasising will be curtailed, not provoked.

Finally, there is the belief that adopted children cannot metabolise or contain more than one version of their birth story; that children 'need' a tidied-up version of their history in order to help them 'move on'. Ongoing letter contact will unsettle and destabilise children's 'need' for a singular account of their history. It is noted in a letter to M's siblings that his life story book and 'daily opportunities to discuss his feelings' are the preferred way to keep M's family involved. In comparison to ongoing letter contact, these are forms that keeps M's birth history open at a safe, remote and static distance. Life story book is a form of open practice that is subject to the interpretations of the adopters, who can represent or translate the birth family to M without any discordant contribution from the birth family themselves.

As I have already emphasised, open practices such as life story work are tools of recollection that situate the past as a source of knowledge for the adopted child. In this case it is clear that the local authority wish to resist an ongoing involvement in present time for M's birth parents, wanting to make them figures of his past. However, it is apparent that M forms himself through fantasising about his birth father, that his self-fashioning is in some way linked to this absent paternal figure. One might argue that the refusal for an ongoing involvement, rather than working to confine the father to the past, actually works to produce him in the 'present' of M's fantasy life. This seems to be confirmed by the addendum, which reports the following conversation with M: 'M was nonchalant when I tried to engage him in discussions regarding his natural family. When I asked him when he had last seen them, he told me it was "yesterday". This was clearly not the time.'

However, in this period, alongside cases of resistance, the local authority also actively defined and implemented letterbox practices, even instituting the skeleton of a system that would eventually become a formalised aspect of adoption work. It is to these adoptions I will now turn. I will divide my discussion into two sections: firstly, a consideration of how letterbox contact was defined and, second, how it was implemented.

Two technologies in opposition: defining the practice of letterbox contact

Whilst there was no clear policy directive in the files about this form of practice, this sample does contain many scattered references to the benefits that letterbox contact should confer. In spite of the paucity of a clearly articulated local authority policy, it is clear from a number of adoptions in this sample that letters and photographs were being sent, and less commonly, exchanged, on a regular basis between adopters and birth family.

Two key benefits are cited: it gives children information about their origins and it gives them a 'link' with their birth parents' contemporary lives. The former benefit speaks to a familiar and enduring concern about the need for knowledge about childhood origins; the latter, more unusually, speaks to a need to sustain those former relationships in present time. Clearly, two quite different technologies of the adopted subject are at play here, one rooted in past knowledge and one in contemporary relationships. I want to now cite some examples.

Past knowledge

An adoption from 1995 has this in a Schedule II: 'in order that J may make sense of his adoption and be able to find out more about his mother as he grows older it would be helpful for letters, photographs and cards to be exchanged via social services twice per year' and the Guardian Ad Litem's (GAL's) report adds 'letterbox would be the most beneficial way of ensuring that J retains knowledge of his origins'. This extract clearly situates the purpose of letter exchange as enhancing the adopted child's knowledge about his origins. Receiving letters will help the child work through his adoptive status. Similar to life story books, letters within this construction are hermeneutical tools, helping the child unravel their dual adoptive identity.

An adoption from 1995 records a need for letterbox contact with the birth mother:

> I am of the opinion that there should be letters and photographs between [the birth mother] and any prospective adopters post-adoption, albeit perhaps through the medium of social services, on an annual basis. This is to acknowledge the children's link with their birth mother and her part in their life story.

A later file note for the same case remarks: 'Although there is no longer any live contact, [the birth mother] is still able to periodically telephone.' This example again understands the letters as archival documents. They facilitate the recollection of the past, the part the children's mother had in their former life, but these letters do not engage with the present. The final file note reflects this with its description of telephone contact as implicitly dead. It is almost as if the birth mother has to be consigned to non-living place, emptied of contemporary significance, in order to be allowed to participate at all in her adopted children's lives.

Contemporary relationships

A case from 1992, involving a large sibling group, has the following brief statement: 'The importance of maintaining links with their brothers and sisters has been explained to G and D in some detail.' This brief comment does not situate the maintenance of links within any kind of kinship history; the implication is that the benefit for G and D resides in keeping in touch with their brothers and sisters in their current lives, the making of history, rather than its recollection.

An adoption from 1998 contains the following plan for letterbox:

> There will be letterbox contact between Birth Mother and T. This means on a yearly basis Ms B will receive information on T's progress and developments from prospective adopters. Also Ms B may send information about T's sisters and herself that is by way of photos, letters.

This plan focuses on the contribution that the current lives of the participants will make to a letter exchange. The birth family will hear about T's progress and development over the year and the adopters will receive information about the birth family's current concerns. This letter exchange is for the sustaining of relationships in present time and not a tool for the recollection of the past.

These two technologies have a very different relationship to knowledge. In the first examples, the letterbox works to supply historical knowledge to the adopted child, facilitating recollection and a process of self-exegesis. In contrast, the second examples supply contemporary information, knowledge about the present lives and circumstances of the adoption participants. Foucault (2005, p. 278) describes the kind of knowledge that this latter technology generates: 'This form of knowledge involves grasping ourselves again here where we are, at the point

where we exist, that is to say of placing ourselves within a … world.'
The technology of the subject that informs this present centred form of
knowledge works in the following way:

> The whole game, precisely what is at stake in this movement, is
> never to lose sight of any of the components that characterize our
> own situation, in the very spot we occupy … And stepping back we
> see the context in which we are placed opening out, and we grasp
> again this world as it is, the world in which we exist. (Foucault 2005,
> p. 282)

This is not, then, an interior knowledge from an interior self, but a
knowledge from the world that maps out and transforms one's position
in that world. There is, I am suggesting, within my study local authority an operative technology of the adopted subject where knowledge is
constructed in this way. If letters are understood as communications
about the present lives of adoption participants, then the knowledge
they transmit works to both map and remap the contemporary territo-
ries that everyone inhabits.

Whilst I said earlier that there are no policy directives for letterbox,
its role as a compensatory practice stands as an implicit policy statement. This was the era when the 1989 Children Act had taken effect,
enforcing local authorities to sustain contact between parents and their
children in foster care. Many of these samples of adoptions detail the
history of visits to foster homes until the adoption decision is taken and
visits are terminated. The following chapter will analyse this in more
detail, but it is clear that there is already a relationship between the end
of foster visits and the establishment of letter contact for children who
will be adopted.

Some of the files offer letterbox contact as a compensation for the termination of visits, a way to soften the lack of a more immediate physical
relationship with the adopted child. There is also the idea that indirect
contact is less 'disruptive' than visits and two cases illustrate this:

> Ms K has been inconsistent in maintaining contact with all her chil-
> dren, because her attitude in the past has had a disruptive effect on
> the children. It was agreed that indirect contact would be better for
> the children in the long-term' (Adoption, 1995). 'There was an objec-
> tion to direct but not to indirect contact. This was because S was now
> placed and becoming settled, also because of the numerous, many
> moves back to [birth mother]. (Adoption, 1996)

There are a number of points to be made here: first, there is a strong association with visits and children being unsettled. In the first example this is because the mother was 'inconsistent' with visiting; in the second example it is because the child had experienced many failed rehabilitations home. Chapter 9 will explore direct contact in more detail, but I mention it here to underline the compensatory role that letterbox contact plays when unfit mothers fail to achieve visiting contact with their children. Second, letters are defined as better contact in the long term, particularly if parents have been unreliable or inconsistent with visiting. Adopted children can better metabolise unreliability in letter writing than with visits. Finally, and following on from the above, letters are not defined as unsettling. One might equally argue that receiving letters every year from someone one never actually meets might be very unsettling and very disrupting. Clearly, there is something about the distance and lack of physical proximity that works to define letter contact as non-disruptive. Interestingly, a case from 1992 shows how letters can unsettle and disturb.

The case involved a baby who was placed for adoption following child protection concerns. There was a one-way letterbox put in place, comprising an annual letter and photograph from adopters to birth mother, with a clear note that the adopters wanted nothing in return. The letters are progress reports on the child, her life summarised into an account of her educational progress, friendships and family activities over the course of a year. It is reported that the adopters became very upset one year when a letter was inadvertently forwarded from the birth mother to them. Having information about her life they find 'unsettling', it is the unscheduled incursion of the birth mother in 'real time' as opposed to 'historic time' that unsettled the adoptive family. They are clearly only comfortable when staying in charge of what is transmitted of their daughter's life; a letter dialogue would unsettle the stable picture they wish to communicate each year.

Clearly, in order to continue to define letters as non-disruptive certain limitations had to be operative in the above case. This was also reflected in other cases, where there was a very evident move to minimise the involvement of the birth family. As in the example above, many of the cases were just one way with the birth family receiving information, but not sending letters themselves. Two examples from 1995 demonstrate this: '...whilst she [birth mother] may not respond to any mail, we should continue to send her information about D to her' and 'she had no maternal feelings...but would like to be informed of her progress'.

In both these cases the mothers are excluded from an exchange with the adopters, but included through receiving information. The second example is implicitly suggesting that the lack of maternal feelings precludes involvement – only 'real' mothers have engagement with their children – but information about her daughter will be provided.

As letterbox contact begins to become defined, there is a sense that the involvements it invites – that of the birth family – need to be contained, curtailed or excluded.

Implementing letterbox: the formalising of a system

In this period in my study local authority there is clearly a tension about the purpose of the adoption archive file as letterbox contact begins to actively emerge. Is it for a practice of archiving, where a history is recorded and stored, or is it for a practice of ongoing letter contact, where new histories are made and exchanged? Increasingly, through the 1990s the files remain 'open' after the adoption order to accommodate letterbox exchanges, a move that increasingly compromises the file's more traditional function as storage for past history. Such tension would eventually lead to the establishment of two different systems in 1999: an archive storage and a letterbox exchange.

There was clearly a formalising of the system emerging throughout this period and many of the files mention some form of letterbox contact. The terms used vary greatly – 'postal contact'; 'indirect contact programme'; 'post-box contact' 'letterbox scheme' – reflecting a system that has still not acquired a stable operative presence. It is often not clear from the files how active the letterbox is, as the files often contain either copies of letters or originals, creating confusion about what has actually been sent through to the families. The emergence of a discreet letterbox system in 1999 will work to clarify this.

This sample of files commonly contained signed agreements for letterbox contact, informal contracts that birth parents and adopters agreed to operate together. This partnership way of working sat uneasily amidst a highly adversarial adoption discourse. As Chapter 6 discussed, open practices emerged in the 1990s as an effect of a complex regulatory situation created by the interface of the Children Act and the Adoption Act legislation. Whilst an adoption order severed the child's legal ties to its family of origin, the notions of both partnership and contact installed by the Children Act worked to reintroduce the presence of that family through open practices. The unfit family is, then, strangely situated. On the one hand, an adoption order has excluded them from their child's life, but on the other hand they are invited back in to negotiate and agree arrangements for their inclusion with their child's new parents. In common with many local authorities, my study local authority had installed these practices of informal agreement for many of their letterbox arrangements.

Some files append a standard written agreement that both adopters and birth parents have signed, detailing what will be sent, by who and when. A case from 1992 is a good early illustration of this. It is the first case where there is a proper letterbox form and where letterbox appears to be an integral part of the adoption. There is a form for recording the number of exchanges that take place, although in this file only one exchange is noted. This was also a reciprocal letterbox, where the birth mother could respond. The file notes that this annual exchange will be 'vetted' by the adoption team. There is no clarification about what vetting may signify, but it presumably alludes to a system of surveillance where correspondence is opened and read before forwarding to assess its suitability. This introduces the local authority as the hidden author behind correspondence, shaping and limiting the parameters of the acceptable communication generated by a specific technology of the adopted subject. This will become a more manifest and explicit part of how the letterbox system operates by the time of its formal inauguration in 1999.

A number of cases mention agreements being signed by both parties: 'Adoption order granted with no access. Explained that an agreement had been signed by the adopter ... to correspond and send photographs to birth mother twice a year at Christmas and birthday also any other significant event' (Adoption, 1992). An adoption from 1997 notes that the birth mother filled in a 'contact agreement form' 'I would write to her once pre-adopters had signed their part of the agreement to confirm this'.

The importance of an agreement being reached is underlined by an adoption from 1995, where it is noted that the birth parents have not signed an agreement form. It is suggested by the social worker that the adopters vet anything they receive from the parents for the child because the birth parents have not 'co-operated' with the local authority and signed any 'postal contact agreement'. Here the contractual and partnership discourse is reworked by a more insidiously coercive discourse, where co-operation is required not freely granted and agreements are compulsory, not freely entered. I will return to this discursive complexity when I discuss the inauguration of the separate letterbox system in the final section.

This contemporary emphasis on negotiating and agreeing arrangements between different sets of parents implies or promotes a very different way of achieving adoption. The impression from this sample of files is of a dynamic and interrelated set of people in an active relationship with each other. The conventional self-enclosed family of the wider culture is here challenged; those boundaries have now become porous and the adopted child, far from being rooted in one singular place, lives between two quite different places. The adopted child's sense of self comes into being through an involvement in the exchanges between its different families; following Foucault, one could say that the adopted subject is formed through activity, and not a historical origin or essence.

Clearly, in this sample of adoptions letterbox practices are beginning to emerge more fully and forcefully into social work accounts. These practices install a different conception of children's welfare through a different technology of the self. The active sending of information and photographs in present time reconfigures the position of the birth family; no longer restricted to a place of historical origin, they enter the present life of the adopted child with the sending of cards and photographs, with the receiving of annual news. It would seem that how social workers care about the adopted child has acquired a different relationship to knowledge. The knowledge that an ongoing letterbox will hold for the adopted child may well contain truths about its original biography, but it will also be an ongoing source of knowledge about its birth family's contemporary life – new, not historic truths. Ongoing letterbox practices unsettle a regime of truth governed by knowledge by installing a regime of truth governed by the transformative potential of relationships in present time.

Final sample 2000

> I can see that you have been very diligent and sent lovely letters twice a year to the birth family, which I know means a huge amount to them. The issue for them seems to be around timing as they appear to be on tenterhooks in the month they expect to receive the information. (Adoption, 2000)

The above extract from a letter sent to adopters by the local authority underlines certain changes in both the status and operation of letterbox contact in my study local authority by the year 2001. What is striking about this letter is the equality between the participants – we are now in the territory where both adopters and birth family can expect a certain level of service from each other. It is also the territory where a worker from the local authority offers support to each party in the sustaining of the letterbox contact, support that continues after the adoption order has been conferred. In this final section, I will be discussing the emergence of a discreet system for letterbox contact and analysing the degree to which its operation destabilised the dominant technology of adoption in my study local authority.

The letterbox system: the reworking of history

My final sample of files consisted of adoptions made in the year 2000. For these adoptions, letterbox contact is routinely arranged, with file reports noting that this is the intended open practice following the adoption order. These archive files do not contain the actual letter exchange, a contrast with my previous sample, where such an exchange was recorded and stored in the archive file. This can be explained by the inauguration of a separate system for letterbox contact in 1999.

The letterbox system was set up to accommodate the letter exchanges between adoptive family and birth family that would be ongoing after the adoption order. As Chapter 7, discussed this system is housed in the adoptions teams' office and not in the basement with the archive files, the geographical location reflecting a very different notion of its historical purpose. However, the files are ordered according to the child's birth name, not their adopted name, suggesting that the system is regarded as belonging to the child's past history. A relationship between the two systems is maintained. If a letterbox exchange becomes 'dormant' – not operative for five years – then all the paperwork is returned to the archive file for its storage as 'dead' history.

The letterbox files are located within a filing cabinet that houses the documentation for the local authority 'post-adoption service', indicating that from 1999 two discreet cultures are now operative: adoption and after adoption. As Chapters 5 and 6 discussed, from the 1970s onwards ongoing support to adoption participants following the adoption order became an increasing feature of adoption work. By the mid- to late 1990s many authorities were creating post-adoption posts or teams to undertake this support work. My study local authority created a position for a post-adoption worker in 1999, whose responsibilities included the administration of the letterbox system.

The newly formalised letterbox system incorporated a number of the practices that adoption workers had been implementing to set up letter exchanges. Negotiated decision-making and signed agreements – practices already in circulation – became part of the new system, with past and present families agreeing together, or separately, the content and form of the letter exchange. The local authority operated like a postal sorting office by forwarding mail to the different parties. The new system recognised that participants might need support with letterbox contact and directed families to the post adoption worker. However, and somewhat against this, there was also a sense that the parties can manage this process between themselves. The letterbox guidance document even suggests that the letter exchange can be carried out independently of the local authority, if families would prefer. What seems important is that 'normal family life' is simulated, that families can perform this exchange without the tutelary intrusions of the local authority worker.

A discourse of co-operation and partnership structures the management of this service, operating in stark contrast to the coercive and adversarial discourse of adoption proceedings prior to the order. Birth parents are here reconfigured from unfit parents requiring exclusion to parents negotiating their invited inclusion. In one sense this difference marks the passage from the archive file to the letterbox file, a passage that remakes the unfit parent into a person who can be included in their child's life. This shift is reflected in the contrasting constitution of these two very different files.

The letterbox file essentially operates as a record of a correspondence, including any social worker action taken to facilitate that correspondence (chasing up letters; managing any dispute or disagreement). At the front of each file is a note of the letterbox agreement – who writes the letters, whether birthday, Christmas cards or photographs are to be included and when these are to be sent. What follows is a chronological record of the letters that are exchanged between the adoptive family and the child's birth family, with any uncollected mail stored at the front of the file. In contrast to the archive files, there is a striking absence of child protection narratives, an absence that frees the adoption participants from their roles in those former histories. One could argue, then, that the letterbox system does not re-centre participants lives in old histories, but is set up to create new history. Consequently, both adopters and birth family are treated in an equal and even-handed way, as the quotation that prefaced this section illustrated. These files record actions, a history of conduct, not reports or assessments about those actions or conducts. I will give an example from an adoption case which figures in both archive and letterbox files.

The archive file of this case documents how birth mother and father consistently failed to parent their son through reported gross inadequacies in their parenting capabilities. There are two dominant and intersecting narratives in the file: a narrative of the child protection concerns that led to the adoption decision and a narrative of parental visits that led to the termination of their visits. Assessments and judgements of the birth family dominate the reports, as the file documents the progressive rewriting of the birth parents from out of their son's life. By contrast, the letterbox file contains none of this previous child protection history and there is a marked absence of any moralising discourse around the issue of contact. This file simply records an account of how the letterbox arrangements between the birth parents and the adopters has progressed. It is striking how the adoption participants speak for themselves without any local authority meta-narrative. The reported conversations of the birth family are not reframed or reinterpreted within the previous child protection history of their unfitness. There appears to be no privilege given to the adopter's perspective and the birth parents wishes and complaints seem to be equally represented.

However, I am not suggesting that this discursive move to make birth parents equal participants has really operated to rework their position. In turning to the referral form for letterbox contact, it quickly becomes apparent that any letter exchange is in the control of the local authority. Whilst 'agreement forms' for both adopters and birth family are mentioned, the social worker clearly has the final say about how the letterbox will be set up. The worker has 'to give a realistic estimate of how often the contact should take place' and has to detail the 'type of post' that will be exchanged. There is also a monitoring question about the birth family and whether there is anything that should be revealed about them that might affect how the letterbox runs. Child protection concerns are quietly present, installing parental unfitness as central to the question of letter exchange. Clearly, the letterbox system is rooted in social worker-imposed decisions, although there is a need to make these decisions appear to be consensual and negotiated.

A policy for letterbox contact

This is the first articulation of a formal policy for letterbox contact and I will examine it in some detail before analysing the actual cases to which it refers. There is a one-page guidance sheet explaining the purpose of letterbox contact:

> The letterbox system exists to pass on information from birth families to children who have been adopted, where no direct contact with birth families can take place. It is also used by adoptive families to pass on information to birth families about the progress of the child.

Here the letterbox system is presented as a compensation for direct contact, a substitute for an arrangement that is to do with physically seeing a child. This has been a latent policy within this authority since the practice first emerged, but here it assumes a clearer directive. It is almost as if the two discrete practices serve the same purpose and where one is not possible, the other is substituted. This policy statement suggests that the purposeful transmission of information is about a keeping in touch, a sustaining of a tie and not necessarily to do with knowledge about past history.

The guidance sheet goes on to cite two reasons for having such an 'exchange of information. First, it can be 'invaluable in answering questions the children might have about their family of birth (emotional, medical and significant updates)' and, second, it reassures the birth family that the children are 'loved and looked after'. These reasons centre the practice in contemporary time, where children have questions about their parent's current lives in response to their own current experiences. Unlike the previous sample, there is no mention here of knowledge of kinship origins or the importance of past histories. This new emphasis for letterbox practice is further elaborated in the two guidance sheets for the writing of letters, one for birth parents and one for adopters. As the local authority do not usually promote any kind of meeting between the two sets of parents, then such guidance becomes important in facilitating these letter exchanges.

The guidance documents reveal two distinctly different cultures around the production of letters: birth parents will have very little latitude in how they write their letters; they will be expected to produce a certain kind of letter within certain clear parameters. In contrast, adopters have the freedom to produce any kind of letter in the knowledge that it will be acceptable to the local authority.

Birth parent letters need to be 'friendly and positive'; the child must be reassured, not frightened, not worried; the child must 'appreciate, enjoy and understand' what is written. There must be nothing to disturb the child in the letter and so parents are asked not to write anything about their history with the child, particularly their failure as a parent in the past. They must not say they miss the child and they must not include any personal address or contact numbers. They must not refer to the child as their son or daughter. The message is very clear: these must be sanitised letters, with any taint of history removed. The birth parent must recreate themselves as someone different from the mother or father that they were once to the child. The document explains 'this is because it could be confusing for them [the children] when they will already know themselves as sons and daughters of their adopters, although of course they will be told about the existence of birth parents'. The document concludes with a list of possible topics that birth parents can write about. This list contains such topics as 'what sort of job you do and what is fun about it; holidays you have enjoyed; any funny things that have happened to you since you last wrote'. And then the list ends with a suggestion that the birth parent writes about 'other members of your family and a few details about them' This 'family' will of course also be the child's family, but they are designated in this list as if they will be of no significance whatsoever to the child.

This document centres the production of a letter on the birth parents' present life. This is not a correspondence about the past, telling the child about its history, communicating the truth of its origins. This is a correspondence that is about the present and the future, creating new history for the child. The self that the family are invited to present is a self produced through the activity of writing, not a self produced from some previous archive knowledge. However, this process of involvement transforms the birth parent into a slightly distant stranger, who has an entertaining life, full of funny moments, a life where the trauma of the loss of the child does not figure. Such a transformation seems to be framed by a familiar theme throughout the reading of the files: the idea that children can only sustain one version of their lives; that a life has one dominant familial narrative and cannot encompass the complexities of other familial narratives within it. The birth family can play a part, provided it is not a part that challenges the adopted child's supposed singular concept of family.

The document for adopters is informative, rather than instructive. Birth parents are addressed in general non-specific ways; there is a stereotype of a birth parent that any adopter can write to in a letter. The document lists key areas 'they will be keen to know about' and these include the child's health, education, family activities, social progress and hobbies. The overriding concern is the provision of a positive and upbeat picture of the child to communicate to the birth parent. It is only 'real' parents who participate in the worries and crises of their children's lives; birth parents are no longer parents and so they should not be expected or encouraged to carry any of these worries and concerns about their children. They will be given a cleaned-up version of their children's lives in the same way that the children will be given a cleaned-up version of their birth parents' lives.

I wondered whether the cautions and controls implicit in these documents are an effect of the local authority not being able to quite manage the implications of the letterbox practice. The documents seem to be caught between two different technologies of the self. They contain a distinct narrative about the formative importance of a singular belonging and cannot easily accommodate the adopted child's other parents except by stripping them of their historical place. Yet here might lay their radicalness; by removing the strictures of the birth parents' role as the child's originating truth, they are freed to become a contemporary and active presence, creating new life in their letters. However, their involvement is only because of their autobiographical significance, a significance that is both endorsed and erased by the local authority policy. In turning to the letterbox system, I was interested in discovering whether the cases revealed the same paradoxical involvement as the above post-adoption documentation. As the following discussion will demonstrate, this final sample of files reveals a practice where birth parents are simultaneously involved and excluded and a local authority resists the formalisation of its own system in two ways: through an inadequately performed letter exchange and through the disappearance of birth mothers from their children's lives.

Established, but resisted

According to information on the archive files all of this sample of adoptions should have had a letterbox arrangement in place. As my study local authority had introduced a separate letterbox system in 1999, I assumed I would locate all these letter exchanges in that system. However, this expectation was not borne out. I only found four active letterbox files for my adoption sample and no record of the other 11 cases in the dormancy file. Some of the archive files contained details about letter arrangements, when there was no corresponding letterbox file. In spite of the local authority establishing a formal letterbox system, the adoption workers appeared to be undermining and compromising its implementation. Furthermore, even in the four cases I did locate, most of the involved participants were confused and/or ignorant about the way the system worked. One notable case involved a grand-mother and adopters taking independent action to set up a letterbox, after the local authority had failed to put in place the necessary let-terbox arrangements. In an angry letter the grandmother explains her position: 'I had not heard from you for about four months and if it had not been for the kindness the foster carer showed to us we would not have known what had happened to N at all.' The adopters are similarly frustrated and infuriated: 'We were led to believe that the department these forms were forwarded to did not complete the formalities of the setting up of the letterbox contact ... We seem to be going around in cir-cle with this simple request.' The local authority response to the inde-pendent action reveals the degree to which they want to stay in charge of contact arrangements and their implementation. They are clearly horrified that 'informal letterbox contact' had been taking place and they reiterate to all parties that letterbox is 'a formal process' and can-not be undertaken outside of the 'official channels'.

Participants were often confused about the status of letterbox contact and the nature of the contract to which they had signed. There seemed confusion about whether it was negotiated or imposed; informal or for-mal; temporary or permanent. Furthermore, there was a wide disparity of practice around the reaching and signing of agreements. A case again involving a grandmother documents how an intended letterbox was never implemented. There is a letter from the grandmother describing how confused she is about whether she ever completed a letterbox form. She is now very worried that she may have lost her contact, but is send-ing in a birthday card anyway. The local authority respond by stating that there is no agreement on record, yet I found in the file a signed agreement from two years earlier.

A further case involved adopters who were very unclear about what kind of commitment they had made with a letter exchange and with whom? The file contains a letter stating that they have written 'on numerous occasions to have arrangements clarified, but to no avail' and asking 'Is it right that there should be a contract in place between us and the local authority?' They have signed an agreement form, but this process does not seem to have clarified for them the nature of the commitment they have made. Is it with the local authority or with the birth parents? Is it a contract or a much more informal process? Such confusions were common in this sample of adoptions.

The purposes that letterbox contact served were not clearly defined in reports or to participants at the point where an arrangement was being implemented. All the adoption files included it as an unexamined post-adoption assumption, but one that had ceased to have any clearly articulated meaning.

As Chapter 9 will elaborate in more detail, many birth mothers disappeared from their children's lives in this sample or were written out of the adoptions by the local authority. There were few instances of birth mothers being actively involved with letterbox and some examples where mother's involvements were prohibited: 'Birth mother was never part of the letterbox contact plan (discussion with family finder, 5/12/2003).'

Whilst imperfectly inaugurated, the emergence of a discreet letterbox system does work to represent birth parents differently within a set-up where child protection narratives are not operative. The system is centred on new history not old, remaking the birth family into able participants with new narratives to communicate to their adopted children. The few files where birth parents were included represented their stories and their views in an equal and forceful way, communicating a sense that redress is possible, even if not successful. This can be seen with the memorable example of a birth father's putative court case against the local authority for 'non-compliance of letterbox contact agreement'. There is then an emergent culture where birth parents can demand and expect a service from the local authority and where that service constructs them as figures of accountability.

Conclusion

This chapter has traced how the emergence of letterbox contact was problematically implemented within two specific technologies – one governed by knowledge of kinship origins and one governed by the transformative potential of relationships in present time. My analysis demonstrated how letter exchange was understood as both a way of providing historic information and a way of keeping a child in touch with birth family in contemporary time. By 1999, with the emergence of a formal service, the tension between these two technologies was resolved in a surprising way. Whilst the child's original history continued to be defined as central, its transmission through letters became an increasingly controversial area, eventually culminating in a practice where all historical information was prohibited. Birth parents could only appear in letters to their child, if all references to their history with that child had been expunged. Paradoxically, then, their autobiographical significance secures an involvement that is then erased by local authority policy, giving birth parents a strangely unreal presence in the letterbox arrangements from the year 2000.

9
Identity through Injury: Unfit Mothers and Direct Contact

> She [the adoption Manager] outlined her position on direct contact more unequivocally, saying that Ryburn's cases were 'artificial' and could not be applied to her local authority families who were 'drug abusers' and 'prostitutes'... 'How can you expect a baby to get on in a new family' if it is having contact... 'I have no trouble with letterbox, but face to face contact is the problem. (Research diary, January 2003)
>
> She arrived unexpected and was very upset and crying, shouting 'I want to see my baby. Why don't those fucking gutless people come out here and see me, they won't fucking face me, will they.' I spoke to birth mother and explained that she could not have contact then but should see her social worker... Mother said 'you're saying I've no fucking rights for my own daughter.' (Adoption, 1996)

I have prefaced this chapter with two very different quotations from my archive study. The first is from an interview I conducted with the adoption manager where she elaborates her views on direct contact after adoption. The second is from a social worker report describing a mother's unscheduled contact visit to her child in foster care at a time when his new adoptive parents were also visiting. By placing them together I am clearly implying a relationship – a manager opposed to direct contact visits for unfit mothers and an unfit mother's anguish at the prospect of losing her direct contact with her soon to be adopted child. Consistent with the account that I gave in Chapter 6, this manager views direct contact as the controversial and problematic open adoption practice, particularly when linked to unfit parenting. In her view unfit parents are disqualified from direct contact with their children, but can remain in touch by letter exchange, a position that the adoption files commonly reflected throughout the period of my study.

The question of the child's prior history shaped and framed how the practice of direct contact was implemented by my study local authority. As this chapter will relate, this practice has been most continuously resisted because of the involvement of unfit parents that it invites. Throughout the 1990s my study local authority mobilised the child's kinship origins as a reason against introducing the practice of direct contact, whilst simultaneously sustaining the significance of that origin in terms of the adopted child's development and identity. As Chapter 8 explored, letters can be reworked to omit or censor prior histories, whilst visits appear to be constructed as more intransigent signifiers of those histories.

This chapter will elaborate the paradoxical position that the unfit mother of contemporary adoption occupies through an exploration of the practice of direct contact in a decade of adoption work in my study local authority. Within the dominant technology of adoption, their kinship relationship to the adopted child is both central and foundational, yet their unfitness as parents makes problematic certain kinds of involvement within moralising discourses about their parenting histories.

The emergence of the unfit mother

For a long time ordinary individuality – the everyday individuality of everybody – remained below the threshold of description … the disciplinary methods lowered the threshold of describable individuality and made of this description a means of control and a method of domination (Foucault, 1977, p. 191).

In the above quotation, Foucault is identifying a transformation in how power operated in the modern era: no longer exercised by the privileged few, it became a dense and multiple network of disciplinary techniques bringing into visibility the ordinary individual as a case for training, classifying and normalising. In his paper 'The lives of infamous men', Foucault beautifully captures the way this power operates to make visible through a transitory encounter the ordinary individual, whose criminality has temporarily raised him to a position of registered and recorded significance: 'All these ingredients of the ordinary, the unimportant detail, obscurity, unexceptional days, community life, could and must be told – better still written down. They became describable and transcribable, precisely insofar as they were traversed by the mechanisms of a political power' (Foucault, 2000d, p. 169).

This bringing of the everyday into discourse – the endless accumulating and recording of details of daily life into reports and archives – is the modern way of governance. Clearly, such a system is in operation in my study local authority, where the archive of adoption files documents the encounter with the statutory authorities of a group of women – unfit mothers – whose lives would otherwise pass unremarked. This constituency of women figure in these files because of a change in how adoption operates in the contemporary era. Paradoxically, the unfit mother's appearance is an effect of her presence being erased from her child's life. As Foucault (1977, p. 191) makes clear, one of the ways that disciplinary techniques operate is to classify and record in order to exclude. As I will analyse, these women are represented in great detail in file reports where assessments about their contemporary and past mothering informs decision-making about post-adoption direct contact. I want to summarise some of the ways that the adoption files represent the strange kind of visibility of this group of mothers:

Unfit mothers are represented in terms of their unfitness and my study local authority documents the myriad ways these women have failed as parents. They are represented in terms of their relationship to their child in the care system. This is documented through accounts of visits made or not made to foster homes. Their contribution to their adopted child's 'life story work' is reported. Finally their involvement in keeping up ongoing contact with their adopted child is represented.

Clearly, some of the ways that these women are made visible reflect certain disciplinary techniques that work to classify them as unfit and to punish them for this unfitness. Visits to foster homes operate as examinations, where the normalising gaze of the social worker will assess, judge and differentiate the unfit mother from the healthy functional foster mother. However, some of these forms of visibility discipline in a different way. Involving the unfit mother in regimes of care for their child – contributing to a life story book, writing letters, having visits – do not construct her as unfit, but as a person who is still capable of participating in her child's life. I will be interested in exploring how far these forms of involvement work to dislodge the dominant representations of the unfit mother.

Alongside the local authority representations of this group, the files do record the women's own narratives. There are conversations with mothers, where their wishes and views are communicated, as well as disagreements and arguments with local authority workers. Their correspondence is sometimes included, letters to children or to social workers.

Whilst the change to open adoption practices has led to a greater representation of birth mothers' lives and experiences, this representation has not so far produced a position from which their invisibility and exclusion can be reworked. I am interested in interrogating the persistent effect of a lack of enduring force and presence of unfit mothers. What works to keep this category of women so eclipsed in spite of an increasing representation in adoption narratives as this decade progresses? Butler, in *The Psychic Life of Power* (1997b, p. 100), writes about the productive possibilities of Foucault's concept of power:

> For Foucault, then, the disciplinary apparatus produces subjects, but as a consequence of that production, it brings into discourse the conditions for subverting that apparatus itself...the law turns against itself and spawns versions of itself which oppose and proliferate its animating purpose.

This chapter will take up the question that Butler (ibid., p. 104) is raising: Can the unfit mother of contemporary adoption, by being represented and given an identity position through open practices, rework the 'injurious interpellations' of that position, making it both a 'site of radical reoccupation and resignification'.[1] The following discussion will focus on the periods 1992–1998 and 2000.

Middle sample 1992–1998

In the early to mid-1990s, adoption in this authority emerged as a coercive and contested discourse bringing into focus the unfit mother. As this decade progressed the lives of birth mothers reported in the files became more troubled, an emerging cast of women with histories far outside the normative social work discourse of mothering – drug addicts, alcoholics, prostitutes, profoundly mentally ill, imprisoned, in violently abusive relationships. As Foucault states (2000d, p. 161), these histories as lived by the women are, of course, not recorded; what we read is the transfigured version of a life told through the disciplinary filter of adoption social work: 'So that it is doubtless impossible to ever grasp them again in themselves, as they might have been "in a free state"; they can no longer be separated out from the declamations, the tactical biases, the obligatory lies that power games and power relations presuppose.'

The adoption files illustrate a sharp rise in children being adopted from care, with voluntarily relinquished babies making up a very small part of the adoption orders. What follows from this is a rise in 'contested adoptions', an increasing phenomenon for this authority in this period. One of the major ways that birth mothers are represented in the files is by contesting the order, thus extending proceedings and their involvements in those proceedings. My discussion will be divided into two sections: how the unfit mother is represented and how direct contact begins to emerge within a coercive adoption discourse of unfit parenting.

Consolidating and representing the unfit mother as a subject of adoption

In this period there were two dominant ways that unfit mothers were represented in file reports: as unfit to parent and subject to their child's removal through adoption and as someone who will continue some kind of contact with their child after adoption. These two categories represent two divergent and competing discourses within adoption work – the coercive removal of a child for adoption and the sustaining of a mother's contact with her child after adoption. In some instances these discourses worked together and whilst children were removed coercively, parents were offered forms of contact. Sometimes one discourse worked to exclude the other, the coercive removal of a child leading to the termination of any ongoing contact. Coercion and support seemed to work alongside social work with unfit mothers creating a strangely contradictory field of operation.

There is little operative agency for an unfit mother in having a child adopted against her wishes. However, the coercive dimensions to this intervention do provide a small arena where the unfit mother can exercise some power. The mother can refuse to concede to the adoption by refusing to sign her consent and in contesting in this way, she forces the local authority to enforce their plan by the imposition of an order to free the child for adoption. In this period the files report needing to cover costs of contested adoptions, indicating that mothers were exercising the small amount of agency produced through this otherwise technology of domination. I will cite two early examples of what I am describing. An adoption report from 1992 states: 'Mr W informed the adoption panel that J's natural mother will seek legal advice for access to J and that the mother will oppose the adoption.' In this example the mother is using her power to withhold consent to pressure the local authority on the matter of her contact with her child.

In a 1995 case there is a long delay with the adoption and the birth mother contests the final hearing on the basis that the authority did not adequately support her at the time of the baby's birth. In this example the mother withholds her consent as a way of attempting to overturn the adoption decision, mobilising the local authority's treatment of her as a resource in her stand against them. As Butler (1997b, p. 100) eloquently explains, power in this instance does not work as an opposition between reactionary and progressive usage, but of 'a progressive usage that requires and repeats the reactionary in order to effect a subversive reterritorialization'.

What is also interesting about the above case is the way that support for an unfit mother has entered the discourse as something that should happen. This reference speaks to a shift in the position of mothers in this period, following the 1989 Children Act, which marked a change in the government of unfit families. Unfit families are now endorsed to shape themselves as partners with rather than victims of the local authority. Disciplinary power works very insidiously here, concealing its more coercive operations under a guise of partnership and equality. However, what this does open up is the possibility for unfit families to work more accessibly the power relations through which they are being worked. As in the example above, families can now use the local authority means of control and surveillance – support, partnership – against them, mobilising those very techniques to mount an opposition to the local authority's plans for adoption. However, what will become a common theme in this analysis is the persistent failure of unfit mothers to reterritorialise themselves as subjects. In spite of documented examples where they draw upon their oppression as a resource against the oppressive social work regime, their position remains unchanged.

A case from 1996 is a good illustration of how unfit mothers' 'unfitness' is defined through foster home visits to her child, working to secure both adoption as a decision and the termination of the mother's visits. S is in and out of care for the first three years of her life due to her mother's solvent abuse. The file records in great detail the efforts that the local authority made to keep S with her mother. Numerous rehabilitation attempts failed, but there is a strong impression that the birth mother cared for S well. She usually returned S to foster care when she knew she was failing as a mother; she also refused contact at these times, in order to sort herself out so she could have S home properly. Unfortunately, her poor history of sustaining visits was a factor when the local authority decides to make the decision for adoption. The Schedule II report states: 'Contact was always actively encouraged, however due to C's solvent abuse arrangements did not always proceed well. She would fail to attend planned contact visits etc.' It is also noted that 'C failed to take the advantage of contact or liaise with the department to arrange such contact'.

Here the local authority mobilise the discourse of partnership and co-operation against the birth mother, underlining how encouraging they have been and how much the birth mother failed to take up the opportunities offered to her. C's solvent abuse is a shorthand communication for all sorts of behaviour and attitude that is incommensurate with visiting a child in foster care. The sense of C as an addict eventually works to overturn the glimpsed sense of her as a responsible mother, who had used the care system to protect her child from her addiction. S was then placed for adoption and a further report concludes:

> As a department we would have objected to direct contact, but not objected to indirect contact. This was because S was now placed and becoming settled also because of the numerous moves, including many moves back to C. It was felt not to be in S's interest to have direct contact.

The securing of C as an unfit mother works to achieve her complete exclusion from her daughter's life through both adoption and the termination of visits. The mother does begin to apply formally for contact through the courts, but is clearly overwhelmed by the local authority judgement on her parenting and withdraws her application. What is interesting in this case is how the visibility accorded to the birth mother through changing practices of support and partnership became further disciplinary techniques, ways of assessing her mothering as unfit and grounds for excluding her from her daughter's life.

In some cases from this period the unfit mother is still progressively excluded, whilst enjoying inclusionary forms of social work support. An adoption from 1997 is striking for the amount of time given to work with birth parents compared to earlier cases. In the file reports the social worker has made very detailed notes about visits and telephone calls to both the adoptive family and the birth parents. There are extensive write-ups of life story work being undertaken by the local authority, detailed records of conversations with the birth parents and a lot of information about the setting up of a letterbox arrangement. There is, overall, a manifest sense that birth parents need to be included in their children's lives. The file documents a number of different narratives that are kept separate, but can clearly be read as interlinked: birth parents meeting up with the adopters of their children; setting up of a reciprocal letterbox arrangement; including the birth mother in life story work with her older child, A.

These narratives apparently include the birth parents in a central way, yet it is an inclusion predicated on them remaining marginal figures. During the meeting between the adopters and the birth parents, the social worker records that the adopters told the birth parents that they will keep their memory alive for the girls, a sentiment usually associated with the death of someone. The first letter the birth parents receive from the adopters includes the phrase 'thank-you for completing our family', a very clear communication about how excluded the birth parents now are. But what is perhaps most striking is how the older girl's relationship with the birth mother has been progressively reinterpreted, so that it is written out of the story. This can be clearly seen in the account in the file about life story work. The GAL is concerned that A will only settle fully into her adoptive family 'if she is given permission' to do so by her birth mother. The birth mother is asked if she will write a letter to her daughter to this effect. The file notes 'we advised how A had been told that her mother hadn't enough care to look after her; we discussed this. Talked about life story book and photos she has. Discussed a draft letter for J to write and discussed what J may wish to say.' This letter is written and given to A by the social worker during a life story session. It is noted: 'A reads it out loud and there is a discussion about her move from home not being her fault and her birthmother wanting her to settle in her new adoptive home.' The GAL notes some weeks later that A is in a state of some distress. Her interpretation is that A is distraught about her damaging history with her mother and she recommends therapy for the girl. It does not appear to occur to any of the involved professionals that A may be distressed because she will not be seeing her mother again; she may have interpreted her mother's letter as a final statement of her mother going from her life. This seems to be corroborated by a file note that states: 'A is very attached to both her parents particularly her mother. She gets very distressed when contact is missed or ends.' However, A's relationship with her mother has been progressively foreclosed and then ended by social worker intervention.[2]

A practice without purpose: the contested emergence of direct contact

This sample of files contains very little in terms of a local authority policy or defined purpose for this form of contact. In Chapter 8 I argued that there were two distinct technologies of the self simultaneously deployed in the practice of letterbox contact, one rooted in past knowledge and one in contemporary relationships. These two technologies gave rise to very different purposes for this form of open practice. However, with respect to direct contact, it was hard to find any actively deployed technologies of the self to promote this form of contact. Unlike letterbox contact, the reports do not usually contain reasons why direct contact might be a beneficial post-adoption practice. I located only a few examples.

It is important that T maintains some links with his birth parent K and I envisage K attending face to face contact once a year. This is dependent on how successful K's farewell contact is and on her willingness to meet prospective adopters. The contact should be formally prescribed as a part of adoption plans and does not need to be supervised unless requested by the adoptive parents. (Adoption, 1998)

In the above the maintaining of links is the cited purpose for the plan for direct contact. Maintaining a link suggests sustaining a relationship in contemporary time, a practice that immediately contests the dominant technology that this authority has embraced. However, this annual inclusion of the mother is dependent on her relinquishing her maternal role. This report is careful to locate the possibility of her seeing her child post adoption, with a properly performed 'final' visit pre adoption, where she will revoke her former status as mother. Paradoxically, then, her inclusion in her son's life will be emptied of maternal significance, whilst it is only because of that significance that the visit has any purpose.

An adoption from 1993 is another rare example where direct contact is planned. A report notes that the direct contact is to 'ensure that the boys keep in touch with their family of origin without unsettling their long-term placement', but there is nothing to explain why such keeping in touch might be beneficial. The report is concerned about this issue of unsettling the adoptive family and places emphasis on the planning and containing of any contact visits. Whilst this is an unusual instance of implementing direct contact, there is a marked sense that the involvement of an unfit mother needs managing and limiting. Clearly, visits from a parent challenge the dominant technology of adoption as a full-replacement family, a new set of attachments. These two examples show the local authority remaking the visiting birth mother into a figure who will not threaten the 'new' attachment foundation of adoption. However, this form of contact does initiate a different kind of involvement for the family of origin. Far from being a source of historic knowledge, a visit invites an immediate engagement, a space where relationships evolve in the everyday and become detached from the biographical history of unfitness documented in such places as life story books.

An adoption from 1998 is a striking example of the local authority providing support to a birth mother to enable her to see her three children. The birth mother has a long history of schizophrenia and has had all four of her children removed. The local authority placed three of the children together and planned an annual visit for the birth mother. The file gives details of how the local authority supported the birth mother in terms of preparing her for the visit. They fund a new outfit for her, provide her with a worker to help her bathe and dress before the visit and give her money for gifts for the children. They undertook to have this level of support in place every year. What interests me with cases such as this is the question of responsibility. There is a sense that in cases where the unfit mother can't be responsible for her unfit mothering through a learning difficulty or a mental health problem, then social workers provide support. Unfit mothers, who are unfit through 'life style choices' such as solvent abuse or prostitution, are undeserving of support and undeserving of the benefits – such as contact with their children – that follow from support.

However, for the majority of these cases there was no direct contact implemented after adoption. As the preceding section made clear, in this period the mother's unfitness was mobilised as a resource to assess a decision about direct contact, mostly with the consequence that it would be terminated. In this sample the local authority commonly facilitate and encourage direct contact during care proceedings in order to assess birth parent capability and then terminate contact once adoption has been decided. The assessment about capacity to parent then informs a very different assessment, capacity to keep in touch with an adopted child. If a birth mother has failed to adequately perform as a parent, then this failure will powerfully inform whether she continues to see the child post adoption order. It is here in the refusal of direct contact that one can see more clearly a distinct technology of the self being consistently mobilised.

There are many examples of inadequate mothering being used as the basis to exclude mothers from contact post adoption. Foster care visits are commonly used as informal examinations to assess the issue of direct contact in terms of mothering capabilities. This is from a report of the final visit a birth mother had with her son in December 1994, where much is made of the child's reluctance to go to her during the visit:

> At the last contact between J and his mother, it was observed that whilst J recognised his mother he did not have a significant attachment to her and in fact has a close bond with his prospective adoptive mother. I believe that face to face contact with his mother is not in his best interests, but that in order that J may make sense of his adoption and be able to find out more about his mother as he grows older it would be helpful for letters, photographs and cards to be exchanged via social services twice per year.

It would appear from the above that direct contact is being assessed on the basis of the level of attachment the child has to his birth mother. It is implied that if the attachment had been more 'significant', then direct contact would continue. But then what would have happened to the bond with the adoptive mother? There is a sense here that bonds are formed unilaterally, either with the adopter or with the birth mother. This view is confirmed by the GAL's comment that face-to-face contact 'will be unsettling ... in the immediate future', destabilising the achievement of a singular attachment with the adoptive parent. So the unfit mother is here caught in a paralysing contradiction. She must exhibit a good attachment in order to see her child after adoption, but in so doing, will so threaten the child's new attachment that visits will not be permitted anyway.

In a further example the unfit mother, T, had her child placed for adoption and her visits to him terminated as simultaneous interventions. The professionals' view in the file is that the boy will not benefit from seeing his birth mother and in a summary report the social worker states: 'I have met the mother on two occasions and found her to be a very self-centred woman who appears to show little concern for Y and much more concern for herself.' Here a normalising discourse of the mother is used to define T as unfit and therefore disqualified for visits with her son. In this example direct contact would sustain a bad attachment with a narcissistic mother, a view that is reached by a worker who has not even witnessed this mother's relationship with her child.

These two cases show how direct contact has been resisted because it promotes a technology of the self rooted in contemporary relationships and contemporary engagements. Clearly, these unfit mothers have to be confined to past knowledge and not current involvement. An adoption from 1996 gives a fuller elaboration of how the local authority understand the relationship between direct contact and adoptive family life. The following extract is from a social worker report explaining the reasons for refusing a birth mother's request for face-to-face contact:

> This request was declined by the LA because it would not be realistic as a) Ms B has not seen W since 1994 and b) would upset and confuse W as he is still a young child and does not fully understand the concept of adoption even though it has been explained to him. Therefore it would not be fair on W as he is very settled in his new family.

In this case the social worker is drawing upon adoption as replacement attachment to refuse the request for direct contact. Whilst kinship origins are considered important – the practice of explaining is cited – there is a familiar argument about those kinship ties remaining 'historic'. A number of reasons are given for not allowing visits with the mother. First, W will be 'unsettled' by her presence in his contemporary life, whilst by implication he is not unsettled when she is a part of his 'past' life. Second, W will be confused and upset by her presence because he has not grasped the concept of adoption and its dual parenting legacy. Such reasoning is informed by a technology rooted in a hermeneutical relation to the self, where forgotten knowledge of childhood origins can be accessed through tools of recollection such as life story books and explaining. Clearly, W's social worker does not regard direct contact as a practice that will facilitate such recollection and it is precisely because of this that she refuses the request. As we saw in an earlier example, visits from an unfit mother are routinely refused on the grounds that such contact would recapitulate traumatic knowledge of a bad childhood. In the example of T above, the social worker thinks that her narcissistic parenting would be repeated if she was to see her child, thus sustaining the child in a historic relationship that was the cause of its removal in the first place. The relationship between unfit mother and child is, then, frozen in the time of unfit mothering, reduced to a re-enactment and not capable of resignification.

Curiously, this technology is challenged by the ways that social workers understand adoptive family life. Clearly, adopted children are capable of transformations within their new adoptive families, becoming different subjects with different parents once freed from their earlier childhood moorings. Foucault (2005, p. 235) is instructive here on the different technology that is suggested by this set-up:

> It is by making us appear to ourselves as the recurrent and constant term of all these relations that our gaze should be directed on the things of the world...it is in this field of the relation between all these things and oneself that knowledge can and must be deployed.

In drawing upon this technology from late antiquity, Foucault points to a contrast with who we are today. This 'relational' knowledge is of a different order to the internalised knowledge through which contemporary subjects are formed. Within this technology the self is transformed through living in the everyday present, acquiring not discovering truths. One might argue that with no originating biography, adoptive families form themselves through such everyday relating. However, this potentiality to remake the adopted child is not used to understand the involvements of unfit mothers, who are consigned to simply repeat their former histories with their children.

It is my contention that direct contact promotes a different kind of knowledge for adopted children, a knowledge that unsettles and puts into question the dominant technology of adoption. Visits in contemporary time work to reconfigure the adopted child's sense of self by remapping that self in relationship to parental figures in an everyday encounter. Far from simply recapitulating traumatic knowledge, visits open up a space for a re-transcribing of past involvements in present time, involvements that destabilise the way that adoption is currently understood.

I want to conclude my discussion of this sample of files by comparing how differently the local authority is positioned when it is a question of sibling direct contact. In this period there were many examples of adopted children being kept in touch with their separated siblings through visits. The files contain a much clearer sense of purpose for direct contact for this group. For example, an adoption from 1999 talks about sibling contact sustaining 'a sense of belonging'. A case from 1998 wants visits to 'preserve the relationship between E and her brother'. Some of these adoptions emphasise the link that adopters make with birth relatives and even mention a 'developing friendship' with an older visiting sibling.

The purposes for direct contact identified above – preserving relationships and keeping a sense of belonging with former kinship circles – seem to operate unproblematically when it is a question of siblings rather than parents. Clearly, the preservation of sibling relationships does not work to destabilise how the local authority understand the adoptive family unit.

Final sample 2000

This last sample of adoptions from 2000 is striking for the number of birth mothers who disappear from their children's lives. The files document how unfit mothers in this period systematically vanish either through the termination of their direct contact or through their own physical withdrawal once the local authority has removed their children. In this sample the unfit mother is barely present and decision-making about her involvements rarely figures; in most cases her narrative presence has gone from the adoption accounts by the time of the adoption order.

Ephemeral presences

> Lives of a few lines or a few pages, nameless misfortunes and adventures gathered into a handful of words... they are examples that convey not so much lessons to ponder as brief effects whose force fades almost at once. (Foucault, 2000d, p. 157)

Compared to my previous samples, birth mothers in the year 2000 had considerably less visibility and presence in file accounts and reports. There was less evidence of their wishes and views being represented and less sense of professional engagement in their lives. This can be partially explained by the far higher incidence in this sample of birth mothers disappearing; in a large number of the adoptions they absented themselves from their children's lives soon after their birth and removal. It is interesting to consider what this might signify about the social work culture of the late 1990s. Is it simply that more contemporary adoptions include a far higher number of birth parents with chaotic, unaligned lives? Or is it that the provision of a service to support their involvement has become a far lower priority?[3] As Foucault captures so well above, birth mothers' appearances in these adoption files are brief, forceful and transitory.

The majority of the birth mothers in these adoptions had troubled histories of prostitution, drug addiction and imprisonment. Many of the women had numerous children, with long histories of local authority involvement. Their identities as mothers are always subsidiary to their identities as addicts with criminal life styles. Most of the women feature only through their fleeting encounter with the authorities at the time of the birth of a child. The files record babies being left in hospital by mothers who disappear, leaving behind a promise with a social worker to be in touch, an intention that is never fulfilled. One file records a typical case of a mother who was a crack cocaine addict and prostitute, who 'abandoned her baby in hospital'. The report goes on to note 'despite efforts by the social worker to arrange contact the mother had no further visits'. She then 'disappeared, not enquiring after child's welfare'. A further case more shockingly describes the death of a birth mother:

> Received a call from JM who told her S [the birth mother] walked into the hospital on Monday and gave birth to a baby girl. S had received no antenatal treatment; the baby was born with severe drug addiction and there is uncertainty about her chances of survival. On Wednesday S was found in the hospital toilets, she had taken drugs and unfortunately died following a drugs overdose.

The most striking aspect of this case is the sense that the death of the birth mother is treated as an expediency. A report notes: 'Adoption hearing likely to be heard in the same court and as no-one now to contest it is likely to be a fairly quick hearing.' The mother's death makes the adoption a tidier and speedier process.

These brief vignettes barely register these women as mothers, describing behaviours and life styles far outside the usual cultural measure of mothering. It is only because of their encounter with power – in this instance social services – that these women fleetingly emerge as mothers, although in the cases above it is their refusal of the maternal role that compels attention and judgement. Furthermore, in the contemporary era discourses of partnership and co-operation structure the way that social workers conduct their relations with mothers, enforcing the recording of maternal failure in all its desolate detail. The need to include and record the unfit mother's communications has been an ongoing practice since the early 1990s in my study local authority. Whilst there was a marked decrease in birth mothers' involvements in these adoptions, there were a few cases where those involvements were well documented. This is illustrated by a case which contains correspondence from a mother citing numerous complaints, including the pending adoption of her daughter, the lack of contact, the way the local authority removed C at birth and the adopters changing C's name. What is interesting about these inclusions is the openness with which the local authority record these complaints. Partly this can be understood as techniques of accountability. Unfit mothers can now contest adoptions, exercising resistance to social work plans on the basis of contact not having been adequately explored or implemented. One might see these inclusions as simply a social work strategy to account for itself, whilst still operating exclusionary and marginalising practices. However, there is a sense that the unfit mother has become a subject to whom the local authority are accountable, a person with whom explanations and plans need to be communicated. Accountability usually operates to limit power, to check its excess. In terms of this instance it is hard to imagine that the unfit mother is a figure that would achieve any curtailment in the way the local authority exercise power, but her representation in this light suggests a system that has opened up a space previously not available, a space of potential and future resignification.

A practice without presence: direct contact with unfit mothers

As Chapter 8 discussed, my study local authority inaugurated a post-adoption service in 1999, but the documentation contained little written guidance or policy on direct contact. One reference is made in a document detailing the role of the post-adoption worker: 'if face to face contact is to occur then it can be organised at a neutral venue and supervised by the Post Adoption worker.' There is nothing written to elaborate why neutral venues are desirable or why supervision is required. The only other reference is contained within the letterbox guidance sheet, where the purpose of the system is being explained: 'The letterbox system exists to pass on information from birth families to children who have been adopted, *where no direct contact with birth families can take place*' (my emphasis).

As Chapter 8 noted, the letterbox system is presented as a substitute for direct contact; it is almost as if the two discreet arrangements serve the same purpose and where one is not possible, the other is substituted. There is also a sense that face-to-face contact is actively considered, but sometimes not possible, when it is clear from reading the files that the local authority rarely put in place such contact for adopted children. Interestingly, there is no information sheet for direct contact in the post-adoption documentation. This glaring omission seems to suggest that as direct contact is so rarely implemented, it needs no specific practice guidelines, an implication borne out by the paucity of arrangements in this final sample.

As previously stated, in the majority of the adoptions direct contact was routinely terminated. In the many cases where mothers 'disappeared', there was little evidence of the local authority wanting to keep open the possibility of direct contact in the future. The following case involves a birth mother who 'disappeared' after the birth of her son, R. The case file contains hardly any information, but there are some details about the termination of visits. 'Despite extensive encouragement by the LA including setting up contact at an independent resource, mother failed to turn up.' The care plan states: 'In view of S's lack of contact it has not been possible to gain her views and wishes.' However, rather than keeping open the possibility of contact, the local authority applies for an order, section 34 (4), to ensure that they can refuse contact in the future.

There are some cases where mothers do remain involved, but direct contact is still refused. In this sample of adoptions there is a clearer sense of direct contact being assessed on the basis of mothering practices. The following case is a good illustration, where throughout the file reports there is a consistent elision of parenting a child and visiting a child. This case involves a young woman who is reported as unable to safely parent her daughter T: 'L was unable to demonstrate an understanding of T's needs and that T would suffer significant harm if she were to be returned to her mother's care.' The local authority therefore plan to have T adopted. However, the birth mother's reported inability to meet her daughter's needs does not just disqualify her from parenting, but also from occasional visiting. The same reasons for T's removal are mobilised to terminate visits: 'At the time of writing L has not attended any planned contact sessions … There has been ongoing concerns about the quality of L's contact with T. L has not demonstrated a good understanding of T's needs or that she is able to adequately meet them.' The above report gives a detailed analysis of L's contact visits, with a whole range of inappropriate behaviours cited as reasons to terminate the visits:

> T appears to respond positively to L when she arrives for contact, but does not seem to show any signs of distress at the end. It also suggested that T sees the contact sessions as playtime. However, L has not been able to demonstrate an understanding of T's physical and emotional needs and thereby meet them.

The foster carer is not positive about the contact visit's either: 'D does not think that T gets anything from the contact visits, they wander round the house and L talks to T in very immature language.' The GAL is also critical: 'L would not always feed T or change her nappies.'

Clearly, the visits are being assessed on the basis of mothering practices, where those in attendance are looking for 'evidence' that L, an already failed mother, will successfully perform maternal tasks such as nappy changing, feeding and age-appropriate interaction. Presumably, if L functioned in these ways, then her daughter would not be a subject for adoption. What L can offer – playing with T in a way she appears to enjoy – is assessed as inappropriate and a further indication of her unfit mothering. Playing as an engagement with T in present time, an activity not linked to the prior history of unfitness, has no discursive place for my study local authority.

The one exceptional case where birth parents have direct contact is unusual in a number of respects. First, it involves a voluntarily relinquished baby; second, the contact plan involves face-to-face visits for a newborn baby and, finally, the birth parents and the adopters worked together to draw up the agreement for contact.

The white middle-class couple that relinquished the baby were clearly unusual birth parents in the contemporary era. The very thick file documents in much detail the period of the pregnancy and the couple's decision to have their baby placed directly for adoption from hospital.[4] The case is striking for the very positive proactive stance the local authority takes on contact. In no other file have I read such a robust support and articulated purpose for the practice of visits: '[The adopters] are keen to have contact. They recognize that M has a need to be in contact with his birth parents and have access to birth information from source. They believe M will grow with an integrated sense of himself if he has meaningful face to face contact.' Direct contact as facilitating an integrated sense of self is emphasised repeatedly as the prime purpose for implementing this practice:

> M will benefit from contact and M and H will benefit in their long-term emotional health through seeing M grow and having access to him on a regular basis. Mr. and Mrs. D will benefit as they have the unselfish wish for M to grow with all he needs to develop an integrated sense of himself.

The negotiation of contact arrangements between both sets of parents is highlighted as important, with annual reviews of the arrangements also planned.

These fit relinquishing parents stand in dramatic contrast to the unfit mothers whose involvements have largely figured in this chapter. Of course, it is precisely the absence of child protection concerns that made possible the direct contact arrangements, arrangements that have been usually absent in the majority of the adoption files. In the above case, integrating the adopted child's adoptive and birth identities was unproblematic, as that process of integration did not need to encompass a history of unfit mothering. Unfit mothers have been habitually excluded because of their unfit histories and where that unfitness is not operative, more inclusionary practices appear to be possible.

Conclusion

> Lives that are as though they hadn't been, that survive only from the clash with a power that wished only to annihilate them or at least to obliterate them. (Foucault, 2000d, p. 163)

Following Foucault, it could be argued that the file accounts that remain of these 'unfit mothers' describe a particular relation to power, one that works to obliterate even as it brings into momentary view the mother in all her unfitness. In tracing how the unfit mother has been represented in a decade of adoption work, it is clear that she has not reworked the injurious address, but has remained condemned and marginalised by it. Discourses of partnership and co-operation have engaged the unfit mother's involvement, but in many instances have simply worked to further exclude her. This chapter has traced how the practice of direct contact provided a platform through which the unfit mother appeared. Throughout the decade, she is seen, assessed and examined at foster home visits, only to vanish again as her visits were routinely terminated following adoption. For my study local authority, the unfit mother is condemned to relive her unfitness; her involvements with her child are reduced to a re-enactment of her unfit mothering, a history deemed incapable of resignification. Although in open adoption practices the unfit mother is given a language and an identity position, it has not proved possible for her to rework the negative terms of the interpellation. This chapter has shown how the possibilities for such a reworking have remained very limited within the prevailing adoption culture of my study local authority, with the consequence that the unfit mother has continued to be sustained in a subjected position by the injurious address of her unfitness.

10
Conclusions

> Any child would be surprised if they knew their parents were going to give you to someone else. Any child would be surprised. (Thomas et al., 1999, p. 33)

Adopted children have been strangely absent from this study, although their presence has been evoked as central to the debates and arguments surrounding open practices. It seems therefore timely to preface this conclusion with the words of a nine-year-old adopted girl, from the recent study *Adopted Children Speaking* (1999). She captures in quite a simple way the problematic place that original kinship occupies in adoption work and how her own position has been forged through and within it. Being adopted is 'surprising' in a culture where original kinship occupies a foundational place in securing the truth of one's sense of self.

This study has been an attempt to trace how the cultural importance of original kinship in founding contemporary subjectivities has made adoption an enduringly problematic form of substitute care. Adopted subjects are irreducibly marked by their original kinship histories, but are also subjects capable of remaking themselves within new adoptive families. Simultaneously freed of and yet tied to a previous historical legacy, adopted subjects are endorsed to form new attachments within a culture that teaches the fundamental importance of original attachment figures. There is, then, a dual and contradictory message at the centre of adoption practices: provide the child with a new foundation, but simultaneously sustain the old foundation of the family of origin. This inaugurating paradox has led to a history where birth family involvements have been invited and contested. It is this contested field that my study has explored, drawing extensively on the genealogical approach of Foucault.

This project arose from a desire to understand the contested status of open adoption, the field in which I worked for most of the 1990s. My professional involvement shaped the research question that has generated this study: What compelled the adoption profession to introduce practices that they then contested? The available commentaries and histories within the adoption field could not address the nature of this enquiry. Most histories characterise adoption within a reductive opposition – adoption developed out of closed practices to become open or adoption was originally open and then became closed. These traditional adoption narratives cannot account for the simultaneous emergence and deployment of both inclusionary and exclusionary forms of practice around the place of the birth family in adoption work. I needed a different way to think about both adoption history and adoption practices and this led me to the work of Foucault. His genealogical approach gave me both a theory and a methodology that have framed the way I have both conducted and written this study. I think Foucault's genealogical method opens up new possibilities for the adoption field and I want to briefly summarise the main contributions such an approach offers.

First, a genealogical approach allowed me to foreground the constitutive and transformative role of practices. Most accounts of the adoption field give adoption an originary and explanatory position from which practices are then understood to emerge. The problem with this kind of approach is how it defines the field of operation in advance of any exploration of that field and leaves unaddressed the way that practices enter, shape and form that field. Second, most commentaries impose a singular, dominant historical reading, whilst my genealogical approach could map the play of different histories in different contexts. By focusing on the present emergence of a practice, I was able to trace the specific and various ways it operated in the field, allowing for the complex play of events, the unexpected or chance occurrence. Third, my genealogical analysis allowed the exploration of discontinuities and exceptions, as well as hidden continuities in adoption history and did not collapse these together into a developmental reading. Fourth, most adoption commentaries do not have an analysis of how power relations work in the field of adoption. Foucault's (1977, 1978) account of power, and Butler's (1997) elaboration of that account, allowed me to identify and map both the disciplinary and productive dimensions of power relations and how they worked together to create an adoption field constituted through self-governance and governance from the outside. Fifth, and following on from above, my analysis has an important emphasis on how subjects are not only formed but form themselves through available regimes of truth/knowledge. Such a focus has enabled me to identify the problematic place that original kinship occupies in how adoptive identities are formed, making the involvements of birth family both irreducibly important and irreducibly unsettling. Finally, I have used Butler's work to explore the productive effects of exclusionary practices, a focus with considerable relevance to an adoption field where such practices have commonly circulated. This approach was useful in a number of key ways: it helped me show how subjugated identities can be reworked and re-territorialised and it allowed me to explore how the public disenfranchising of certain forms of love and loss operated to simultaneously endorse and exclude certain kinds of attachments. The genealogical analysis I have conducted makes an original methodological contribution to the adoption field and establishes a new way of theorising adoption history and practices.

This genealogy of adoption took as its starting point a problem in the present, the contested status of contemporary open adoption, then read the history for how this contestation emerged at critical points in that history. Part I of this study documented this process. Following Scott (1996) I elaborated a strategy for the reading of this history through identifying the paradox of original kinship that has operated to both secure and destabilise adoption's substitute status. Part I traced how adoption practices have consistently produced the adopted child's biological origin as a prior truth and knowledge for the adopted child, whilst simultaneously installing a new set of truths in a new adoptive family, thus establishing adoption as a paradoxical form of substitute care. Whilst excluded narratives were brought into the heart of adoptive family life through open practices, there remained in operation a cultural prohibition on the forms of parenting and forms of love these narratives represented; illegitimacy and infertility in the 1950s and 1960s; unfit mothering in the contemporary era. This has created a paralysing field of deployment where secrecy and disclosure work together within a field where original kinship has to be simultaneously accepted and refuted. I showed that this constitutive paradox has produced an enduring terrain of controversy and contestation throughout the history of adoption's implemented practice.

Part I concluded with an analysis of the emergence of open adoption at the end of the 1980s that marked both a continuity and a break with preceding adoption traditions. With the advent of open adoption two distinct forms of practice were instituted, letterbox or indirect contact and visits or direct contact, both involving the birth family in an ongoing relationship with the adopted child. What distinguishes these two forms from previous open practices is their relationship to history; these practices were creating history, not simply archiving it, thus installing the possibility of a different technology of the adopted subject. In this part of my study I turned to Foucault's late work on technologies of the self, wanting an approach that could help me identify the challenges that open adoption practices posed for the dominant technology of adoption. I drew upon the distinction Foucault makes in *Hermeneutics of the Subject* (2005) between a technology where truth is rediscovered and a technology where truth is transformative, arguing that both these technologies of the self are problematically at play in how the adopted subject was formed in the era of open adoption. Part I of this study had explored how historically open practices had emerged within a regime of truth that emphasised the discovery of an explanatory and originating kinship history and certainly letterbox and direct contact emerged within those concerns. However, these open practices also instituted a different kind of involvement for the birth parent that installed a very different regime of truth. Far from being rooted in some originating history, letterbox and direct contact operate in contemporary time, potentially transforming the relationships they engage. I wanted to explore how far in actual adoption work these practices were implying or promoting a different technology of the self to that of earlier periods of adoption. Part II of this study was an interrogation of this question through an analysis of one local authority adoption files between 1989 and 2000.

In turning to my archive study, Foucault's work was an invaluable guide in helping me trace how both letterbox and direct contact are practices that operate within two different regimes of truth – one governed by self-knowledge and one by self-transformation.

In the implementation of letterbox contact my study local authority were clearly at times 'refusing' the traditional technology of adoption at least in how they theorised the purpose of this form of contact. My analysis revealed an operative technology rooted in the transformative potential of relationships in contemporary time, a technology that puts into question the paralysing grip that original kinship has upon the field. In contrast, direct contact as a practice was usually resisted precisely because of the involvements in contemporary time that it invited. The figure of the unfit mother was central to how my study local authority both understood and implemented these open practices. Letter involvement in contemporary time did not engage the participation of an unfit mother in the same way as visiting contact. By the year 2000 the presence of unfit mothering, in either letters or visits, was increasingly refused by my study local authority, as their practice worked to confine such mothers to a history of unfitness, incapable of resignification. File reports could only understand an unfit mother's involvement with her adopted child as a repetition of her unfit mothering; she had no other role to perform.

One of the central questions that this analysis poses for childcare work is whether there is a potentially different technology of self that marks a contemporary adopted child and effects a different kind of self-production to that of children in biological families. From my own archive study I would suggest that such practices do mount a challenge to the dominant technology of adoption. The documented resistances to birth family involvements that I encountered in the files certainly strengthened my view that open adoption practices invite a radical re-thinking of the place of original kinship, a remaking of familial ties.

Implications for practice

> What continues to be a major problem is the lack of a theoretical bridge allowing links to be made between the empirical evidence currently available on contact and the need to make specific decisions in particular cases. (Neil and Howe, 2004, p. 3)

I have prefaced this section with a quotation from a recent book that argues for new approaches in the implementation of contact for adopted children. In the above extract, the authors discuss a continuing professional reluctance in adoption work to translate empirical research evidence about contact into individual plans for children. The authors address this problematic by drawing together a number of research studies that explore the benefits of contact and their concluding chapter is an attempt to weave together these research insights into a 'developmental calculus', a 'transactional model' for thinking about contact (ibid., p. 224 onwards). There are two points that I want to make. First, the authors do not analyse why we have an adoption profession reluctant and resistant to the research evidence and, second, their response to such resistance is to further promote the research and to generate another working model for contact.

Whilst this is a very worthwhile publication in both circulating research and promoting new ways of thinking, it fails to address what this study has attempted to interrogate: the contested status of open adoption. This study has shown how the professional opposition to open practices is an enduring effect of how original kinship operates in the field of adoption. Adoption has always worked to simultaneously install a new family origin, whilst sustaining the centrality of previous kinship history. Adoption, then, is constituted through a paralysing paradox, where it has to contest the involvements that it invites. Better research or better working models will not assuage a resistance which is an integral part of how adoption is constituted. Furthermore, the generation of further research to resolve the contested status of contact works to achieve the opposite effect. Far from reassuring practitioners, more research simply fuels the contestation, as its production is inextricably tied to the contestation itself. It is, then, not a question of liberating practice into a more open and enlightened place, but of understanding the ways that adoption's peculiarly paradoxical nature has produced a contested and controversial status for openness. This study is an attempt to help the field of adoption better understand the contested status of its contemporary open practices. Unless practitioners can grasp how the field is constituted, they will continue to contest the very practices that they implement.

The issue is not to resolve the paradox that original kinship founds, but to understand how it has produced conflict and contestation at the heart of adoption as a form of family life. Scott (1996, p. 175) makes this point very clearly: 'Subjecting our own paradoxes to critical scrutiny is a way of appreciating the enormity of the problems ... faced ... and the need for ways of thinking that do not insist on the resolution of opposites.' It is through an understanding of how this conflict has been produced that the possibility of less conflict-driven practices emerge. By appreciating the fundamental place that original kinship occupies culturally, we can become less bound by the terms that it sets and more conscious of how it operates reductively within the field of contemporary adoption. Adoption is a radical questioning of kinship ties, as well as a conformism with that familial form of belonging. My archive study illustrated how open adoption as a set of practices potentially reworks the paralysing place that original kinship occupies by extending the traditional parameters of family belonging. The involvements of birth family in contemporary time challenge and remake the usual ties of family, producing a new technology of the adopted subject, an identity position less bound by original kinship and the hermeneutical knowledges that it inscribes. This finding has an immediate bearing on how professionals might reconceptualise the welfare of adopted children within such a new technology.

I have intended this study to reinvigorate and renew thinking on an issue in the field of adoption that has proved peculiarly intransigent to change. My final words are Foucault's: 'As for what motivated me, it is quite simple...it was curiosity...not the curiosity that seeks to assimilate what it is proper to know, but that which enables one to get free of oneself' (Foucault, 1986, p. 8).

Notes

1 Introducing the Study

1. As a rare counter to this dominant modernist aesthetic, the University of East London set up the Centre for Adoption and Identity Studies (CAIS) in the mid-1990s 'to develop a new agenda of research, debate and policy making around issues of identity, childhood and family life, especially as these affect the fields of fostering, adoption and community care' (Cohen 1995, p. 7). In a paper elaborating this new initiative, Cohen (ibid., p. 3) reflects upon the dominance of essentialist discourses around identity in adoption work and a consequent resistance in the field to post-structuralist challenges to those discourses. In considering the contribution that CAIS may make towards reworking the grip of identity politics on the field, Cohen (ibid., p. 4) writes:

   > In the field of adoption it is likely to encounter fierce resistance, since for various reasons and often from opposed standpoints there is a strong emotional and ideological investment in the reparative power of self-identity and 'positive role models' in overcoming the early trauma of abandonment. The assumption is that a sense of security, stability and roots can only be achieved if it is anchored within some kind of centred narrative in which there are no loose ends.

   Sadly, CAIS had only a brief presence in the field, and its research programmes were never carried through. One of its co-directors, Amal Treacher, did go on to co-edit a collection of papers on adoption (Treacher and Katz, 2000), but the collection was not framed within the same critique that CAIS had promised, although narrative perspectives are included (ibid., pp. 13–14).

4 Differences Denied: The Normalisation of Adoption

1. Heywood (1965, p. 65) points out that the levels of poverty and material deprivation in working-class housing made preventive work with families impossible until twentieth-century improvements in quality of living arrangements.

2. This reconfiguration of the pre-war culture of rescue and severance was not, however, reflected in the reported practices from the period (see particularly Trasler, 1960; Parker, 1966; George, 1970). Over two decades, research revealed how fostering continued to be a long-term form of care for children, eschewing any contact with the natural parents, thus sustaining continuity with the preceding era's traditions of childcare. In spite of new discursive conditions for the emergence of new practices, working-class children in care remained estranged from their families of origin. Whilst clearly the post-war period marked a transformation in how family life and substitute family life was understood, these new understandings did not substantially change the

ways that working-class children in care were kept in touch with their natural families.

3. Goodacre (1966) notes that in the period 1959–1960 a third of all adoptions were to legitimate illegitimate children. Mothers were often in the bizarre situation where they adopted their own child! These were an unusual category of women because against the social attitudes of the day they had kept their children by them, suffering the prejudice of being an unmarried mother of an illegitimate child (ibid., p. 139). Adoption always followed the marriage and was seen as a need to regularise family life for the child, particularly if there were other step children or a baby born of the newly married couple (ibid., p. 143).

4. The Hurst Report (1954) reflected this tension between regulated and autonomous practice. For example, the committee is very happy to let adoption societies 'make rules for their own guidance' regarding matters to do with the placement of children and decisively advocates for a more under-regulated approach (1954, p. 33), whilst also recommending a number of legislative changes that further regulated adoption practices.

5. The 1949 Adoption Act allowed the child to remain in the adoptive family if the biological parent withdrew her consent to the adoption, unless a court ruled otherwise. Previously the child would have been returned to her care or removed to an institution.

6. The 1949 Adoption Act introduced the 'unreasonable withholding of consent' clause. The 1958 Act added a clause about failure to discharge parental obligations. It is this broadening of the grounds for dispensation of consent that has made some commentators (Heywood, 1965, p. 185) see the post-war adoption legislation as circumscribing 'more than ever before the rights of natural parents in a way which is intended to facilitate the process of adoption'. The broadening of local authority involvement, alongside the extension of the grounds for dispensing with parental consent, laid the foundations for the adoptions of older children from care that characterised the permanency movement of the 1970s and early 1980s (see Chapter 5).

7. Triseliotis et al. (2005, p. 4) note that under Scottish adoption law access to birth records was an effect of adopted children having inheritance rights with their birth family. In order to inherit, knowledge about their birth family was fundamental. Even after inheritance rights were abolished in 1964, the open access to records remained. There was never this link in English adoption law, raising questions about how successfully an adopted adult would have accessed any inherited monies in the pre-war era where that was still allowed.

8. The committee made two suggestions to this effect: that there is an entry on the form of application for an adoption order which expressly requests the adopters to confirm that they will bring the child up in the knowledge he or she is adopted and that 'a duty be laid on the court to satisfy itself before making an order that the adopters have told or intend to tell the child of his adoption' (Hurst Report, 1954, p. 152).

5   Differences and Identities: The Making of Contemporary Adoption

1. Packman (1975) comments that local authorities had been able to operate as adoption providers since 1949, initially of children in their own care and by

1958 of any child. However, local authority placements still only accounted for 3,000 of all adoptions by the mid-1960s (ibid., pp. 91–3).
2. The influence of 'pioneering' American adoption work was considerable in this period, with British social workers visiting the United States and American project leaders, such as Kay Donley, invited to Britain to disseminate the new role of adoption (see Triseliotis, 1980b, for a number of accounts).
3. Adoption from care made up 7 per cent of the total in 1975, but 40 per cent by 1990 (Parker, 1999, p. 3). Thoburn (1990, p. 35) cites the following statistics for such adoptions: 1978, 1,300 from care; 1983, 1,897.
4. Lambert (1994, p. 78) cites the 1971 survey of adoption by Grey and Blunden, where they report that 98 per cent of UK adoptions were consensual.
5. Ryburn cites the survey by Murch et al. (1993) where 26 per cent of agency placements were contested and 75 per cent of freeing applications were contested. Additionally, Ryburn (1998, p. 56) cites a personal communication from Lord Chancellor's department, stating that in 1995 30 per cent adoptions and 57 per cent of freeing orders were contested.
6. See in particular Rowe and Lambert (1973, p. 72), whose study showed that adoption placements were more commonly made when parents were in agreement and Vernon and Fruin (1986, p. 92) who found in their study sample that social workers did not choose adoption if parents were in opposition to the plan. This latter research showed social workers resisting an adversarial adoption practice (ibid., p. 147). The local authority who participated in Part II of this study were still largely operating adoption as a consensual practice as late as the 1980s/early 1990s, showing the enduring force of the consensual discourse in constructions of adoption work.

6 Contested Attachments: The Controversial Emergence of 'Open Adoption'

1. See Quinton et al., 1997; Ryburn, 1998; Quinton and Selwyn, 1998; Ryburn, 1999; Quinton et al., 1999.
2. See chapters 4 and 5 in Fratter et al. (1991) regarding the emergence of open adoption practices.
3. Parton (1991, pp. 54–78) highlights how the decade was punctuated by a series of child deaths, Jasmine Beckford (London Borough Brent, 1985), Tyra Henry (London Borough Lambeth, 1987) and Kimberley Carlisle (London Borough Greenwich, 1987), which worked to sustain the discursive momentum for more interventionist ways of working. This was reflected in an increased use of emergency interventions into family life (Place of Safety orders), from 5,207 in 1984 to 8,055 in 1987 (ibid., p. 54).
4. Atherton (1986b, pp. 98–9) argues that the technology of attachment always works against contact. In the same collection, she also argues that direct contact facilitates children's development in substitute care (1986a, pp. 14–15). For a further articulation of the pro-contact position see 'Natural parent contact – a theory in search of practice' (Kelly 1984).
5. The Cleveland case emerged in June 1987 and centred on the large numbers of Cleveland children who had been taken into care on the grounds of sexual abuse. Both the investigating social services and the paediatrician Marietta Higgs became the focus of a scandal that revolved around the activities of an

intrusive and authoritarian state unnecessarily intervening into the privacy of family life. (See chapter 4 in Parton (1991) for a fuller discussion.)

6. During the 1990s there was a proliferation of independent specialist projects emerging to support adoptive families in their parenting of attachment disordered children. Keys and Family Futures are two good examples. Other independent agencies, such as the Post-Adoption Centre, developed therapeutic programmes based on attachment theory, to incorporate into their more general post-adoption services.

7. See note (1).

8. My own work at the Post-Adoption Centre certainly reflected this move towards informal and co-operative initiatives in the facilitation of contact arrangements. Between 1994 and 2001, I co-co-ordinated a Contact and Mediation Service, set up to support the making and managing of contact arrangements between adopters and birth family members. The tensions that arose as an effect of using mediation within an adversarial intervention such as adoption inevitably complicated and compromised the equalities that such an approach promised. For a fuller account see authors' unpublished report (1999) and Kedward et al. (1999).

7   Introducing the Archive Study

1. Chapter 6 discusses how before the 1976 Adoption Act, there was not the same emphasis on the keeping of adoption records. Consequently, records were either brief, with little information, or missing. In the case of third-party and direct adoptions, records were often not even kept.

2. All extracts from the adoption files in Chapters 8 and 9 will be in italics to more clearly differentiate these quotations from the main body of the text.

3. A form E records details of the child to be adopted and its birth family; a form F records details of the prospective adopters. These forms are completed as part of the adoption planning process. A Schedule II report is compiled for the final adoption hearing.

4. My analysis of the adoption files does not foreground gender or race. This omission is certainly not because I consider race and gender insignificant in structuring how adoption operates, but reflects more the need to limit this study to a more general analysis of open practices. Therefore, in Chapters 8 and 9 I have not usually identified the race or gender of the children in my sample and when it is identified I have not usually drawn upon it to inform my analysis. My sample included a high percentage of children from black or mixed-race families, with gender fairly evenly represented. It seemed that decision-making around contact did not operate differently according to race or gender differences, but this area would reward a further dedicated analysis of its own.

9   Identity through Injury: Unfit Mothers and Direct Contact

1. During the 1990s there have been some instances of support services for unfit mothers beginning to enter adoption work. These services usually include

group or individual counselling and advocacy work. Charlton et al. (1998) document, in the powerfully titled publication *Still Screaming*, the work of two projects in Manchester and Durham where support was actively offered to non-consenting birth mothers. The work of the Post-Adoption Centre in London was pioneering in offering unfit mothers regular individual and group support in addition to the service of an advocacy project (1997–1999). The recent Adoption and Children Act (2002) makes support to unfit mothers a compulsory practice for adoption workers. These emergences, whilst providing clearer validation for the position of unfit mothers, have not yet contributed to a reworking of that position.

2. Clearly, the case of A is an example of disavowed love, a love which cannot be mourned because there are no social forms available for its acknowledgement. Judith Butler, in the context of homosexuality and race, has written extensively on the effects of such foreclosure. She explores how certain forms of desire become ungrievable within certain public discourses (Butler, 1999, p. 170). Butler's notion of a culturally produced melancholic identification could be fruitfully transposed to think about the field of adoption, where birth parents are situated as the 'unlovable' and so the disavowed other for the adopted child. If adoptive mothering is 'naturalised' through an insistence on the 'otherness' of the unfit birth mother, then the state of being adopted is purchased through a melancholic incorporation of the love that has to be disavowed (Butler 1997b, p. 139). 'It is an identity based upon the refusal to avow an attachment, and hence the refusal to grieve' (ibid., p. 140).

3. The authors of *Adoption: The Modern Law* (2003) argue that from the mid- to late 1990s there was a shift in judicial thinking around the importance accorded to birth family in terms of child welfare. Whereas the Children Act had made the maintenance of blood ties of fundamental importance, the authors contend that in more recent years the 'psychological parent' has acquired a far greater importance in terms of child welfare (Bridge and Swindells, 2003, pp. 52–3). It is interesting to consider how far this shift may be apparent in the adoption culture of my study local authority from the late 1990s onwards.

4. This was, of course, very common practice in an earlier era, but today babies are placed in short-term foster care before adoption to enable birth parents time to consider. This case was most unusual in that the baby was placed directly with the adopters when only a few hours old, albeit adopters who were approved short-term carers.

Bibliography

Official Documents and/or Parliamentary Papers

Adoption of Children Act 1926
Adoption of Children (Regulation) Act 1939
Adoption of Children Act 1949
Adoption Act 1958
Children Act 1975
Adoption Act 1976
Adoption Agencies Regulations 1983
Health and Social Services and Social Security Adjudications Act 1983
Children Act 1989
Adoption and Children Act 2002
Hopkinson Committee (1921) *Report of the Committee on Child Adoption*, Cmd. 1254, London: HMSO
Tomlin Committee (1925) *Child Adoption Committee: First Report*, Cmd. 2401, London: HMSO
Tomlin Committee (1926a) *Child Adoption Committee: Second Report*, Cmd. 2469, London: HMSO
Tomlin Committee (1926b) *Child Adoption Committee: Third Report*, Cmd. 2711, London: HMSO
Horsburgh Committee (1937) *Report of the Departmental Committee on Adoption Societies and Agencies*, Cmd. 5499, London: HMSO
Curtis Report (1946) *A Report of the Care of Children Committee*, Cmd. 6922, London: HMSO
Gamon Report (1947) *In Loco Parentis: A Report with Recommendations on Existing Legislation Governing the Adoption of Children*, London: HMSO
Hurst Committee (1954) *Report of the Departmental Committee on the Adoption of Children*, Cmd. 9248, London: HMSO
Houghton Committee (1972) *Report of the Departmental Committee on the Adoption of Children*, Cmd. 5107, London: HMSO
Secretary of State for Health (1993) *Adoption: The Future*, Cmd. 2288, London: HMSO
Department of Health (1995) *Moving Goalposts: A Study of Post-Adoption Contact in the North of England*, London: Department of Health
Department of Health (1996) *Adoption – A Service for Children*, London: Department of Health
Department of Health (1998) *Adoption – Achieving the Right Balance*, LAC (98) 20 and CI (99) 6, London: Department of Health
Performance and Innovation Unit (2000) *The Prime Minister's Review of Adoption*, London: Performance and Innovation Unit

All other sources

Adcock, M. (1980) 'Social Work Dilemmas', in M. Adcock and R. White (eds.) *Terminating Parental Contact: An Exploration of the Issues Relating to Children in Care*, London: ABAFA

Adcock, M., White, R. and Rowlands, O. (1983) *The Administrative Parent: A Study of the Assumption of Parental Rights*, London: BAAF

Aries, P. (1996) *Centuries of Childhood*, London: Pimlico

Argent, A. (ed.) (2002) *Staying Connected: Managing Contact Arrangement in Adoption*, London: BAAF

Atherton, C. (1986a) 'The importance and purpose of access', in *Promoting Links: Keeping Children and Families in Touch*, London: Family Rights Group

Atherton, C. (1986b) 'The family's difficulties in access' in *Promoting Links: Keeping Children and Families in Touch*, London: Family Rights Group

Barn, R. (2000) 'Race, Ethnicity and Transracial Adoption', in A. Treacher and I. Katz *The Dynamics of Adoption*, London: Jessica Kingsley

Barret-Ducrocq, F. (1992) *Love in the Time of Victoria: Sexuality and Desire among Working-Class Men and Women in Nineteenth Century London*, London: Penguin

Beck, U. (1992) *Risk Society: Towards a New Modernity*, London: Sage

Beck, U. and Beck-Gernsheim, E. (2002) *Individualization*, London: Sage

Benet, M. (1976) *The Character of Adoption*, London: Jonathon Cape

Bouchier, P., Lambert, L. and Triseliotis, J. (1991) *Parting with a Child for Adoption*, London: BAAF

Bowlby, J. (1990) *Childcare and the Growth of Love*, London: Penguin

Borland, M., O'Hara, G. and Triseliotis, J. (1991) 'Adoption & Fostering: The outcome of permanent family placements'. In *Adoption & Fostering* 15 (2), 18–28

Bridge, C. and Swindells, H. (2003) *Adoption: The Modern Law*, Bristol: Jordan

British Agencies for Adoption and Fostering (1999) *Contact in Permanent Placement: Guidance for Local Authorities in England & Wales and Scotland*, London: BAAF

Brodinsky, D. (1984) 'New perspectives on adoption revelation'. In Adoption and Fostering, 8 (2), 27–32

Brodinsky, D. and Schecter, M. (eds.) (1990) *The Psychology of Adoption*, New York: Oxford University Press

Burlingham, D and Freud, A (1942) *Young Children in Wartime: A year's work in a Residential Nursery*, London: George Allen & Unwin

Burnell, A (1990) 'Explaining adoption to children who have been adopted: how do we find the right words?', London: Post-Adoption Centre Discussion Paper

Butler, J. (1997a) *Excitable Speech*, London: Routledge

Butler, J. (1997b) *The Psychic Life of Power*, Stanford: Stanford University

Butler, J. (1999) 'On Speech, Race and Melancholia: An Interview'. In *Theory, Culture and Society*, Vol. 16 (2), 163–74

Butler, J. (2005) *Giving an Account of Oneself*, New York: Fordham

Chambon, A. (1999) 'Foucault's Approach: Making the Familiar Visible', in A. Chambon, A. Irving and L. Epstein (eds.) *Reading Foucault for Social Work*, New York: Columbia Press

Charlton, L., Crank, M., Kansara, K. and Oliver, C. (1998) *Still Screaming*, Manchester: After Adoption

Clapton, G. (2002) *Birth Fathers and Their Adoption Experience*, London: Jessica Kingsley

Cohen, P. (1994) 'Yesterday's Words, Tomorrow's World: from the racialisation of adoption to the politics of difference', in I. Gaber and J. Aldridge (eds.) *Culture, Identity and Transracial Adoption*, London: Free Association Books

Cohen, P. (1995) *Frameworks for a Study of Adoptive Identities*, London: University of East London

Cretney, S. (1998) *Law, Law Reform and the Family*, Oxford: Oxford University Press

Deleuze, G. (1999) *Foucault*, London: Continuum

Derrida, J. (1996) *Archive Fever*, Chicago: University of Chicago

Donzelot, J. (1979) *The Policing of Families*, London: Hutchinson

Dreyfus, H. and Rabinow, R. (1982) *Michel Foucault: Beyond Structuralism and Hermeneutics*, Brighton: Harvester Press

Diduck, A. (1999) 'Justice and Childhood: reflections on refashioned boundaries', in M. King (ed.) *Moral Agenda's for Children's Welfare*, London: Routledge

Dutt, R. and Sanyal, A. (1998) 'Openness in adoption or open adoption – a black perspective', in M. Hill and M. Shaw (eds.) *Signposts in Adoption*, London: BAAF

Dyson, D. (1947) *The Foster Home and the Boarded-out Child*, London: Allen and Unwin

Farmer, E and Owen, M (1995) Child Protection Practice: Private Risks and Public Remedies, London: HMSO

Fearnley, S. (1996) *The Extra Dimension*, Rawtenstall: Keys Attachment Centre

Ferguson, H. (2004) *Protecting children in Time*, Basingstoke: Palgrave

Foucault, M. (1972) *The Archaeology of Knowledge*, London: Tavistock

Foucault, M. (1977) *Discipline and Punish*, London: Penguin

Foucault, M. (1978) *The History of Sexuality volume I An Introduction*, London: Penguin

Foucault, M. (1980) 'Two Lectures', in C. Gordon (ed.) *Power/Knowledge*, Harlow: Longman

Foucault, M. (1986) *The Use of Pleasure*, New York: Vintage

Foucault, M. (1988) 'Technologies of the Self', in L. Martin, H. Gutman and P. Hutton (eds.) *Technologies of the Self*, University of Massachusetts

Foucault, M. (1997a) 'Sexuality and solitude', in P. Rabinow (ed.) *Essential Works of Foucault Volume I* London: Penguin

Foucault, M. (1997b) 'Subjectivity and Truth', in P. Rabinow (ed.) *Essential Works of Foucault Volume I* London: Penguin

Foucault, M. (1997c) 'The ethics of the concern for self as a practice of freedom', in P. Rabinow (ed.) *Essential Works of Foucault Volume I*, London: Penguin

Foucault, M. (1997d) 'An interview by Stephen Riggins', in P. Rabinow (ed.) *Essential Works of Foucault Volume I*, London: Penguin

Foucault, M. (1998a) 'Nietzsche, Genealogy, History', in J. Faubion (ed.) *Essential Works of Foucault Volume II*, London: Penguin

Foucault, M. (1998b) 'Different Spaces', in J. Faubion (ed.) *Essential Works of Foucault Volume II*, London: Penguin

Foucault, M. (1998c) 'Structuralism and post-structuralism', in J. Faubion (ed.) *Essential Works of Foucault Volume II*, London: Penguin

Foucault, M. (2000a) 'Questions of Method', in J. Faubion (ed.) *Essential Works of Foucault Volume III*, London: Penguin

Foucault, M. (2000b) 'Governmentality', in J. Faubion (ed.) *Essential Works of Foucault Volume III*, London: Penguin

Foucault, M. (2000c) 'About the concept of the "dangerous individual" in nineteenth-century legal psychiatry', in J. Faubion (ed.) *Essential Works of Foucault Volume III*, London: Penguin

Foucault, M. (2000d) 'The lives of infamous men', in J. Faubion (ed.) *Essential Works of Foucault Volume III*, London: Penguin

Foucault, M. (2000e) 'The subject and power', in J. Faubion (ed.) *Essential Works of Foucault Volume III*, London: Penguin

Foucault, M. (2005) *The Hermeneutics of the Subject,* New York: Picador

Franklin, S (1997) *Embodied Progress: A Cultural Account of Assisted Conception*, London: Routledge

Fratter, J., Rowe, J., Sapsford, D. and Thoburn, J. (1991) *Permanent Family Placement: A Decade of Experience*, London: BAAF

Fratter, J. (1991a) 'Towards more openness in adoption: the perspectives of 22 voluntary agencies', in J. Fratter, J. Rowe, D. Sapsford and J. Thoburn *Permanent Family Placement: A decade of experience*, London: BAAF

Fratter, J (1991b) 'Postscript: a personal perspective, 1980–1990', in J. Fratter, J. Rowe, D. Sapsford and J. Thoburn *Permanent Family Placement: A decade of experience*, London: BAAF

Fratter, J. (1996) *Adoption with Contact*, London: BAAF

Gaber, I. and Aldridge, J. (1994) *Culture, Identity and Transracial Adoption*, London: Free Association Books

George, V. (1970) *Foster Care Theory and Practice*, London: Routledge

Gibbons, J., Gallagher, B., Bell, C. and Gordon, D. (1995) *Development after Physical Abuse in Early Childhood: A Follow-Up Study of Children on Child Protection Registers*, London: HMSO

Giddens, A. (1991) *Modernity and Self-Identity*, Cambridge: Polity

Gill, O. and Jackson, B. (1983) *Adoption and Race*, London: Batsford

Goldstein, J., Freud, A. and Solnit, J. (1973) *Beyond the Best Interests of the Child*, New York: Free Press

Goodacre, I. (1966) *Adoption Policy & Practice*, London: Allen & Unwin

Grey, E. and Blunden, R. (1971) *A Survey of Adoption in Great Britain*, London: HMSO

Haimes, E. and Timms, N. (1985) *Adoption, Identity and Social Policy*, Aldershot: Gower

Heywood, J. (1965) *Children in Care: The Development of the Service for the Deprived Child*, London: Routledge

Hollway, W. and Jefferson, T. (2000) *Doing Qualitative Research differently: Free Association, Narrative and the Interview Method*, London: Sage

Hook, D (2007) *Foucault, Psychology and the Analytics of Power*, Basingstoke: Palgrave MacMillan

Howe, D., Sawbridge, P. and Hinings, D. (1992) *Half a Million Women*, London: Post-Adoption Centre

Howe, D. and Feast, J. (2000) *Adoption, Search & Reunion*, London: The Children's Society

Howe, D., Brandon, M., Hinings, D. and Schofield G. (1999) *Attachment Theory: Child Maltreatment and Family Support*, Basingstoke: Macmillan

Inglis, K. (1984) *Living Mistakes: Mothers Who Consented to Adoption*, Sydney: Allen & Unwin

James, A. and James, A. (2004) *Constructing Childhood*, Basingstoke: Palgrave Macmillan

James, A., Jenks, C. and Prout, A. (1998) *Theorising Childhood*, Cambridge: Polity

James, M. (1980) 'Home-finding for Children with Special Needs', in J. Triseliotis (ed.) *New Developments in Foster Care & Adoption*, London: Routledge

Jenks, C. (1996) *Childhood*, London: Routledge

Jordan, B. (1994) 'Contested adoptions and the role of the state in family matters', in M. Ryburn (ed.) *Contested Adoptions: Research, Law, Policy and Practice*, Aldershot: Arena

Kedward, C., Luckward, B. and Lawson, H (1999) 'Mediation and post-adoption contact: the early experience of the Post-Adoption centre contact mediation service'. In *Adoption and Fostering* 23 (3), 16–26

Kelly, G (1984) 'Natural parent contact – a theory in search of practice', in *Substitute Families – Security or Severance*, London: Family Rights Group

Kellmer Pringle, M. (1967 *Adoption – Facts and Fallacies*, London: Longmans

Kirk, D. (1964) *Shared Fate*, London: Collier Macmillan

Kornitzer, M. (1952) *Adoption in the Modern World*, London: Putnam

Kornitzer, M. (1968) *Adoption and Family Life*, London: Putnam

Lambert, L. (1994) 'Contested proceedings: what the research tells us', in M. Ryburn (ed.) *Contested Adoptions: Research, Law, Policy and Practice*, Aldershot: Arena

Lawler, S (2008) *Identity: Sociological perspectives,* Cambridge: Polity

Lloyd, M. and Thacker, A. (2005) 'Still Thinking Differently: Foucault Twenty Years On'. In *New Formations*, 55, 44–53

Lowe, N., Murch, M., Borkowski, M., Weaver, A., Beckford, V. and Thomas, C. (1999) *Supporting Adoption: Reframing the Approach*, London: BAAF

Lowe, N. (2000) 'English adoption law: past, present and future', in S. Katz, J. Eekelaar and M. MacLean (eds.) *Cross Currents: Family Law Policy in the United States and England*, Oxford: Oxford University Press

Macaskill, C. (2002) *Safe Contact*, London: Random House

Mason, K. and Selman, P (1998) 'Birth parents' experience of contested adoption', in M. Hill and M. Shaw (ed.) *Signposts in Adoption,* London: BAAF

May, T. (2006) *The Philosophy of Foucault*, Chesham: Acumen

Milham, S., Bullock, R., Hosie, K. and Haak, M. (1986) *Lost in Care: The Problems of Maintaining Links between Children in Care and Their Families*, Aldershot: Gower

Milham, S., Bullock, R., Hosie, K. and Little, M (1989) *Access Disputes in Childcare* Aldershot: Gower

Murch, M., Lowe, N., Borkowski, M., Copner, R. and Griew, K. (1993) *Pathways to Adoption: Research Project*, London: HMSO

Neil, E. (2000) *Contact with birth relatives after adoption: a study of young, recently placed children,* Norwich: University of East Anglia, unpublished PhD Thesis

Neil, E. and Howe, D. (eds.) (2004) *Contact in adoption and permanent foster care: research, theory and practice,* London: BAAF

Newman, R. (1995) 'From access to contact in a local authority setting', in H. Argent (ed.) *See You Soon: Contact with Children Looked After by Local Authorities*, London: BAAF

O'Leary, T. (2002) *Foucault and the Art of Ethics*, London: Continuum

Packman, J. (1975) *The Child's Generation*, Oxford: Blackwell
Packman, J., Randall, J. and Jacques, N. (1986) *Who Needs Care? Social Work Decisions about Children*, Oxford: Blackwell
Parker, R. (1966) *Decision in Child Care*, London: Allen and Unwin
Parker, R. (1990) *Away from Home: A History of Childcare*, London: Barnados
Parker, R. (1999) *Adoption Now: Messages from Research*, Chichester: Wiley
Parton, N. (1985) *The Politics of Child Abuse*, London: Macmillan
Parton, N. (1991) *Governing the Family*, London: Macmillan
Parton, N., Thorpe, D. and Wattam, C. (1997) *Child Protection: Risk and the Moral Order*, London: Macmillan
Parton, N. (1999) 'Reconfiguring Child Welfare Practices: Risk, Advanced Liberalism and the Government of freedom', A. Chambon, A.Irving and L. Epstein (eds.) *Reading Foucault for Social Work*, New York: Columbia Press
Piper, C. (1999) 'Moral Campaigns for Children's welfare in the nineteenth century' in M. King (ed.) *Moral Agendas for Children's Welfare*, London: Routledge
Quinton, D. and Rutter, M. (1988) *Parenting Breakdown: The Making and Breaking of Intergenerational Links*, Aldershot: Avebury
Quinton, D., Rushton, A., Dance, C. and Mayes D. (1997) 'Contact between children placed away from home and their birth parents: Research issues and evidence'. In *Clinical Child Psychology & Psychiatry*, 2 (3), 393–413
Quinton, D., Rushton, A., Dance, C. and Mayes, D. (1998*) Joining New Families: A Study of Adoption & Fostering*, Chichester: Wiley
Quinton, D. and Selwyn, J. (1998) 'Contact with birth parents after adoption: a response to Ryburn'. In *Child & Family Law Quarterly* 10 (4), 1–14
Quinton, D., Selwyn, J., Rushton, A. and Dance, C. (1999) 'Contact between children placed away from home and their birth parents: Ryburn's 'reanalysis' analysed'. In *Clinical Child Psychology & Psychiatry*, 4 (4), 519–531
Raynor, L. (1971) *Giving Up a Baby for Adoption*, London: BAAF
Rall, M. (1961) *Casework with Parents of Adolescent Unmarried Mothers*, New York: Child Welfare League
Reich, D. (1988a) *Working with Mothers Who Lost a Child to Adoption*, London: Post-Adoption Centre Discussion Paper
Reich, D. (1988b) *Preparing People to Adopt Babies and Young Children*, London: Post-Adoption Centre Discussion Paper
Riley, D. (1983) *War in the Nursery,* London: Virago
Roberts, R. (1966) *The Unwed Mother*, New York: Harper & Row
Rockel, J. and Ryburn, M. (1988) *Adoption Today: Change and Choice in New Zealand*, Auckland, New Zealand: Heinemann Reed
Rose, N. (1989) *Governing the Soul*, London: Free Association Books
Rose, N (1998) *Inventing Ourselves: Psychology, Power and Personhood*, Cambridge: Cambridge University Press
Rowe, J. (1959) *Yours by Choice* (1st edition), London: Routledge
Rowe, J. (1966) *Parents, Children and Adoption*, London: Routledge
Rowe, J. (1982) *Yours by Choice* (2nd edition), London: Routledge
Rowe, J. and Lambert, L. (1973) *Children Who Wait*, London: BAAF
Rowe, J. (1980) 'Fostering in the 1970s and beyond', in J. Triseliotis (ed.) *New Developments in Foster Care & Adoption*, London: Routledge
Rowe, J., Cain, H., Hundleby, M. and Keane, A. (1984) *Long Term Foster Care*, London: Batsford

Rowe, J. (1991) 'An historical perspective on adoption and the role of voluntary agencies' in J. Fratter, J. Rowe, D. Sapsford and J. Thoburn *Permanent Family Placement*, London: BAAF

Rutter, M. (1972) *Maternal Deprivation Reassessed*, London: Penguin

Ryan, M. (1986) 'The law on access', in *Promoting Links: Keeping Children and Families in Touch*, London: Family Rights Group

Ryan, M. (1994) 'Contested Proceedings: Justice and the Law', in M. Ryburn (ed.) *Contested Adoptions: Research, Law, Policy and Practice*, Aldershot: Arena

Ryburn, R. (1992a) 'Advertising for Permanent Placements'. *Adoption and Fostering*, 16 (2), 8–15

Ryburn, M. (1992b) *Adoption in the 1990s: Identity and Openness*, Royal Leamington spa: Leamington Press

Ryburn, M. (1995) 'Adopted children's identity & information needs'. In *Children & Society*, 9 (3), 41–64

Ryburn, M. (ed.) (1994) *Contested Adoptions: Research, Law, Policy and Practice*, Aldershot: Arena

Ryburn, M. (1996) 'A study of post-adoption contact in compulsory adoption'. In *British Journal of Social Work*, 26 (5), 627–46

Ryburn, M. (1998) 'In whose best interest? Post-adoption contact with the birth family'. In *Child & Family Law Quarterly*, 10 (1), 53–70

Ryburn, M. (1999) 'Contact between children placed away from home and their birth parents: a reanalysis of the evidence in relation to permanent placement'. In *Clinical Child psychology & Psychiatry*, 4 (4), 505–18

Sants, H. (1964) 'Genealogical bewilderment in children with substitute parents'. In *British Journal of Medical Psychology* 37, 133–41

Sawbridge, P. (1980) 'Seeking new parents: a decade of development', in J. Triseliotis (ed.) *New Developments in Foster Care & Adoption*, London: Routledge

Schofield, G. and Beek, M. (2006) *Attachment Handbook for Foster Care and Adoption*, London: BAAF

Scott, J. (1996) *Only Paradoxes to Offer*, Cambridge, Mass: Harvard University Press

Seglow, J., Kellmer Pringle, E. and Wedge, P. (1972) *Growing Up Adopted*, Windsor: National foundation for Educational Research in England and Wales

Shawyer, J. (1979) *Death by Adoption*, Auckland: Cicada Press

Smith, C. L. (1980) 'The New Families Project', in J. Triseliotis (ed.) *New Developments in Foster Care & Adoption*, London: Routledge

Smith, C. and Logan, J. (2004) *After Adoption: Direct Contact and Relationships*, London: Routledge

Strathern, M (1995) *After Nature: English Kinship in the Late Twentieth Century*, Cambridge: Cambridge University Press

Steedman, C. (1994) *Strange Dislocations: Childhood and the Idea of Human Interiority 1789–1930*, Cambridge, Mass: Harvard University Press

Tamboukou, M. (1999) Writing genealogies: an exploration of Foucault's strategies for doing research'. In *Discourse: Studies in the Cultural Politics of education*, 20 (2), 201–17

Teague, A. (1989) *Social Change, Social work and the Adoption of Children*, Aldershot: Gower

Thoburn, T., Murdoch, A. and O'Brien, A. (1986) *Permanence in Childcare*, Oxford: Blackwell

Thoburn, J. (1990) *Interdepartmental Review of Adoption Law Background Paper Number 2: Review of Research Relating to Adoption*, London: Department of Health

Thoburn, J. (1996) 'Psychological parenting and child placement: but do we want to have our cake and eat it?', in Howe, D (ed.) *Attachment and Loss in Child and Family Social Work*, Aldershot: Avebury

Thoburn, J., Norford, L. and Rashid, S. (2000) *Permanent Family Placement for Children of Ethnic Minority Backgrounds*, London: Jessica Kingsley

Thomas, C. and Beckford, V., with Lowe, N. and Murch, M. (1999) *Adopted Children Speaking*, London: BAAF

Tizard, B. (1977) *Adoption: A Second Chance*, London: Open Books

Tizard, B. and Phoenix, A. (2002) *Black, White or Mixed Race? Race and Racism in the Lives of Young People of Mixed Parentage*, London: Routledge

Trasler, G (1960) *In Place of Parents*, London: Routledge

Treacher, A. and Katz, I. (eds.) (2000) *The Dynamics of Adoption*, London: Jessica Kingsley

Triseliotis, J. (1973) *In Search of Origins*, London: Routledge

Triseliotis, J. (1980a) 'Counselling Adoptees', in J. Triseliotis (ed.) *New Developments in Foster Care & Adoption*, London: Routledge

Triseliotis, J. (ed.) (1980b) *New Developments in Foster Care & Adoption*, London: Routledge

Triseliotis, J., Sellick, C. and Short, R (1995) *Foster Care: Theory and Practice*, London: Batsford

Triseliotis, J., Shireman, J. and Hundleby, M. (1997) *Adoption: Theory, Policy & Practice*, London: Cassell

Triseliotis, J. (1998a) 'Adoption – Evolution or Revolution?' in M. Hill and M. Shaw (ed.) *Signposts in Adoption*, London: BAAF

Triseliotis, J. (1998b) 'Perceptions of Permanence', in M. Hill and M. Shaw (ed.) *Signposts in Adoption*, London: BAAF

Triseliotis, J., Feast, J. and Kyle, F. (2005) *The Adoption Triangle Revisited: A Study of Adoption, Search and Reunion Experiences*, London: BAAF

Vernon, J. and Fruin, D. (1986) *In Care: A Study of Social Work Decision-Making*, London: National Children's Bureau

Veyne, P. (1997) 'Foucault revolutionizes history', in A. Davidson (ed.) *Foucault and His Interlocutors* Chicago: University of Chicago

Weeks, J. (1981) *Sex, Politics and Society: The Regulation of Sexuality since 1800*, London: Longmans

Weeks, J. (1985) *Sexuality and Its Discontents*, London: Routledge

Wells, S. (1993) 'What do birth mothers want?'. In *Adoption & Fostering* 17 (4), 22–6

White, R. (1993) 'Adoption and contact: the legal framework', in M. Adcock, J. Kaniuk, J and R. White (ed.) *Exploring Openness in Adoption*, Croydon: Significant Publications

Williams, F. (1989) *Social Policy: A Critical Introduction: Issues of Race, Gender and Class*, Cambridge: Polity Press

Winnicott, D.W. (1984) *Through Paediatrics to Psychoanalysis Collected Papers*, London: Karnac Books

Winkler R. and Van Keppel, M (1984) *Relinquishing Mothers in Adoption*, Melbourne: Institute for Family Studies

Yelloly, M. (1965) 'Factors relating to an adoption decision by the mothers of illegitimate infants'. In *Sociological Review* 13 (1), 5–14

Young, L. (1954) *Out of Wedlock*, New York: McGraw Hill

Index